Legal Aspects of Special Education

Kurt E. Hulett

Merrill
is an imprint of

Upper Saddle River, New Jersey
Columbus, Ohio

Library of Congress Cataloging in Publication Data

Hulett, Kurt.
    Legal aspects of special education / by Kurt Hulett. —1st ed.
        p. cm.
    Includes bibliographical references and index.
    ISBN 978-0-13-117346-0 (pbk. : alk. paper)
    1. Special education—Law and legislation—United States.   I. Title.
KF4209.3.H85 2009
344.73'0791—dc22   2007045118

Vice President and Executive Publisher: Jeffery W. Johnston
Executive Editor: Ann Castel Davis
Senior Managing Editor: Pamela D. Bennett
Editorial Assistant: Penny Burleson
Production Editor: Sheryl Glicker Langner
Production Coordination: Kelly Keeler/GGS Book Services
Design Coordinator: Diane C. Lorenzo
Cover Designer: Jason Moore
Cover Art: Super Stock
Cover Concept: H. Jennings Sheffield
Production Manager: Laura Messerly
Director of Marketing: Quinn Perkson
Marketing Manager: Kris Ellis-Levy
Marketing Coordinator: Brian Mounts

This book was set in Garamond by GGS Book Services. It was printed and bound by RR Donnelley & Sons Company.
The cover was printed by R.R. Donnelley & Sons Company.

Pearson® is a registered trademark of Pearson plc
Merrill® is a registered trademark of Pearson Education, Inc.

Pearson Education Ltd., London
Pearson Education Singapore, Pte. Ltd.
Pearson Education Canada, Inc.
Pearson Education–Japan
Pearson Education Australia PTY, Limited

Pearson Education North Asia, Ltd., Hong Kong
Pearson Educación de Mexico, S.A. de C.V.
Pearson Education Malaysia, Pte. Ltd.
Pearson Education Upper Saddle River, New Jersey

Merrill
is an imprint of

10 9 8 7 6 5 4 3
ISBN 13: 978-0-13-117346-0
ISBN 10:   0-13-117346-4

This book is dedicated to my wife,
H. Jennings Sheffield.

PREFACE

This text is intended for undergraduate and graduate students in regular and special education teaching programs. Additionally, the text is intended to serve as a desk reference for practitioners—for regular and special education teachers, school and district administrators, psychologists, social workers, and all related service providers of students with disabilities.

The purpose of this book is to provide the practitioner (or practitioner-in-training) with pertinent, current, and easy-to-read guidance regarding special education law. The intent is also to provide the practitioner (nonlawyer) with a reference tool for developing and implementing legally and educationally sound special education programs and policies.

Although the Individuals with Disabilities Act (IDEA) is the major focus of the text, other related pieces of legislation—the No Child Left Behind Act of 2001, Section 504 of the Rehabilitation Act of 1973, and the Americans with Disabilities Act of 1990—are covered in individual chapters. Unique features of the text include (1) case studies throughout the text with follow-up questions to help the reader apply the law to everyday situations, (2) a "Facts at a Glance" section at the beginning of each chapter, (3) analysis of the 2004 IDEA amendments and implementing regulations, (4) extensive analysis of the No Child Left Behind Act, (5) an in-depth interview with Joseph Ballard, and (6) the link between the Civil Rights movement and special education law.

ACKNOWLEDGMENTS

Although I will acknowledge several individuals for their support of and significant contributions to this project, one individual deserves credit, thanks, accolades, and appreciation beyond words. B. Joseph Ballard, affectionately known as "Joe," contributed to the development of this text from day one. As you will soon read, I began the research process for this book by interviewing Joe—one of the most diligent and respected advocates for children with disabilities since the passage of Public Law No. 94-142. Joe chose to contribute to this world by fighting for—and subsequently enhancing and protecting—laws for children with disabilities.

Within a month of the completion of the final draft of this text, Joe passed away. Joe was extremely committed to this project and provided his support in the same way he approached everything—with great thought, kindness, passion, and resolve. I remember sitting at Joe's kitchen table during the spring of 2006.

We were watching the nightly national news and the broadcaster ended the show with a quick human-interest story.

The story was about a young man with autism who had been a dedicated and beloved manager for his high school's varsity basketball team. As a measure of appreciation for his support of and service to the team, the coach put the young man in the game during the waning moments of the last game of the season. Moments after entering the game and with the student body cheering loudly and zealously, he launched a shot from three-point range. I don't think anyone in the gym expected him to make the shot, but everyone wanted to see him play and take a shot. Against odds, and followed by the explosive cheer of the crowd, the young man made it. Had the story stopped there, it would have been newsworthy—but it didn't. In the final two minutes or so, the young man made three-point shot after shot. Following every shot the crowd erupted louder and louder—aware they were all a part of an amazing, inexplicable moment. Joe and I sat together, with the rest of the American viewing public, in utter amazement. I will never forget Joe's words following the story. With uncharacteristic tears in his eyes and a slight crack in his voice, Joe said, "That's why, Kurt. That's why we worked so hard and refused to give up. That's why you have to continue to fight and tell the story. That boy and his classmates are an example of what can happen when *all* children are given a chance." He never said it, but I think that one story validated his life's work and purpose.

My wife, H. Jennings Sheffield, has been an amazing support throughout this project. Her moral support and continual encouragement provided me with the fortitude and motivation necessary to complete this text. I owe an incredible debt of gratitude to Aileen Colorado for inviting me to be a counselor at the Muscular Dystrophy Association summer camp. Aileen is my inspiration and the reason I became an advocate and a special educator. Without Aileen, this book would not exist.

I would like to recognize the following colleagues for their intellectual input and support through different stages of this text: Travis Hicks, Theresa Lee, and Terry Overton.

Additionally, I would like to thank all of the wonderful educators and children with whom I have worked over the years. My true education came from all of you—not books. The following reviewers also contributed greatly to this book: Paula Adams, Sam Houston State University; Sharan E. Brown, University of Washington; Steve C. Camron, Eastern Michigan University; Mike Cass, Sull Ross State University/Rio Grande College; Terry Cox-Cruey, Northern Kentucky University; Daryl Eason, San Diego State University; Ronald Felton, Florida International University; Dan Fennerty, Central Washington University; Helen Hammond, University of Texas at El Paso; Ken B. Heinlein, University of Wyoming; Kristine Jolivette, Georgia State University; Kristina Krampe, University of Kentucky; Carl Lashley, University of North Carolina at Greensboro; Norbert K. Ohlendorf, University of Houston, Clear Lake; Jane M. Williams, Towson University; and Yaoying Xu, Virginia Commonwealth University.

Last, but certainly not least, I recognize my entire family—both Hulett and Sheffield—for all of the support, love, and encouragement I have received throughout my life.

BRIEF CONTENTS

CONTENTS

CHAPTER 4

SECTION 504 OF THE REHABILITATION ACT OF 1973   43

CHAPTER 5

THE AMERICANS WITH DISABILITIES ACT   61

CHAPTER 6

IDEA 2004 MEETS NO CHILD LEFT BEHIND   70

CHAPTER 7

FREE AND APPROPRIATE PUBLIC EDUCATION   90

CHAPTER 8

LEAST RESTRICTIVE ENVIRONMENT   106

CHAPTER 9

EVALUATION AND ASSESSMENT   123

CHAPTER 10

THE INDIVIDUALIZED EDUCATION PROGRAM   144

CHAPTER 11

PROCEDURAL SAFEGUARDS   164

EPILOGUE

FUTURE IMPLICATIONS   190

PROLOGUE

The following is an interview with Joseph "Joe" Ballard. As the reader will soon learn, Joe was instrumental in the development and protection of the Individuals with Disabilities Education Act (IDEA) from the very start. Joe committed his life's work to the protection of individuals with disabilities through public policy and advocacy. Joe's commentary provides tremendous insight into the original intent of and historical circumstances surrounding the IDEA. This interview was conducted in the fall of 2003 at Joe's home in Delaware.

Q: Can you tell me about your background?

A: All right. I had come to Washington, D.C., in the now ancient year of 1967 to work as an intern for a member of Congress. Her name was Edith Green and her district was Portland, Oregon. As it happened, she was the ranking Democrat—that means the most senior Democrat other than the Chair—on the U.S. House Education and Labor Committee, which means that before awfully long, I was becoming fairly immersed in federal education legislation, as we knew it in the early years. In those days, members of Congress had patronage positions to fill as they became more senior: police positions, doorperson positions, elevator operator positions, mail distribution positions. This provided a prized opportunity for young persons like myself to learn legislative process and content literally from top to bottom. You worked part-time in your patronage job (I was a doorman at the House chamber) and the balance of your time in your member's office as one more staff person. Well, I didn't stay on patronage very long before Edith Green decided I should be full-time staff. I did that for five years and in the process learned quite a bit about most legislation coming under the jurisdiction of the committee—whether education, labor, or poverty.

For instance, Edith Green had the higher education subcommittee at a time when some of the critical higher education legislation was being enacted. Parenthetically, she was always doing college commencement speeches, so I learned more than I ever really wanted to know in speech writing for that audience. Most importantly for the future, however, I was becoming familiar with the Elementary and Secondary Education Act of 1965 (ESEA). Edith was very involved in the Lyndon Johnson years in the development of that landmark bill. So she knew it well, and she taught me well. And the heart and soul of the ESEA, then and now, is its Title I.

Q: They often talked about that being one of the biggest pieces or one of the first pieces of major federal legislation that addressed special education. Would you say that's true?

A: Actually, yes and no. Though I was not around yet, after they enacted Title I, the Congress realized that nothing had been done for children with disabilities. The focus of Title I of the ESEA was incidence of poverty and economic disadvantage in the schools, with an overall mantra of educational disadvantage for the specific targeted students. So the Congress enacted an amendment to the ESEA, which is known as the 89-313 program, derived from its legislative numbers—P.L. 89-313. This will show you the limited knowledge that Congress had at that time about the scope and depth of deprivation for children with disabilities. The program was directed almost solely to children in institutional and other residential settings. Though it was our first major direct service program, and though it was directed at many of those children with the most severe disabilities, it was quite limited in both scope and dollars.

Q: That was an add-on, an addendum to the ESEA?

A: Correct. It was a later amendment placed within Title I of the ESEA. It should be noted that indirect educational support programs for children with disabilities in the areas of training and research date back to the Eisenhower administration. Also, modest state-level direct support was inaugurated after enactment of the ESEA and before the full legislative mandate for all children with Public Law No. 94-142 in 1975 (now known as the IDEA). But very modest, indeed, compared to what would come in 1975.

   Brown v. Board of Education set the stage for Title I and also for the IDEA by making the equal protection clause of the Constitution an underlying principle for the education of all America's children. What you give to the majority you must give to all, which translated into equal educational opportunity for all. Beyond the very serious matter of desegregation of the schools, *Brown* had broad and deep implications, which govern policy to this day, and I hope forever.

   We clearly saw that Title I of the ESEA was our golden opportunity. What we found ourselves conceptualizing was a possible, let's say, first cousin—no, better yet, a twin—for Title I that would have basically an equal stature over time with Title I, but would address children with disabilities rather than the trigger of poverty/educational disadvantage. Interestingly, this is reflected to this day in the funding distribution formula for the IDEA, which is borrowed from the formula for Title I—namely, the number of children served times a certain percentage of the national average per pupil expenditure. That formula in the IDEA—which as we speak now produces an authorization of, what, $35 billion—is a match-up with Title I. But more importantly, Title I, making equal educational opportunity national policy, led us to assert, "Why not the same for children with disabilities?" Lyndon Johnson had been up in the hollows of West Virginia asking "What are we doing for poor kids?"

We took hold of that message and ran with it on behalf of another oppressed group of young Americans. We envisioned two central programs federally in elementary and secondary education—Title I of the ESEA, which is still in place, though it has now become the umbrella for educational reform with the No Child Left Behind Act, and the IDEA, also still alive and vibrant. But it would take ten years.

Q: You were already planning it back then?

A: Let me clarify. It would be ten years between the enactment of the ESEA and the passage of Public Law No. 94-142. When the Council for Exceptional Children (CEC) began planning for the eventual IDEA, I was still on Capitol Hill. I came to CEC in 1972. I wanted to specialize and I was utterly captivated by what CEC was calling the Right to Education Movement. The goal of that movement was to end the outright exclusion of vast numbers of children with disabilities from the public schools—a staggering number—and the inappropriate education programs for another vast cohort. Yes, it was just that awful. Since I am a mission-oriented guy, CEC was inviting me to discover my mission. *They* have a right to an education, too. When I observe all the young teachers today who may oftentimes think of the IDEA as an unnecessary headache, I wish I could transport them back to that time in history. I think they would embrace the need for the IDEA. After all, what was going on then could happen again. That is one of the lessons that history teaches.

Q: So this is sort of a mini–civil rights movement for special education kids?

A: Absolutely. In its earliest development, this was already the most consumer-intensive education legislation that we have, even to this day. What do I mean by consumer-intensive? It required parent involvement from the very inception, and with special educators as advocates—and what a wonderful marriage. Because one of the first things I learned is that there is no discipline within education that gets closer to parents than special educators, because they have to. And special educators by their very nature, at least in the old days and I am certain even today, have to be advocates. They are advocates within the schools. They are advocates within the community. For instance, if a young person is going to be successfully employed after the school years, special educators need to be hustling within the business community to guarantee some onsite school-supervised job training before matriculation. So a determined parent/special educator partnership went to work to achieve passage of the IDEA.

At the same time, CEC was promoting various court cases to end exclusion in courtrooms across the nation. When Public Law No. 94-142 was passed, there were something like 34 to 36 court cases pending or completed in the United States. Moreover, state-level mandatory legislation to end exclusion and inappropriate education had been enacted in some states and was under consideration in the legislatures of other states. There was a problem, though. No law yet existed to embrace the rights of all children in the nation. We lacked what I like to call a national minimum floor of responsibility.

Q: And that's what the literature seems to say: The reason Congress stepped in was because you had *Pennsylvania Association of Retarded Citizens v. Pennsylvania*, you had *Mills v. Board of Education of the District of Columbia*, and basically you had all these cases occurring. So Congress came in to come up with an overall rule for all the states.

A: Correct. And we found that we had interesting groups who were willing to join us from the larger general education community. And let me give you the two prime players, in my judgment, from that community: the National School Boards Association (NSBA), representing the local boards of education, and the Council of Chief State School Officers (CCSSO), representing the state commissioners of education. Why? Not because they were feeling particularly warm and cuddly toward our population of children with special learning needs, but because they were showing signs of frenzy coping with different court decrees emanating from different benches around the country, as well as mandatory laws in certain states that differed in specifics and details from those of other states.

Q: What about money?

A: Ah, yes, money. What will the U.S. Treasury contribute to the cost of the education of these children?

Q: They were hoping the federal government would provide some of that?

A: We all agreed that a major federal fiscal partnership with the states would now be required. Further, we had a delicate understanding with the general education interests, which I just mentioned. We, CEC, and other advocacy groups representing the children and families would defer to the folks in the general education community on exactly what kind of a fiscal formula and funding distribution package would be developed if they would leave us to attend to the nature of an appropriate educational program and the guarantee of rights and protections for the children and their families. The latter is our business and our area of expertise. So, as examples, the language on student evaluations, the triggers for parent due process, the nature of least restrictive environment, the IEP, all of these fell in our domain. By the way, the requirement of an IEP is the very heartbeat of the IDEA, and a critical policy now firmly established in American education.

Q: Can you explain that though? They didn't want you too involved with general education, and what you were saying is that we won't get too involved with what you do so long as you let us put in some measures to protect our children, our special education kids. Is that right?

A: Let me try this a bit differently. We also are interested in and support an infusion of federal money into this program. However, we will leave the policy details of how that is done, how the fiscal arrangements are made, to you folks because you are the superintendents and the keepers of the local school budgets. After all, our people worked for these administrators. On the other hand, you will leave to us the determination of how to guarantee an appropriate program for each student. Leave to us the definition of FAPE, a free appropriate public education. For us, money was an important issue, but the constitutional right to an education was the overriding issue. I need to add, though, that all the years after enactment of the IDEA we worked vigorously with the general education community to achieve full funding of the IDEA.

Q: And you figured that probably what they really wanted was the money and would allow you to control substantive and procedural guarantees?

A: *Control* might be too strong a verb; let's try *shape*. But as I mentioned before, they also wanted that national minimum floor of responsibility. A family moves from Missouri to Maine, for example, and the parents say, "What has happened? I had these related services for my child in Missouri, but I don't have them in Maine." They rightly perceived that they were heading into a programmatic nightmare because of the lack of what only the federal government can do by legislation—namely, set the floor of uniform responsibility.

Q: And that's when the *Rowley* case came in and said you don't have to provide the maximum—you have to provide what is appropriate or reasonable.

A: That is a different take on the word *minimum* than my usage. For us, *minimum floor* means an IEP for each child that includes all that the child needs to thrive educationally. The Supreme Court held in *Rowley* that the child must have a program reasonably calculated to benefit the child. Actually, we did not think that *Rowley* was a particularly good case to bring to the High Court because it involved the denial of a related service only. The specific instructional program was not at issue in the case. Trying to steer the right cases to the Supreme Court is a very chancy matter. It is not easy to do. Though not the best case, the principle of "benefit" was established. Does that clarify the two usages of *minimum*?

Q: Oh, yes, very much so. So you were there for five years working for Congresswoman Green. And then you moved to CEC in 1972. And what position did you assume there?

A: I immediately assumed the position of having primary responsibility—we were a very small shop—for federal issues and content. We were a three-man team. Fred Weintraub, who hired me, was our leader as the director of what was then called CEC Governmental Relations. The fact that Fred brought me on board means that he will have my lifelong gratitude. Al Abeson, the third in our little triumvirate, had charge of state and local issues and content. They wanted someone who had experience on the Hill, who was known on the Hill, and who had worked primarily in the arena of education legislation. We were a good team, always ready to learn from each other. Interestingly, the area of education I did not know much about was special education. On that matter, Al and Fred said, in effect, "Joe, don't worry. We will give you your informal degrees in special education." By the way, Fred and Al eventually went on to make other important contributions to the disability movement and the profession of special education. I remained in the public policy domain through my entire career at CEC and thus attended to the protection and further nurturing of the IDEA for some 22 years beyond its enactment.

On that matter of hiring someone who had been a congressional staff person, CEC knew what it was doing—better than I did myself at the time. Once you have shed blood and tears as a Hill staffer, you are in the special brother/sisterhood for the rest of your life. When, now a CEC person, I would say to a Hill staff person, "Hey, I know what this is like. I was up here once myself, so let me see if I can help," I could literally feel the sudden bonding. Even now, when I mention to a Hill person that I was one of them for five years back in times that must seem like the Bronze Age to them, I sense that same magic bonding. The underlying message: You had to have been working here in the Congress to truly understand that it is like no other village on the planet.

Q: What would you say were the driving forces behind special education advocacy?

A: I presume you mean toward achieving the passage of Public Law No. 94-142. Key advocacy groups were involved, though mighty few compared to today. But I would single out one for special mention, the National Association for Retarded Citizens, which is now ARC. I would give the ARC credit for having been involved with us from beginning to end. There were also key parent groups who were able to make an impact with the Congress—for instance, the Ohio parent coalition. These were the progenitors of the vibrant national parent network existing now.

Q: CEC and ARC are the two I have cited so far because all of the literature talks about these two groups.

A: I affirm your research. Our CEC threesome worked as a team with Paul Marchand, a deeply committed advocate and director of ARC governmental relations to this day. Paul, Fred, and I wore out a lot of shoe leather walking the halls of Congress. In the meantime, Al Abeson was providing essential back-up through extensive data gathering and research.

Q: And so it was actually a very small band of individuals that helped engineer the law. I mean, all of you wrote a great deal of this legislation, didn't you, for Congress to then pass?

A: It was, indeed, a relatively small band of determined brothers and sisters in Washington and around the country. Today you would have to rent the Hollywood

Bowl to bring together all the stakeholders in an IDEA reauthorization. Also, a very small number of key Hill staff persons worked hand and glove with CEC from as early as 1972 to final enactment. Themselves deeply committed, they included Lisa Walker, Martin LaVor, and Jack Duncan. We were able to develop their trust because, in my opinion, they knew that we at CEC were professional educators and advocates for children at the same time; and they knew that we would be open, frank, and honest—even when the message was not what they wanted to hear regarding a particular fact, opinion, or proposal. The story of their true grit still needs telling.

Q: And Ford's administration was fine with it?

A: It was, to say the least, a reluctant embrace. Though Gerald Ford signed Public Law No. 94-142 into law, we like to say he accompanied his signature with a veto message.

Q: How did Ford convey this message?

A: With a separate statement sent along with the signed legislation. Though he did not veto the bill, he stated the legislation was a false promise, especially with respect to funding.

Q: Why do you think he signed it? Was there enough support and pressure?

A: We like to think so. For instance, CEC had created in 1973–1974 its own political action network, made up of members from its state federations and professional divisions, now known as the CEC Children's Action Network. By sheer luck or calculation—I can't remember—the network was meeting at headquarters at the very time the legislation was awaiting presidential action at the White House. So members of the network were on every phone that could be found in the five-story CEC headquarters. They were deluging the White House with calls on behalf of their particular states and localities and generating further calls from colleagues and parents back home.

Q: They took it seriously enough and felt the numbers were great enough. Do you think he would have signed it without that?

A: My guess is probably. Along with a growing community of support for the bill in the nation, the legislation enjoyed heavy support at final passage in the House and Senate. Very few voted against the final House–Senate conference agreement. By the way, only about ten in the House of Representatives voted against final passage, which leads me to say something to you, you Virginian. Four of that group voting against final passage represented contiguous congressional districts in southwestern Virginia.

Q: Did they not want federal involvement?

A: You are on target. "Don't tread on me." The legacy of old Virginia.

Q: Hasn't changed a whole lot today. They still don't like the federal government.

A: Yes, especially when observing that Senator Strom Thurman of South Carolina, a legendary states-rights man, voted for final passage. He wasn't going to be caught out. By the way, even if your ideology argues against a bill, sometimes simply the title of the bill causes you to take pause. Call it the power of words. "Am I going to vote against legislation entitled 'The Education for All Handicapped Children Act of 1975'?"

Q: And was that very intentional on your part?

A: No, not really. The title was chosen simply because it stated the precise purpose of the legislation. But the title may have been helpful for this additional reason, as well. The Lord provides in mysterious ways.

Q: When you look back nearly 30 years from its original passage, is it overwhelming? Did you know how all-encompassing this would be? And if you were to look back and then look to where you are now, to think that you were one of the key people in the engineering of this, is it overwhelming to think of your impact?

A: Well, I think in the first moments, when we realized that the President had in fact signed it, we were in a suspended state of both shock and relief. In the next moments, I distinctly recall thinking to myself, "This is the most important thing I will do in my life." Though now having nearly doubled my years from the ripe old age of 33 at that time, I still believe it was "the most important thing." And then a few moments later I thought, "Life does not get any better than this. They will never get rid of our children now."

Q: What did you intend for this legislation to do?

A: In the most compact statement of purpose, to guarantee a free appropriate public education for children with disabilities in the least restrictive educational environment commensurate with the educational needs of the individual child, accompanied by a due process mechanism for family redress of grievance. Most of us can do that statement in our sleep, and probably frequently do. And what is the heartbeat of the IDEA toward the achievement of that purpose? The written individualized education program (IEP) for each child. For early-twentieth-century political conservatives, the ultimate nightmare of unprecedented federal intervention in education had arrived with the requirement of an IEP for every child.

Q: So you didn't push for that?

A: Quite the contrary.

Q: You did push for the IEP?

A: Yes, absolutely, from the very beginning. Since the IEP would be the essential mechanism for providing what is *appropriate* for each child, we pushed the IEP as the critical mass of the legislation. Incidentally, many people wanted to call it a *plan*. We insisted, and do to this day, and the legislation says it: The IEP is not a *plan*; it is a *program*. We wanted to signal that the days of engaging in long-range state and local planning for some as yet unrealized educational future for these children was over. Kaput. The individualized education *program* must be implemented now for each child.

Q: My question is, now that we are approaching another reauthorization—I guess the sixth—what would you say looking back are the most unintended outcomes?

A: Despite all the many achievements for children and families realized through the IDEA, we certainly did not intend that the IEP should become in many places such a complex and bureaucratic process. We need to return to a more fundamental concept of the IEP as originally intended in the IDEA of 1975. To wit, the parents, the teachers, someone who speaks for school authority, and, where appropriate, the child will meet to develop and implement an IEP for the child. The parents and the hands-on teachers and other providers were and are intended to be placed at the pinnacle of the educational pyramid. Everyone else in the educational system was intended to follow the lead of this core, instructionally based grouping.

It was not intended that every word uttered would have to be placed in notes, that special education teachers and others would have such a burden of plain old paperwork, that everyone would be looking over their shoulder about what they might be faced with, that so many bells and whistles of legal accountability would encircle providers to the point of becoming fear-producing. The underlying problem, unseen at the enactment of Public Law No. 94-142, is that American society in the last quarter of the twentieth century had become enslaved by its own penchant for litigation. This development under the IDEA, in my opinion, simply reflects the litigious mania of our larger society. I know many will say, "Get over it, Ballard. Times have changed." Well, I refuse to get over it. Let's journey to a more gentle climate.

Q: The due process was there just to protect the kids from unilateral removal from school, to make sure they had a process through which they could be protected and heard, and look at what was going on.

A: Right. But disagreements would be resolved in a reasonable manner by persons who had the background to make informed educational judgments. Due process was not intended to be confrontational as it is all too often now, nor so highly legalized, nor populated by lawyers throughout educational process and administrative due process. Hearings were not intended to evolve into administrative law courts. In fact, at the time of enactment of the IDEA, judges were encouraging us to get these cases out of the courts and into nonjudicial resolution settings. And the original procedural safeguard mechanisms of the IDEA were designed to do that.

Q: So you did not envision IEP meetings with multiple lawyers at the table?

A: We did not envision any attorneys at the table. Never.

Q: So you put into place something where educators and families could work through problems together and keep it out of the courts?

A: That is exactly right. Courts were acknowledged in the law as an unfortunate last resort, though clearly a necessary ultimate option for parents. I would add, though, that we are gradually making our way back to that more gentle climate with, for instance, the inclusion of authority for voluntary mediation in the 1997 IDEA amendments and with discussion of voluntary arbitration and other approaches in the current reauthorization.

Q: Please provide some insight into the passage of the 1997 amendments.

A: Two political realities affected that reauthorization. First, in 1995, we found ourselves with the largest cohort of new members of Congress since the post-Watergate election, which required a comprehensive education on the IDEA for these freshmen. Second, the Republicans captured both the House and the Senate for the first time since the early years of the Eisenhower administration, which meant new elected and staff committee leadership to get to know on a very large scale. Both of these factors contributed to an unusually long and protracted reauthorization. Also, something unprecedented occurred. Since the House reported from subcommittee a perfectly ghastly bill, and since there commenced a universal howl of protest from virtually all of us stakeholders, the House leadership ordered us to gather together and produce our own bill. So we sat across from each other for an intensive two weeks and hammered out an alternative, *we* being general education groups, special education interests, parent groups, other advocacy groups, and lawyer interests.

A majority of the most important provisions that we agreed to among ourselves are reflected in the 1997 IDEA amendments. Our only major issue of disagreement centered around discipline in the schools, with CEC and other groups adamantly opposed to the expelling of students for any discipline infractions, that is, no alternative program whatsoever. Begone, kid! Congress ultimately embraced our demand for no cessation of services. Major refinements in the 1997 amendments include strengthening of the relation to the general curriculum, an overhaul of the evaluation and reevaluation provisions, critical stipulations regarding state- and districtwide tests, and the inclusion of controversial, but vital requirements in the domain of behavior and discipline.

Q: If, in the current authorization, the Congress goes with the three-year IEP, it will be interesting to see what safeguards or requirements they put in place.

A: It will, indeed. Both the House and the Senate are moving out on some form of the three-year IEP, though the Senate is being much more cautious. Caution is in order. Currently I understand that the parent groups are adamantly opposed. CEC has recommended a pilot only in specific locations in the country. Should it be simply a parent option, which they can accept or reject? That is my inclination. Simplification of IEP requirements is an underlying goal here, with an attendant reduction in unnecessary procedural paperwork. Interestingly, in the 1997 reauthorization, the Congress would not listen to us, or the administration, on the paperwork issue. At last, they see that this burden is driving people out of the profession of special education teacher. But in addressing this issue, a bit of advice from the ancient Romans: "Hurry. But slowly."

Another of my larger concerns in this reauthorization is what No Child Left Behind (NCLB) has done to us by making academics the overwhelming measure in determining student proficiency. Granted the goal of appropriate cross-fertilization of the IDEA and NCLB, but not at the risk of burying attention to the comprehensive educational needs of the child.

Q: But that is what you see as the biggest issue with No Child Left Behind impacting special education. Ignoring the whole child?

A: Yes, though not my only concern with NCLB. Leaders in the school reform movement need to be periodically reminded that the special education student cohort is composed not just of children with moderate learning and behavior issues. The population includes a large cluster of very involved children with very severe challenges, as you well know. In some of the draft language circulating in the current reauthorization, one observes the phasing out of the word *developmental*. Further, the word *academic* takes center stage in the IEP provisions. Academic achievement is vital, but it is not and never will be the sole objective of education. While attending to academic proficiency in the IEP, we must never let slip away the statutory language focused on the "other educational needs of the child."

In that it provides a strong commitment to high-stakes educational achievement for students with disabilities, NCLB is laudatory overall. However, another major policy feature must be further addressed conceptually. The IDEA is about the achievement of each child on an individual basis, whereas NCLB focuses on the achievement of groups of children, including that group receiving the support of special education. Problematic consequences are thus developing that must be worked through so that the desired intersection of the two laws does not become a train wreck.

Q: Why, in a nutshell, is advocacy so important for organizations like CEC and ARC and from a rights standpoint for children with disabilities?

A: Because, in our case, national policy had to be instigated—and then protected and nurtured—by a grassroots movement of the citizenry. Otherwise, children with disabilities would be languishing, and too often hidden, to this day. Further, political reality for the Congress gets down to some very basic arithmetic. How many children are designated for special education today? Let's say approximately 8 million. If you have 8 million children, you have 16 million parents. Then you have four grandparents apiece. And then you have the further millions of friends of these families. Ultimately, in this country, numbers count because politicians have to win elections. Now we might have wanted Congress to enact and now maintain the IDEA out of the goodness of their collective hearts and minds. But given the multitude of national priorities and the endless struggles in the carving up of the fiscal pie, let us be realistic. Grassroots advocacy must be created, and it must be sustained on a permanent basis.

Q: The one thing I have never understood about special education is that it is known to have a very powerful interest base group. What I have seen is that there is a correlation between children with disabilities and low socioeconomic status parents. When you look at gifted children, they do not have a big advocacy group. They do not receive a whole lot of services in my school. Most of my gifted parents, though, are very affluent, very involved, and very educated. So where does this large advocacy group get its power? Who are these people?

A: Very perceptive base for that question. Yes, there is a known correlation between disability and economic disadvantage. But at the same time, our children are present in all strata of our society. They cut across all economic, social, geographical, and educational strata. You will find them in the affluent mansions of Pacific Palisades in California, in the farming towns of Iowa, and in the most distressed sections of the Bronx. It constitutes a sort of national biological equalization. I found, time and again, that we could find parents to talk with a member of Congress from that member's district, whether a rich or poorer district. Also, bear in mind that those parents with the greater education and greater resources will, in effect, also be speaking for the children and families with the least education and resources.

CEC also advocates for gifted children, but a separate interview with you would be required to address the limited success we have realized at the national level for these children. That is my one great disappointment.

Q: When we look at the history of African Americans in this country, we see that they went through years of slavery, oppression, all the way through the first half of the twentieth century. And then all of a sudden, one group was able to have profound influence. I'm wondering, was CEC able to, in a similar vein with some of these other groups, empower and all of a sudden have a great deal of influence?

A: A wonderful question, about which a book could be written. There are threads that tie our movements together, whether it be African-American civil rights, women's rights, or disability rights. Look, two world wars, only 20 years apart, with the Great Depression to live with in between, changed the fabric of America. Like never before, we found that we are all in the soup together and that we had to take care of each other. The era of rugged individualism was dead and buried.

But these movements still take time. And they require the right people taking action at the right time and in the right circumstance and the right band of brothers and sisters, willing to maintain a life-long passion toward the achievement of a clearly defined objective. What better objective is there than the educational well-being of a very vulnerable group of children? You must accompany all of this with good timing and thorough strategic and tactical planning. Beyond that, advocacy is simply grinding work— to borrow from Thomas Edison or whomever, 99 percent perspiration and 1 percent inspiration.

Q: As far as the future goes in the reauthorization, from what you have seen and what you hope, what would you like to see with the reauthorization? At the same time, what do you think the future holds for special education and what direction do we need to move toward for children?

A: For one matter, time must be allowed for major policy from the previous reauthorization to be internalized, to gel. For example, an important step was taken in the 1997 amendments to strengthen progress in the general curriculum. Thus, we had addressed serious implications for greater involvement of general education teachers and overall educational administration at the school level. We are barely into meaningful implementation of such directions as this, and it is time for another reauthorization. That has always been a problem, and I have always felt that, short a crisis, we need a longer time span between reauthorizations. It reminds me of the U.S. presidency; we have barely sworn in one President before we are busily deciding on the next President.

In any event, we are now into our first reauthorization for the twenty-first century. It seems to me that one area we need to address is undue designation for special education, which requires systems and resources for the delivery of early intervening services for children prior to formal referral for special education. In that same terrain, we must continue the struggle to end the failure syndrome—that is, no interventions until demonstrable learning failures around the third and fourth grades. Also in the same terrain, we must candidly grapple with issues surrounding learning disability, including earlier detection and alternatives to the discrepancy formula. Scientific advances should help.

In this reauthorization, I think we must also continue work on the accountability nightmares, which I mentioned previously, as well as de-bureaucratization of special education process. Also, accommodations, modifications, and decision making with respect to state-level and districtwide testing should be revisited. The other side of me says leave all of the preceding alone for a few more years and allow overwhelmed families and exhausted professionals to catch their breath and exercise their common sense.

May I add that no issue should command our attention more throughout the twenty-first century than the changing ethnic and cultural tapestry of America? This will be a better nation because of this ever more colorful tapestry, I have no doubt. But unless we are vigilant, aggressive, and creative in our approaches to teaching and learning, we will find ourselves with a whole new population of vulnerable children, both with and without disabilities.

Q: Do you see the federal government taking a serious role in funding for the states and localities, and what that would take?

A: I don't know if it is going to reach the levels of that famous Title I–borrowed authorization formula, which I previously cited. But finally, in the last ten years, we are making notable progress in funding.

Q: I have never understood the discrepancy.

A: For the first 15 years of the IDEA, we had modest, but respectable increases in the level of funding. But the appropriations committees of the Congress always knew they were essentially off the hook since the combination of Public Law No. 94-142 and Section 504 mandated that education be provided even if Congress offered not even a dime of support.

Q: What changed?

A: The original commitment under Public Law No. 94-142 was that the federal government would pay the excess cost of special education, that higher cost for special education programming beyond the average cost for each student in our schools. Bear with me. Proposition: For some 15 to 20 years, the federal government has not met its part of the bargain, so the states and localities have had to make up the difference, most often through local property taxes designated for local school finance. So let's inaugurate local tax relief under the IDEA. Members of Congress could push for dramatic increases in funding for the IDEA and declare, by so doing, that they were providing significant local tax relief. We initiated this policy in the 1997 IDEA amendments. This supplanting provision will almost certainly be further enhanced in the latest reauthorization.

Further, by the late 1980s, we were embroiled in a serious national backlash on the costs of special education and the alleged manner in which that cost was a drain on local school budgets. As evidence, *60 Minutes* did a piece hosted by Leslie Stahl that opened with a child being transported at public school expense each day by private jet to his special education program site. This and other rumblings focused the minds of advocacy groups more seriously on the money issue, about which they had been previously rather cavalier. They joined up more vigorously with CEC and the other education associations to promote increased funding. Thus, dramatic funding increases over the last eight to ten years. Did I answer you?

Q: Oh, you did, indeed. Do you have a closing comment?

A: Yes, Kurt, I do. And permit me to compliment you on the quality of your questions. The IDEA, like any landmark legislation, can be viewed both positively and negatively. In the negative, it can be treated as an annoying headache and something to simply get around, manipulate, sidestep. In the positive, it can be used as a set of legal tools, weapons, to be used by families and professionals to enhance, in this case, the growth and well-being of a cohort of precious infants, children, and youth. Attitude is everything. I love to quote the observation of one of the former members of the U.S. Supreme Court whom I most admire, Justice Benjamin Cardozo: "The law never *is*. The law is always *about to be*."

1

The Basics of the Law

Facts at a GLANCE

- The U.S. Constitution separates the federal government into three distinct branches: the legislative, executive, and judicial branches.
- The United States has four basic types of law: constitutional, statutory, regulatory, and case law.
- Drafted in 1787 and put into effect in 1789 after nine states had ratified it, the U.S. Constitution comprises the Preamble, 7 articles, and 27 amendments.
- The first ten amendments to the Constitution are known as the Bill of Rights.
- Education is never specifically mentioned in the U.S. Constitution.
- Article 1, Section 8 and the Tenth and Fourteenth Amendments to the U.S. Constitution provide the constitutional basis for federal involvement in American education and the rights of students with disabilities.
- Once a state undertakes the responsibility of educating children, that education becomes a property right.
- Statutory law consists of the enactments of legislative bodies.
- The U.S. Department of Education is responsible for developing specific regulations for the practical implementation of special education legislation.
- Case law is the cumulative body of decisions handed down by the judicial system. Courts interpret the laws enacted by legislative bodies.

The United States is governed by federal, state, and local governments. The U.S. Constitution separates the federal government into three distinct branches: the legislative, executive, and judicial branches (see Figure 1.1). The Founding Fathers developed this system, referred to as *separation of powers*, to ensure the presence of checks and balances that would limit any component of government from wielding too much power. The process they designed would stand the test of time, allow for changes, empower the people, and provide the protection necessary for all individuals to live and thrive in a free and democratic federal republic.

In its purest form, the legal system that guides and protects the citizens of the United States of America is a straightforward, simple, and solid process. In a

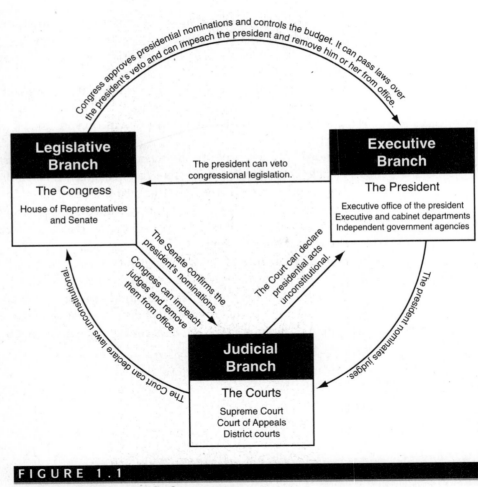

FIGURE 1.1

The Branches of the U.S. Government

nutshell, the American legal system consists of 1 federal legal system and 50 separate state legal systems. Hudgins and Vacca (1999) note:

> Law may be defined as a body of principles, standards, and rules that govern human behavior by creating obligations as well as rights, and by imposing penalties. Different from equity (e.g., the system of justice and fairness intended to supplement and complement the legal relief granted by courts of law), law in our nation is made up of constitutional provisions, legislative enactments, court precedents, lawyers' opinions, and evolving customs. (p. 2)

In reality, the American legal system seems to consist of big, confusing words; lengthy, meandering processes; an enormous, intricate court system; multiple sources of law; and lawyers and politicians who do not make the system any easier to navigate or understand. For most nonlawyers, including educators, the terms *law* and *legal aspects* generally tend to engender a middle to high level of anxiety. As Morris (1989) notes, "The legal systems of the United States baffle most foreign visitors. And not a few American citizens stand in awe of them. There is such a multiplicity of courts, laws and jurisdictions that even the perceptive nonprofessional observer can become lost in the legal maze" (p. 4.). The law seems very complex, confusing, tricky, and convoluted to the layperson.

Adding to the complexity is the fact that the United States has four basic types of law: constitutional, statutory, regulatory, and case law. However, this text will make the legal system more understandable by demonstrating and explaining how the four types of law interact and regulate behavior at the federal, state, and local levels. To begin, this chapter will explain the basic tenets of the American legal system. In order to understand the symbiotic relationships among special education advocacy, legislation, reauthorizations, and resulting litigation, one must have a firm understanding of the basic legal process.

CONSTITUTIONAL LAW

The Constitution of the United States of America is the single most important document in American law. Drafted in 1787 and put into effect in 1789 after nine states had ratified it, the U.S. Constitution comprises the Preamble, 7 articles, and 27 amendments. It is a tremendous testimony to the strength of the document that it has been amended only 27 times in over two hundred years.

The Preamble serves as a road map of sorts, providing the basic contents and purpose of the document.

> WE THE PEOPLE of the United States, in Order to form a more perfect Union, establish Justice, insure domestic Tranquility, provide for the common defense, promote the general Welfare, and secure the Blessings of Liberty to ourselves and our Posterity, do ordain and establish this CONSTITUTION for the United States of America.

The first ten amendments to the Constitution are known as the Bill of Rights. At the time the Constitution was drafted, several anti-Federalists refused to sign it unless it guaranteed specific rights for individuals. Fallon (1996) suggests: "The addition of the Bill of Rights to the Constitution is perhaps the most significant event in American government history, since it was the reason that opponents to the Constitution agreed to ratify the Constitution in the first place" (p. 17). The Bill of Rights guarantees individual rights, which were of great concern at the end of the eighteenth century.

The Constitution is intended to be the broad basis from which all other law is derived. The Founding Fathers understood that change would be needed and inevitable; however, they wanted to ensure that certain timeless principles would endure. Although other sources of law exist in the United States, no single statute, regulation, or case can violate the Constitution. The Constitution, as ultimately interpreted by the U.S. Supreme Court, is the supreme law of the land.

Although education has been increasingly heralded as one of the most important factors in the development and continued prosperity of the United States, nowhere in the Constitution is education mentioned. Three components of the Constitution have been identified to justify federal statutes covering education and to provide direction to states in regard to actual educational authority—as well as to guarantee equal protection for all individuals under the law. It is critical for students of education law to be aware of the three constitutional components that affect American education.

First, Article 1, Section 8 states: "The Congress shall have Power To lay and collect Taxes, Duties, Imposts and Excises, to pay the Debts and provide for the common Defence and general Welfare of the United States. . . ." *General welfare* is a broad term that provides for the involvement of the federal government in passing federal legislation such as the No Child Left Behind Act (NCLB), the Individuals with Disabilities Education Act (IDEA), and Section 504 of the Rehabilitation Act of 1973. The IDEA and Section 504 are the two federal statutes that most affect special education law. Both statutes will be discussed in detail throughout this text. Federal statutes have provided billions of dollars of financial support to state and local education agencies. Many states and localities, however, have argued that certain legislation—the IDEA, for example—has imposed a fiscal burden greater than the support it provides. The IDEA is often referred to as an unfunded mandate, since Congress has never funded more than approximately 17.8 percent of the cost of its implementation.

Second, the Tenth Amendment states: "The powers not delegated to the United States by the Constitution, nor prohibited by it to the States, are reserved to the States respectively, or to the people." Since the Constitution does not identify education as a federal responsibility, nor does it deny it to the states, each state has taken responsibility for educating children through its state constitution. Education has generally been considered a state responsibility, and most states have taken a great deal of ownership and developed a sense of autonomy. Increased federal involvement in education (e.g., through NCLB, with its prescriptive provisions and national accountability measures) has created consternation over the federal government's role in education. Nonetheless, since education is not denied to the states, it is considered a state responsibility.

Third, the Fourteenth Amendment, Section 1 states: "No State shall make or enforce any law which shall abridge the privileges or immunities of citizens of the United States; nor shall any State deprive any person of life, liberty, or property, without due process of law; nor deny to any person within its jurisdiction the equal protection of the laws." This Amendment is possibly the most important for special education rights and laws.

Due process of law and equal protection of the laws are the basis for many critical precedents set through case law—*Brown v. Board of Education* (1954), *Tinker v. Des Moines Independent Community School District* (1969), *Mills v. Board of Education of the District of Columbia* (1972), *Pennsylvania Association for Retarded Citizens v. Pennsylvania* (1972), and *Goss v. Lopez* (1975)—as well as through resulting legislation such as the IDEA, which provides procedural and substantive due process measures. Once a state undertakes the responsibility of educating children, that education becomes a property right. "Today, education is perhaps the most important function of state and local governments. . . . Such an opportunity, where the State has undertaken to provide it, is a right which must be made available to all on equal terms" (Hudgins & Vacca, 1999, p. 18). Therefore, education cannot be taken away without due process. As well, based on this Amendment, no child can be denied access to education based on any unalterable characteristic. Thus, Article 1, Section 8 and the Tenth and Fourteenth Amendments provide the constitutional basis for federal involvement in American education and the rights of students with disabilities.

STATUTORY LAW

Statutory law includes those policies created by legislative bodies. Laws passed by Congress and state legislatures are considered statutes. Hudgins and Vacca (1999) contend: "A statute refers to a legislative law; it is derived from the action of a legislature. It may refer to a state or a federal law" (p. 27). The IDEA and Section 504 of the Rehabilitation Act of 1973 are examples of federal statutes. Statutes can also be written by cities and counties, but are called ordinances.

Federal statutes are referred to as public laws. When a law is enacted, it is provided a number. For instance, in 1975 Congress passed and President Ford signed into law the Education for All Handicapped Children Act of 1975 (renamed the IDEA in 1990). That law was assigned the legislative number Public Law No. 94-142 (abbreviated Pub. L. No.; see Figure 1.2). The number 94 refers to the 94th Congress, and 142 means it was the 142nd piece of legislation to be enacted during that session.

Statutes are found in the United States Code (U.S.C.). It consists of 50 titles that are further organized by chapters and sections. (Note that the United States Code title and section numbers are included in legal citations, but the chapter

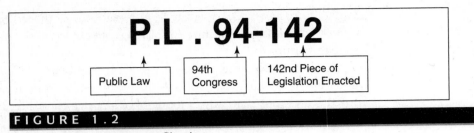

FIGURE 1.2

Understanding Statutory Citations

numbers are not.) The IDEA, along with other education-related statutes, appears in Title 20. Citations are primary law sources which indicate where laws are located. The IDEA legal citation 20 U.S.C. § 1400 indicates the statutory provision located at Section 1400 (the symbol § represents section) in Title 20 of the United States Code (Figure 1.3). The U.S. Government Printing Office (GPO) publishes the United States Code every six years. When additions or changes are made to statutes during the six-year period, the GPO publishes supplements. A time gap might exist between enactment and actual codification of the statute. During this time period, the reader should refer to the actual statute signed by the president. See Figure 1.4 showing the steps followed to create a statute.

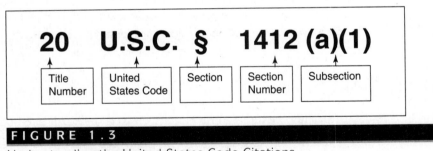

FIGURE 1.3

Understanding the United States Code Citations

REGULATORY LAW

Administrative agencies—which are part of the executive branch—create regulatory law. Once a statute is passed by Congress and signed by the president, the appropriate agency assumes responsibility for developing federal regulations for the practical implementation of the statute's provisions. Since members of Congress cannot feasibly specialize in all areas covered by a statute, they typically pass broad statutes that require specific detail for state and local implementation. The appropriate executive agency then develops regulations to further develop the specifics of the statute.

FIGURE 1.4

The Creation of a Statute

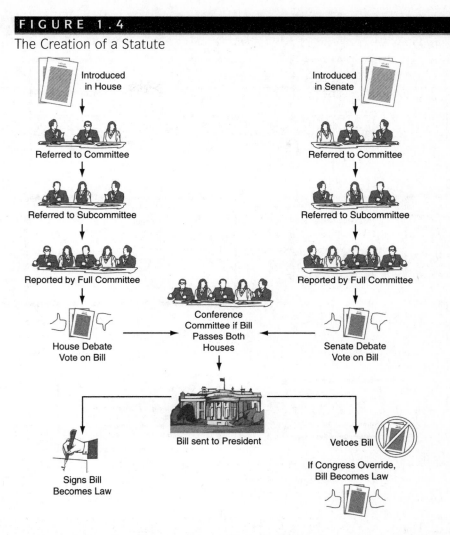

As noted earlier, in regard to special education, for example, Congress created Public Law No. 94-142, the Education for All Handicapped Children Act of 1975. After the legislation was signed by President Ford, the responsibility for developing its regulations was delegated to the Bureau of Education for the Handicapped (BEH) within the former U.S. Department of Health, Education, and Welfare (HEW). (See Figure 1.5.) Today the development of such regulations is the responsibility of the U.S. Department of Education.

Once these regulations are established, they are referred to as administrative or regulatory law. The regulations are sent to the states once they are complete. The amount of time that an agency needs to complete regulations varies considerably. Section 504 of the Rehabilitation Act of 1973 did not have regulations until 1977, whereas the regulations for the Education for All Handicapped Children Act of 1975, which was passed two years later, were completed in the same year, 1977.

FIGURE 1.5

The Implementation of PL94–142

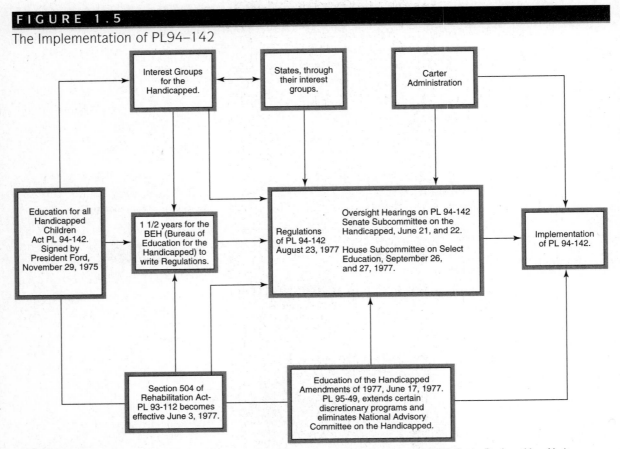

Source: Levin, E and Wexler, M. (1981). *PL94–142: An Act of congress.* Prentice Hall Prof. Tech. Review, New York.

CASE LAW

The first example of common law can be traced back to the Battle of Hastings in 1066. It is often referred to as "judge-made law" or case law. This form of law is critical because it interprets statutory law and often serves as an impetus to the passage of new or refined statutory law.

When the meaning of a statute is contested, it is the obligation of the courts to determine the intent of Congress or other legislative body. For instance, the U.S. Supreme Court interpreted Public Law No. 94-142 (statutory law) through the *Board of Education of Hendrick Hudson Central School District v. Rowley* case in 1982. Specifically, the Court interpreted the term "appropriate" in regard to a free and appropriate public education (FAPE) and related services. FAPE is a substantive right under the IDEA and one of the most important components of the law. This principle ensures that all children with disabilities are provided an education designed to meet their individual educational needs at no extra cost to the family. By interpreting this statute, the Court set a precedent for the rest of the United States in relation to this substantive component of the IDEA. Until the Court rendered the decision, localities had a great deal of discretion in the interpretation and implementation of FAPE.

Multiple courts in multiple situations might interpret a single statute. For example, given the all-encompassing nature of the IDEA, with both substantive rights and procedural safeguards, courts in many localities have interpreted the intent of Congress in very different ways.

Not all precedents set by courts, however, apply to all states and localities. For instance, a precedent set by a local district court will apply only to that district; the decision of a state court will apply only to that state; a federal circuit court of appeals decision will apply only to the states in that circuit. Once a case reaches the U.S. Supreme Court and a decision is rendered, the precedent applies to every state in the United States. For example, the mandate of education in the least restrictive environment (LRE), another substantive component of the IDEA, has never been considered by the U.S. Supreme Court. However, it has been considered by a number of the 13 federal circuit courts of appeals (Figure 1.6). The Court

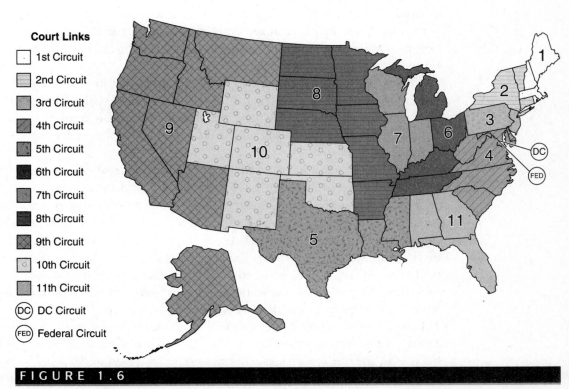

FIGURE 1.6

The United States 13 Circuit Courts of Appeals Map

of Appeals for the Fourth Circuit has established a three-part test for determining the LRE of a child with a disability. This test, however, applies only to the five states in the court's jurisdiction—Maryland, North Carolina, South Carolina, Virginia, and West Virginia. The Third and Eleventh Circuits utilize a different test—the *Daniel* two-part test (see Chapter 8) to determine LRE.

Understanding the legal system and which court decisions apply is integral to implementing special education law and regulations appropriately. The multiple levels of the judicial system can make understanding and applying precedents difficult. It is essential that every special educator have knowledge of how the major principles of the IDEA and related special education legislation have been interpreted and whether these interpretations apply to their locality or state.

SUMMARY

The Constitution of the United States is the supreme law of the land. All laws created by Congress must be in compliance with the Constitution. Although the Constitution does not specifically take ownership of education, nor does it deny ownership to the states, an interesting federal role in American education has evolved. Traditionally providing support for disadvantaged children, children with disabilities, and specialized areas of education, the federal government has begun to take more of a national governance or umbrella approach with the No Child Left Behind Act.

The three components of the U.S. Constitution that most directly affect education are Article 1, Section 8 and the Tenth and the Fourteenth Amendments. Essentially, these components give the responsibility of education to the states, ensure due process of law, and mandate equal protection under the law for all individuals.

There are four major forms of law in the American legal system: constitutional, statutory, regulatory, and case law. It is critical for students of special education to understand the interrelationships that exist among the different types of law. It is equally important to comprehend the cyclical nature of the law. The periodic reauthorization process (see Chapter 3) encompasses every component of law and involves the forces (e.g., advocacy and politics) that contribute to the continuous refinement of law. It is essential to understand each type of law in isolation; however, all of the components operate together and affect one another in the development, implementation, interpretation, and reauthorization of special education law. Therefore, the component most essential to understanding special education law is a grasp of the cyclical process as a whole. Only when the student is able to understand what the role of each spoke of the wheel is, and then see how the entire wheel rolls as a function of each spoke, will he or she have a comprehensive understanding of special education law.

CRITICAL THINKING QUESTIONS

1. Why might the Founding Fathers not have included education in the Constitution?
2. Did the Founding Fathers intend for education to be only a state responsibility? Discuss the current status of federal involvement in education and the intent of the Founding Fathers.
3. Why is it necessary for Congress to pass broad statutes that need more prescriptive information and measures prior to implementation?
4. Since the Constitution does not explicitly assume responsibility for education and the Tenth Amendment provides the states with the authority to undertake the responsibility of education, does a possible conflict exist between state and federal authority in relation to special education law?
5. Is a statute to be strengthened? How does advocacy play into the process of reauthorizing the IDEA?
6. Draw a diagram depicting how the four types of law in the United States interact to create and interpret special education law.

REFERENCES

Board of Education of Hendrick Hudson Central School District v. Rowley, 458 U.S. 176 (1982).

Brown v. Board of Education, 347 U.S. 483 (1954).

Fallon, S. L. (1996). *The Bill of Rights: What it is, what it means, and how it's been misused.* Irvine, CA: Dickens Press.

Goss v. Lopez, 419 U.S. 565 (1975).

Hudgins, H. C., & Vacca, R. (1999). *Law and education: Contemporary issues and court decisions.* New York: Matthew Bender. Levine, E. L., & Wexler, E. M. (1981). *PL 94-142: An act of Congress.* New York: Macmillan.

Mills v. Board of Education of the District of Columbia, 348 F. Supp. 866 (D.D.C. 1972).

Morris, A. A. (1989). *The Constitution and American education.* Durham, NC: Carolina Academic Press.

Pennsylvania Association for Retarded Citizens v. Pennsylvania, 334 F. Supp. 1257 (E.D. Pa. 1971), 343 F. Supp. 279 (E.D. 1972).

Tinker v. Des Moines Independent Community School District, 393 U.S. 503 (1969).

Yell, M. L. (1998). *The law and special education.* Upper Saddle River, NJ: Merrill/ Prentice Hall.

2

History and Advocacy

- The field of special education is rooted in the work of physicians—not professional educators.
- Jean-Marc-Gaspard Itard is credited with the first notable, recorded attempt (in the early nineteenth century) to educate a child with severe limitations in a structured manner.
- Edouard Seguin continued Itard's work with children with mental challenges into the latter half of the nineteenth century.
- Itard's and Seguin's ideas and practices are integral components of current special education practices.
- "The 13th Amendment abolished 'slavery' and 'involuntary servitude.' The 14th Amendment guaranteed the right to 'life,' 'liberty,' and 'property.' In addition, it guarantees all persons the equal protection of the laws. The 15th Amendment guaranteed all American citizens the right to vote no matter what their 'race, color, or previous condition of servitude." (Loevy, 1997, p. 3).
- In order to subvert and undermine the Civil War Amendments, Southern state legislatures began passing Black Codes in 1865.
- The Congress responded quickly by passing the Civil Rights Act of 1866, which made it illegal to discriminate against individuals on the basis of prior servitude, race, or color.
- The *Civil Rights Cases* (1883) delivered a crippling blow to the rights established and the progress made during and immediately following the Civil War.
- In the case of *Plessy v. Ferguson* (1896), the Supreme Court declared it was legal to segregate individuals and have separate facilities so long as they are equal.
- Advocates of special education point to the *Brown v. Board of Education* (1954) decision as the springboard for litigation and legislation that provided

12

individuals with disabilities equal access to a free and appropriate public education.

■ Two major organizations stand out as pioneers in the advocacy for children with disabilities: the Council for Exceptional Children (CEC) and National Association for Retarded Citizens (now simply referred to as ARC).

■ "*Mills* and *PARC* provided a legal basis for numerous challenges to state and local policies denying equal educational opportunity for handicapped persons" (Goldberg, 1982, p. 3).

■ On November 29, 1975, the advocates for students with disabilities celebrated the greatest triumph in the history of special education advocacy. On this date, President Ford signed Public Law No. 94-142—The Education for All Handicapped Children Act—into law.

Prior to the study of any academic discipline or topic, it is incumbent upon the student to seek a thorough knowledge and understanding of the events that contributed to the development of the specific discipline or topic. Students at every level of the educational process often ask, "Why is history important? Why is it relevant?" Great questions. There are several good, multitiered answers to these questions. It is arguable that a knowledge of history is more critical in certain content areas than in others. As well, a knowledge of history helps to prevent us from repeating mistakes, which is most critical in special education.

In relation to special education law, knowledge of the historical events, factors, and variables is critical to understanding the current status, iterative nature, and future of special education law. "We cannot understand today's difficulties very well if we assume they emerge from present circumstances alone. Although knowledge of history is no guarantee that we will not repeat our mistakes, ignorance of history virtually ensures that we will make no real progress" (Kauffman & Smucker, 1995). Without a basic understanding of the history of special education, it is nearly impossible to fully comprehend and appreciate current trends, political issues, legislation, litigation, and pending reauthorizations.

Understanding the history of special education and the current laws that apply is analogous to understanding the relationships among the history of slavery, the Civil Rights movement, the current status of affirmative action, and current issues relating to race and the American culture. Konnert and Augestein (1995) note that history is an ongoing and continuous dialogue that connects the present and the past. Without knowledge of history, one is unable to fully understand why laws, policies, issues, and practices have been created regarding race and discrimination. Furthermore, as noted above, knowledge of the past enables individuals and organizations to keep from repeating mistakes along the road of history.

THE BIRTH OF A FIELD

The beginnings of special education can be traced back to the eighteenth century. The field is rooted in the work of physicians—not professional educators. Although the United States has made the greatest strides in nearly every facet of educating children with disabilities since the latter half of the twentieth century, it was the work of non-Americans that initiated the humane treatment and education of children with disabilities. Several European scientists engaged in the observation and study of deviant behavior and gross abnormalities. These individuals broke from the traditional thought and practices of the era and attempted to educate children who were considered uneducable. As Kanner (1964) contends, these European physicians questioned the practices of their contemporaries and colleagues through their revolutionary ideas and practices.

The first notable, recorded attempt to educate a child with severe limitations in a structured manner occurred in the early nineteenth century. A French physician, Jean-Marc-Gaspard Itard, known for his work with deaf children, discovered a child in his preteens who had been living without clothing, shelter, or a family in the forests of France. This child—named Victor, but known throughout history as "The Wild Boy of Aveyron"—was taken under the wing of Dr. Itard and became his personal and professional project (Humphrey, 1962; French, 2000). Through consistent support, behavior management, and education, Dr. Itard was able to improve measurably Victor's abnormal and antisocial behavior. His work resulted in the first account of someone using education and behavioral modifications to alter the behavior of a child with a disability. Several physicians followed in Itard's footsteps, working with children with mental challenges. His protégé, Edouard Seguin, continued Itard's work with children with mental challenges into the latter half of the nineteenth century. The work of these physicians who deviated so greatly from the norm provided the foundation for current special education legislation and practices. According to Hallahan and Kauffman (1997), the following ideas and practices drawn from Itard's and Seguin's work have become integral components of current special education practices:

- *individualized instruction*, in which the child's characteristics, rather than prescribed academic content, provide the basis for teaching techniques;
- *a carefully sequenced series of educational tasks*, beginning with tasks the child can perform and gradually leading to more complex learning;
- *an emphasis on stimulating* and awakening the child's senses, the aim being to make the child more aware of and responsive to educational stimuli;
- *meticulous arrangement of the child's environment* so that the structure of the environment and the child's experience of it lead naturally to learning;
- *immediate reward for correct performance*, providing reinforcement for desirable behavior;

- *tutoring in functional skills*, the desire being to make the child as self-sufficient and productive as possible in everyday life; and
- *belief that every child should be educated to the greatest extent possible*, the assumption being that every child can improve to some degree. (p. 26)

In further support, Gaynor (1973) notes, "This work was the first example of an IEP (Individualized Education Program), and the beginning of modern special education" (p 34.). The work of Itard provided the foundation on which today's special education practices are built and implemented.

THE CIVIL WAR AMENDMENTS

On January 1, 1863, President Lincoln issued the Emancipation Proclamation in order to free American slaves. When the Union ultimately triumphed over the Confederacy, Congress acted swiftly to pass what are arguably three of the most important amendments to the Constitution, making slavery and other forms of discrimination unconstitutional. Loevy (1997) recalls:

After the Civil War was over, large Republican majorities in the national Congress passed and sent to the states for adoption the three great "Civil War Amendments." The 13th Amendment abolished "slavery" and "involuntary servitude." The 14th Amendment guaranteed the right to "life," "liberty," and "property." In addition, it guarantees all persons the equal protection of the laws. The 15th Amendment guaranteed all American citizens the right to vote no matter what their "race, color, or previous condition of servitude." (p. 3)

In order to subvert and undermine the Civil War Amendments, Southern state legislatures began passing Black Codes in 1865. These Black Codes were intended to limit significantly the rights of African Americans. The Congress responded quickly by passing the Civil Rights Act of 1866, which made it illegal to discriminate against individuals on the basis of prior servitude, race, or color. As was the case during the Civil War, the federal government continued to fight issues of racial discrimination; however, the weapons were statutes, and the fields of battle were the floors and halls of Congress.

The federal government worked hard from 1865 to 1875 to pass legislation to protect the rights of African Americans; unfortunately, the political winds shifted, and by the end of the century, most of these laws had been nullified or repealed (Loevy, 1997). The *Civil Rights Cases* (1883) delivered a crippling blow to the rights established and the progress made during and immediately following the Civil War. "In *the Civil Rights Cases of 1883*, the Supreme Court ruled that the protection of rights guaranteed by the 14th Amendment applied only to the states and not to individuals." Although intended to provide all individuals protection under the laws, the 14th Amendment was sharply limited by these cases. "Thus an 1875 act of Congress prohibiting discrimination against blacks in the inns, public conveyances, theaters, and other public accommodations or amusements was declared unconstitutional because it was limiting *private* behavior rather than state behavior" (Loevy, 1997, p. 6). In effect, in 1883 the Supreme Court made it legal for private individuals to continue to discrimate against African Americans, doing immeasurable damage to the rights of thousands of Americans.

The Democratic Party gained control of both houses of Congress in 1892. Within two years, nearly every civil rights law had been nullified. The strong shift in the political winds was strengthened by the Supreme Court. In a decision that had possibly the most debilitating effect on civil rights and special education in the history of the United States, the Supreme Court established the "separate but equal" doctrine in 1896. In the case of *Plessy v. Ferguson* (1896), the Court declared it was legal to segregate individuals and have separate facilities so long as they were equal. Of course, separate facilities for African Americans were seldom equal. Nevertheless, the decision provided legal backing for blatant segregation and discrimination based on individual differences. Furthermore, the doctrine reinforced the practice of segregating and discriminating against students who deviated from the norm (e.g., children with disabilities). The *Plessy* decision ensured that the Fourteenth Amendment would not be able to provide all Americans "equal protection of the laws." The Court would not correct its decision until 58 years later in its decision in *Brown v. Board of Education* (1954).

THE CIVIL RIGHTS MOVEMENTS

The beginning of the twentieth century found groups in the United States becoming intensely engaged in civil rights movements. Many separate, individual movements sought to secure equal protection of the laws for all individuals. For instance, the movements for women's rights (beginning with the right to vote), children's rights (beginning with child labor laws), workers' rights, protections based on creed and national origin, and, of course, African Americans' rights were all in motion.

Perhaps the most notable civil rights movement in the second half of the twentieth century—that addressing the civil liberties and rights of African Americans—began to gain considerable momentum during the 1950s. Further, not only did the *Brown v. Board of Education* (1954) decision have sweeping implications for African Americans, but also the precedent opened the door of opportunity for all individuals with unalterable characteristics to receive the full protections of the Fourteenth Amendment, especially in the area of education. Kane (1967) notes:

When handed down in May 1954, the landmark decision, *Brown v. Board of Education of Topeka, Kansas,* called for the desegregation of all public school systems in the nation "with all deliberate speed." The court unanimously ruled that separate facilities were, by definition, unequal and, therefore, unconstitutional. Most important, however, was the breadth of the decision. In outlawing segregation in *all* public education throughout the entire nation, the court thereby implied that all forms of segregation were illegal. It could now be assumed that the court would uphold new civil rights legislation banning all forms of public discrimination, provided, of course, Congress could be persuaded to pass such legislation. (p. 13)

Advocates of special education point to the *Brown* decision as being the springboard for litigation and legislation that provided individuals with disabilities equal access to a free and appropriate public education. Goldberg (1982) notes:

In the early part of the 1970s, parents of persons with disabilities began to assert a legal right to an education similar to that offered other children. These parents based their claims on legal victories achieved by civil rights activists advocating on behalf of black students who had been similarly segregated and provided with inferior education or none at all. . . . But in *Brown*, the Court held that separate facilities for black students denied the Constitution's requirement that all persons be treated equally under the law. In language that is frequently cited by advocates representing children who require special education—known today as "exceptional children"—the Court in a unanimous opinion stressed the importance of education to society. (p. 1)

In support, Ballard (personal communication, Oct. 4, 2003) notes:

Brown v. Board of Education set the stage for Title I and also for [the Individuals with Disabilities Education Act] by making the equal protection clause of the Constitution an underlying principle for the education of all America's children. What you give to the majority you must give to all, which translated into equal educational opportunity for all. Beyond the very serious matter of desegregation of the schools, *Brown* had broad and deep implications which govern policy to this day, and I hope forever.

Although the *Brown* decision was handed down in 1954, it took many years for it to be implemented. "It was originally hoped that state and local governments in the South would comply voluntarily with the *Brown* decision. In many areas, however, the decision was met with 'massive resistance'" (Loevy, 1997, p. 18). It was the lack of progress following the *Brown* decision that served as a catalyst for Congress to act a decade later. (See Figure 2.1.)

FIGURE 2.1

Brown v. Board of Education National Historic Site

The U. S. Supreme Court decision in *Brown v. Board of Education* (1954) is one of the most pivotal opinions ever rendered by that body. This landmark decision highlights the Supreme Court's role in [effecting] changes in national and social policy. Often when people think of the case, they remember a little girl whose parents sued so that she could attend an all-white school in her neighborhood. In reality, the story of *Brown v. Board* is far more complex.

In December, 1952, the United States Supreme Court had on its docket cases from <u>Kansas</u>, <u>Delaware</u>, the <u>District of Columbia</u>, <u>South Carolina</u>, and <u>Virginia</u>, all of which challenged the constitutionality of racial segregation in public schools. The Court had consolidated these five cases under one name, *Oliver Brown et al. v. the Board of Education of Topeka*. One of the justices later explained that the Court felt it was better to have representative cases from different parts of the country. They decided to put Brown first "so that the whole question would not smack of being a purely Southern one."

This collection of cases was the culmination of years of legal groundwork laid by the National Association for the Advancement of Colored People (NAACP) in its work to end segregation. None of the cases would have been possible without individuals who were courageous enough to take a stand against the segregated system.

Source: Retrieved from www.nps.gov/brvb/pages/thecase.htm, January 14, 2008.

ADVOCACY

Special education law is the result of the hard work of many concerned parents and individuals who strongly believe that individuals with disabilities should have a free and appropriate public education (FAPE) in the least restrictive environment (LRE). FAPE and LRE are two pillars of the Individuals with Disabilities Act of 1975 (IDEA). They are both substantive safeguards that ensure students with disabilities receive educational services specific to their individual needs at no cost to their parents and are educated with regular education students as much as possible, respectively. Although the history of special education involves many professionals and individuals working on behalf of children with disabilities, advocacy groups did not truly become organized and established until the early to mid-twentieth century. The role of advocacy is among the most crucial components of the development of special education. Without the immeasurable role of advocacy, the history, current practice, and future of special education would be drastically altered.

In explaining the role of advocacy groups, Levine and Cornwell (1979) state: "An interest group is any collection of people organized to promote some common objective that somehow relates to the political process" (p. 68). In addition, according to Levine and Wexler (1981), "An interest group (or pressure group), in a political sense, is composed of people with likeminded interests who are represented by their own members or by a professional staff in the corridors of executive and legislative halls" (p. 11). Interest groups were the first driving forces behind a collective movement to educate children with disabilities. Two major organizations stand out as pioneers in the advocacy for children with disabilities: the Council for Exceptional Children (CEC) and the National Association for Retarded Citizens (NARC, and now simply referred to as ARC).

Recognized as the first advocacy organization for children with disabilities, CEC was founded in the summer of 1922 in New York City at Columbia University. The group was established by students and faculty members concerned with the education of children with disabilities. CEC is recognized today as one of the largest and most influential disabilities-related advocacy organizations for children in the world. CEC has played an integral role in the development of the field, the design and advocacy of special education legislation, and the passage of six successful reauthorizations of IDEA. The main foci for CEC have historically been (1) advocacy at all levels of government to ensure that all children with disabilities receive a free and appropriate public education in the least restrictive environment and (2) the promotion and development of the profession of special education.

The National Association for Retarded Citizens was established in 1950, the result of the combined efforts of 23 separate organizations. During the passage of the IDEA in 1975, ARC had a total membership of 218,000 members. In contrast to CEC, which represents the special education profession and learners with exceptionalities, ARC represents a far larger constituency base with similar concerns, but also with concerns beyond education. "Most of the several million handicapped children in the nation are surrounded by family, teachers, and friends who are concerned about obtaining the optimum benefits from society for them. ARC and CEC are two of the many organizations that represent these interests in government and played a major role in bringing PL 94-142 to fruition" (Levine & Wexler, 1981, p. 16).

As noted above, CEC and ARC have played important roles in the development and passage of major special education legislation. CEC is best known for its grassroots and national advocacy of procedural and substantive safeguards to ensure that children with disabilities receive a free and appropriate public education. Whereas CEC is best known for its activity with legislation, ARC is best known for its litigation. The two organizations proved to be formidable powers, with CEC helping to establish statutory and regulatory law via the legislative labyrinth and ARC setting critical precedents through the judicial process.

Pennsylvania Association for Retarded Citizens v. Pennsylvania

The Pennsylvania Association for Retarded Citizens (PARC) brought a class-action lawsuit against the Commonwealth of Pennsylvania in 1971. The plaintiffs named 13 specific school districts and Pennsylvania's Board of Education and Secretariats of Education and Public Welfare in the case. PARC asserted that students with mental retardation were being denied their constitutional right to equal protection of the laws under the Fourteenth Amendment. "Children who were deemed unable to benefit from education could be excluded from school upon the certification of a psychologist. Furthermore, the compulsory attendance law, which required children from eight to seventeen to attend school, was used to exclude retarded persons who were outside that age group" (Goldberg, 1982, p. 2).

The federal district court found in favor of PARC in *Pennsylvania Association for Retarded Citizens v. Pennsylvania* (1972) and mandated that children with mental retardation be provided a free public education similar to that provided to their peers without disabilities (Zettel & Ballard, 1982). Goldberg (1982) continues: "The PARC case resulted in an agreement (the 'PARC Consent Decree') recognizing the legal right to education for retarded chldren in Pennsylvaia. The agreement required that retarded children be provided with a free and appropriate public education to meet their individual needs" (p. 2). This case was instrumental in establishing the precedent that all children have a constitutional right to public education, without regard to disability.

Mills v. Board of Education of the District of Columbia

By setting the above-described precedent, the *PARC* case served as an impetus for further litigation that eventually led Congress to take statutory action. After *PARC*, similar cases began to emerge throughout the country. "The 'PARC' procedures set a detailed model for future advocates. In another now-famous case, an attack was mounted on the exclusion of children with disabilities from appropriate classes in the District of Columbia" (Goldberg, 1982, p. 3). In 1972, a class-action suit was filed in federal district court against the District of Columbia.

The class comprised seven students who represented a wide range of disabilities. The parents claimed that their children were being illegally excluded from school and the District of Columbia was in violation of the Fourteenth Amendment by denying their children public education without due process of law (Zettel & Ballard, 1982). While finding for the plaintiffs in *Mills v. Board of Education of the District of Columbia* (1972), the court established due process procedures to ensure all students equal protection under the laws. "*Mills* and *PARC* provided a legal basis for numerous challenges to state and local policies denying equal educational opportunity for handicapped persons" (Goldberg, 1982, p. 3). These cases served as a blueprint and a launching pad for the substantive and procedural protections that were later included in Public Law No. 94-142.

THE PINNACLE OF SPECIAL EDUCATION ADVOCACY

On November 29, 1975, the advocates for students with disabilities celebrated the greatest triumph in the history of special education advocacy. On this date, President Ford signed Public Law No. 94-142—The Education for All Handicapped Children Act—into law. Strongly supported by the Council for Exceptional Children and by parents and families across the United States, it was the single most important piece of legislation to secure a free and appropriate education in the least restrictive environment for all children with disabilities. The statute contains all of the procedural and substantive safeguards necessary to ensure equal access to public education for all children with disabilities.

SUMMARY

The field of special education has been evolving for over two hundred years. European physicicans were the first to apply behavioral modification strategies to train and educate children with disabilities. The physicians were truly pioneers— going against the traditional thought, practice, and professional opinions of their peers. Their endeavors set a clear precedent for educating children with disabilities. The work of Itard, Seguin, and their students helped to develop the foundation for current practices and philosophies.

The Civil Rights movement had a profound impact on the passage of key special education legislation and the setting of key precedents for nondiscriminatory practices in schools. Not only did the case of *Brown v. Board of Education* (1954) overturn *Plessy v. Ferguson* (1896) and make it illegal to provide "separate but equal" schools for African Americans, but also it protected students with disabilities from similar treatment. The *Brown* case served as a springboard for special education advocacy. Although it would take many years and struggles to implement the *Brown* case, in time schools were desegregated, and further legislation and litigation followed to continue to protect students with disabilities.

The Council for Exceptional Children (CEC) and the National Association for Retarded Citizens (NARC, and now ARC) were two of the most inflential advocacy groups during the twentieth century. CEC ensured that appropriate legislation was passed to provide substantive and procedural safegards for children with disabilities. ARC played a critical role in bringing lawsuits that set important precedents, such as that in *Pennsylvania Association for Retarded Citizens v. Pennsylvania* (1972). This case guaranteed FAPE for all children regardless of disability. The two groups proved to be formidable forces in the advocacy for all children with disabilities.

The pinnacle of special education advocacy occurred in 1975 with the passage of Public Law No. 94-142—the Education for All Handicapped Children Act. This act ensured a free and appropriate public education in the least restrictive education for all children with disabilities. Public Law No. 94-142 provided prescriptive procedures to prevent discrimination against children with disabilities. At the time of its passage, eight million children with disabilities were being inappropriately educated, and over one million were not receiving services at all. The Education for All Handicapped Chidren Act—renamed the Individuals with Disabilities Education Act in 1990—is the centerpiece of and driving force behind the effort to secure substantive and procedural safeguards for American children with disabilities.

CRITICAL THINKING QUESTIONS

1. Develop a time line of critical events, litigation, and legislation that impacted the development of current special education law.
2. Compare and contrast the Civil Rights movement and the advocacy movement for the education rights of children with disabilities.
3. Why is a knowledge of history so important when navigating the issues of today and planning for the future?
4. Explain the role of advocacy groups in the development of special education law. Discuss two of the most important special education advocacy groups and describe their functions.
5. Discuss the impact and importance of *Brown v. Board of Education* (1954) for special education law. Why was this case so pivotal for students with disabilities?

REFERENCES

Brown v. Board of Education, 347 U.S. 483 (1954).

French, J. E. (2000). Itard, Jean-Marie-Gaspard. In A. E. Kazdin (Ed.), *Encyclopedia of psychology*. Oxford, England: Oxford University Press.

Gaynor, J. F. (1973). The "failure" of J.M.G. Itard. *Journal of Special Education, 7*(4), 439–445.

Goldberg, S. (1982). *Special education law: A guide for parents, advocates, and educators.* New York: Plenum Press.

Hallahan, D., & Kauffman, J. (1997). *Exceptional learners: Introduction to special education* (7th ed.). Needham Heights, MA: Allyn & Bacon.

Humphrey, G. (1962). Introduction. In J. M. G. Itard, *The wild boy of Aveyron.* New York: Appleton-Century-Crofts.

Kane, Peter E. (1967). *The Senate debate on the 1964 Civil Rights Act.* Unpublished doctoral dissertation, Purdue University, Lafayette, IN.

Kanner, L. (1964). *A history of the care and study of the mentally retarded.* Springfield, IL: Charles C. Thomas.

Kauffman, J. M. (1981). *Historical trends and contemporary issues in special education in the United States.* Englewood Cliffs, NJ: Prentice-Hall.

Kauffman, J. M. (1993). How we might achieve the radical reform of special education. *Exceptional Children, 60,* 6–16.

Kauffman, J. M., & Smucker, K. (1995). *The legacies of placement: A brief history of placement options and issues with commentary on their evolution.* Hillsdale, NJ: Erlbaum.

Konnert, M., & Augenstein, J. (1995). *The school superintendency: Leading education into the 21st century.* Lancaster, PA: Technomic.

Levine, E., & Cornwell, E. (1979). *An introduction to American government* (4th ed.). New York: Macmillan.

Levine, E., & Wexler, M. (1981). *PL 94-142: An act of Congress.* New York: Macmillan.

Loevy, R. D. (1997). *The Civil Rights Act of 1964: The passage of the law that ended racial segregation.* Albany: State University of New York Press.

Mills v. Board of Education of the District of Columbia, 348 F. Supp. 866 (D.D.C. 1972).

Pennsylvania Association for Retarded Children v. Pennsylvania, 334 F. Supp. 1257 (E.D. Pa. 1971), 343 F. Supp. 279 (E.D. 1972).

Plessy v. Ferguson, 163 U.S. 537 (1896).

Zettel, J. J., & Ballard, J. (1982). The Educaton for All Handicapped Children Act of 1975 (P.L. 94-142): Its history, origins, and concepts. In J. Ballard, B. Ramirez, & F. Wentraub (Eds.), *Special education in America: Its legal and governmental foundations* (pp. 11–22). Reston, VA: Council for Exceptional Children.

3

The Individuals with Disabilities Education Act

- The Individuals with Disabilities Education Act (IDEA) is organized in a logical structure—Parts A–D—that has remained basically the same since its original enactment in 1975.
- Part A is titled General Provisions.
- Part B is titled Assistance for Education of All Children with Disabilities.
- Part C is titled Infants and Toddlers with Disabilities.
- Part D is titled National Activities to Improve Education of Children with Disabilities.
- The IDEA defines *special education* as "specially designed instruction, at no cost to parents, to meet the unique needs of a child with a disability" (Pub. Law No. 94-142, § 602(25)).
- Six elements of the IDEA constitute the law's essential support structure: the individualized education program (IEP), the guarantee of a free appropriate public education (FAPE), the requirement of education in the least restrictive environment (LRE), appropriate evaluation, active parent and student participation in the educational mission, and procedural safeguards for all participants.
- The confidentiality regulations of the IDEA have their foundation in comprehensive legislation enacted by the Congress in 1974 (the year before enactment of Public Law No. 94-142) titled the Family Educational Rights and Privacy Act (FERPA).
- As both a professional and a legal responsibility, special and general educators are expected to be conversant with what can be called the behavioral sequence: (1) determination that a behavioral intervention plan or BIP (positive behavioral intervention strategies and supports) is needed; (2) development of the BIP, following a functional behavioral assessment (FBA); and (3) implementation of the BIP, with periodic review and modification, as needed.

More than thirty years after the 1975 passage of Public Law No. 94-142, now commonly known as the Individuals with Disabilities Education Act (IDEA), the objectives outlined in the law's preamble remain essentially the same:

> It is the purpose of this Act to assure that all handicapped children have available to them . . . a free appropriate public education which emphasizes special education and related services designed to meet their unique needs, to assure the rights of handicapped children and their parents or guardians are protected, to assist states and localities to provide for the education of all handicapped children, and to assess and assure the effectiveness of efforts to educate handicapped children. (Pub. L. No. 94-142, § 601)

Other than the term *handicapped children*—now superseded by *children with disabilities*—this declaration of purposes is still a valid and cogent statement of intent nearly a decade into the twenty-first century. This chapter will summarize the major elements of the IDEA.

STRUCTURE OF THE IDEA

The IDEA is organized in a logical structure—Parts A–D—that has remained basically the same since its original enactment in 1975. Let's take a look at that structure.

PART A, GENERAL PROVISIONS

This part includes

- findings and purposes;
- definitions of terms used throughout, such as *special education*, *native language*, *child with a disability*, and *free appropriate public education*;
- requirements for employment of individuals with disabilities; and
- requirements for individualized family service plans (IFSPs) and procedural safeguard mechanisms.

PART B, ASSISTANCE FOR EDUCATION OF ALL CHILDREN WITH DISABILITIES

This portion of the law contains the largest number of program requirements and represents the very core of the IDEA, including

- matters related to fiscal policy and money management among federal, state, and local jurisdictions, including federal funding arrangements;

- responsibilities at the state level, usually directed to the state education agency;
- responsibilities of local education agencies, commonly meaning local school districts, but also directed to other organizational units such as a collaboration of school districts for special education purposes;
- rights, protections, and responsibilities in the educational process, including evaluations, eligibility determinations, individualized education programs, and educational placements;
- procedural safeguards, also known as the due process provisions;
- federal administration and ongoing national data-gathering responsibilities of the states and local school districts; and
- preschool grants, directed to children three through five years of age.

PART C, INFANTS AND TODDLERS WITH DISABILITIES

This is a national program that provides early intervention services to children from birth to age three who manifest or are at risk of developmental delay. This part includes

- a definition of the eligible population,
- a listing of authorized services,
- requirements for a statewide system in each state, and
- requirements for an individualized family service plan (IFSP) and procedural safeguard mechanisms.

PART D, NATIONAL ACTIVITIES TO IMPROVE EDUCATION OF CHILDREN WITH DISABILITIES

This part, now including the Education Sciences Reform Act, Part E, comprises two major clusters of generally highly valued support programs—two of which (research and training of professionals) were created in the 1950s. These programs are administered at the national level, where awards are made to a wide array of eligible recipients in the form of grants, contracts, and cooperative agreements. The major components are

- coordinated research and innovation;
- professional preparation;
- studies, evaluations, and an ongoing national assessment of the IDEA's effectiveness;
- parent training and information centers, including community parent resource centers;

■ coordinated technical assistance and knowledge/information dissemination through regional resource centers, including institutes, and clearinghouses; and

■ technology development and utilization and educational media services.

As part of the 2004 amendments, Congress transferred the research functions from the Office of Special Education Programs (OSEP) to the Institute of Educational Sciences. The National Center for Educational Research, one of four centers under the institute's umbrella, directly administers the IDEA's research efforts.

EVOLUTION OF THE LAW

A review of the evolution of the IDEA requires attention to the programs authorized *before* Public Law No. 94-142, as well as the numerous amendments to the IDEA that occurred *after* its enactment in 1975—although Public Law No. 94-142 established the basic framework of rights and responsibilities that remains in place to this day. Pre–Public Law No. 94-142 legislation helped develop an infrastructure of effective early intervention and special education practice while inaugurating a very modest, but useful direct program managed at the state level. Post–Public Law No. 94-142 legislation attended to further refinements of the IDEA.

A bit of historical trivia aids in reducing the confusion commonly surrounding the titles used for the law. From 1970 to 1990, the law was known as the Education of the Handicapped Act (EHA). In fact, Public Law No. 94-142 was actually a massive amendment, amounting to a "top to bottom" rewrite of the earlier core segments of the EHA. In the 1990 reauthorization to the EHA, Congress changed the title from the EHA to the IDEA. For the reader's peace of mind, simply remember that the EHA became the IDEA and this text will consistently lead with "the IDEA."

What is a reauthorization? Put simply, the Congress traditionally affixes an end date to a great many pieces of legislation; this action is popularly known as "sunsetting" the legislation. This means that the Congress must revisit and "reauthorize" (or not "reauthorize," depending on the circumstances) such legislation. Because policy makers agreed that Public Law No. 94-142 constituted a bill of rights for children with disabilities and their families, Part B of the IDEA was and remains permanently authorized. (Consult Structure of the IDEA, beginning on page 25.) However, Parts, A, C, and D (definitions, early intervention, and the national support programs administered at the federal level) require periodic reauthorization. Can Part B still be amended at the periodic reauthorization of the other parts? Yes, but to make the point that Part B constituted permanent civil rights legislation, the policy makers left Part B unaltered for an unprecedented 20 years, except for minor refinements.

What follows is a brief history of the IDEA. The reader is advised that this segment represents nothing more than the evolution of the IDEA and does not address the universe of other national legislation—such as the Rehabilitation Act of 1973 and the Americans with Disabilities Act of 1990 (ADA)—affecting the education of special-needs children. The Rehabilitation Act and the ADA are addressed later in this text.

BEFORE PUBLIC LAW NO. 94-142

Cooperative Research Act of 1954, Public Law No. 83-531

Was the first federal research program in special education.

Training of Professional Personnel Act of 1959, Public Law No. 86-158

Was the initial federal program focusing on professional preparation for educating children with mental retardation.

Teachers of the Deaf Act of 1961, Public Law No. 87-276

Trained educational personnel for hard of hearing and deaf children.

Mental Retardation Facilities and Community Health Centers Construction Act of 1963, Public Law No. 88-164

Expanded support for professional preparation to teach a wider population beyond mental retardation and further expanded the research program.

Federal Assistance to State Operated and Supported Schools for the Handicapped, Public Law No. 89-313

Was passed in 1965 as an amendment to Title I of the Elementary and Secondary Education Act (ESEA); was the first major direct program supporting the education of children and youth with disabilities; stood as the largest fiscal program for instruction until Public Law 92-142, with the assistance primarily directed toward state-run institutions and schools.

Elementary and Secondary Education Act Amendments of 1966, Public Law No. 89-750

Created the Bureau of Education for the Handicapped (BEH), which later became the administering agency for the EHA and the IDEA. The agency was later titled the Office of Special Education Programs (OSEP), which still exists today.

Elementary and Secondary Education Act Amendments of 1967, Public Law No. 90-247

Was the first national commitment to technical assistance and dissemination, with the creation of centers for deaf-blind children in response to the rubella epidemics of 1964; also created regional resource centers (RRCs) for special education.

Handicapped Children's Early Education Assistance Act of 1968, Public Law No. 90-538

Authorized the first early childhood model programs, focusing on children ages three through nine, but emphasizing the preschool years for children ages three through five.

Extension of Programs of Assistance for Elementary and Secondary Education Act Amendments of 1970, Public Law No. 91-230

Decoupled special education programs from the ESEA and consolidated them in a separate and independent EHA.

Education Amendments of 1974, Public Law No. 93-380

Is considered the "early warning" legislation for Public Law No. 94-142; required full-service goals and timetables, as well as assurances that such elements as due process and least restrictive placements were in development; set no dates for actual implementation, however.

PUBLIC LAW 94-142

Education for All Handicapped Children Act, Public Law No. 94-142

Is the landmark legislation requiring a free appropriate public education for all children with disabilities—the heart of which is contained in Parts A and B of the IDEA.

AFTER PUBLIC LAW NO. 94-142

Education of the Handicapped Amendments of 1977, Public Law No. 95-49

Extended authority for the discretionary programs and eliminated the National Advisory Committee on the Handicapped.

Education of the Handicapped Act Amendments of 1983, Public Law No. 98-199

Strengthened the support programs under Part D (grants and contracts managed and awarded at the national level) to promote integration of children with severe disabilities, including creation of severely handicapped institutes; also promoted transitions from school to adult living and a change in statewide service systems; required least restrictive environment as well.

Handicapped Children's Protection Act of 1986, Public Law No. 99-372

Reversed a U.S. Supreme Court decision requiring exhaustion of IDEA due process procedures before filing a civil action under any other statute, such as Section 504 also authorized the awarding of attorney fees to the prevailing party in administrative due process if approved by a court.

Education of the Handicapped Act Amendments of 1986, Public Law No. 99-457

Completed the age mandate of Public Law No. 94-142 by establishing a phase-in of FAPE for preschool children from three through five years of age under Part B; created an early intervention program for infants and toddlers from birth to three years of age, now Part C; also authorized a state-of-the-art program for technology and for educational media and materials.

Education of the Handicapped Act Amendments of 1990, Public Law No. 101-476

Added transition services to the required content of the individualized education program (IEP), which was viewed only as a statutory clarification of an existing requirement; added traumatic brain injury and autism to the disability categories; changed the name of the EHA to the Individuals with Disabilities Education Act (IDEA); and established the parent training and information center (PTIC) system on a nationwide basis.

Individuals with Disabilities Education Act Amendments of 1997, Public Law No. 105-17

Opened Part B to needed adjustments more than 20 years after the enactment of Public Law No. 94-142; included major refinements that strengthened the relationship to the general curriculum, overhauled the evaluation and reevaluation provisions, added new stipulations in the IEP regarding state- and districtwide tests, and designed controversial procedures related to behavior and discipline.

Individuals with Disabilities Education Act Amendments of 2004, Public Law No. 108-446

Coordinated the policy and procedures of the IDEA with those of the No Child Left Behind Act (NCLB); further amended eligibility procedures, IEP requirements, and procedural safeguards; streamlined discipline procedures; and consolidated special education research with other federal research in the Institute for Education Sciences.

SPECIAL EDUCATION

In the definitions of diagnostic categories given in the IDEA regulations, the reader should note the use of the phrase "that adversely affects a child's educational performance." Further, the statutory definition of a *child with a disability* reads: ". . . . and who, by reason thereof, needs special education and related services." These two clauses are critical for determining (1) precisely which children will be served under the IDEA and (2) precisely what makes this educational program partially different from the general education program.

The IDEA defines *special education* as "specially designed instruction, at no cost to parents, to meet the unique needs of a child with a disability" (Pub. L. No. 94-142, § 602(25)). The IDEA regulations, published in the Code of Federal Regulations, or C.F.R., further define *specially designed instruction* to mean "adapting, as appropriate to the needs of an eligible child under this part, the content, methodology, or delivery of instruction to address the unique needs of the child that result from the child's disability" (34 C.F.R. § 300.39(b)(3)).

The policy makers—in both Congress and the administering federal agency—have not further defined *special education* in the IDEA. They continue, wisely, to respect the fact that the parameters of special education are a professional matter that continually evolves through professional research, training, and advances in practice. What they do say through the IDEA, however, is that special education *must be provided* to a defined group of America's children.

THE SIX PILLARS OF THE IDEA

In essence, six elements of the IDEA constitute the law's essential support structure—with no single element complete without the presence of the other five. These six elements are the individualized education program (IEP), the guarantee of a free appropriate public education (FAPE), the requirement of education in the least restrictive educational environment (LRE), appropriate evaluation, active participation of parent and student in the educational mission, and procedural safeguards for all participants.

INDIVIDUALIZED EDUCATION PROGRAM

The cornerstone of educational planning and implementation under the IDEA is undoubtedly the requirement of individualized programming for each student. In fact, the action of placing such a requirement in law in 1975 may be viewed as nothing less than one of the most far-reaching actions undertaken in federal education policy. The mechanism for delivering this requirement is known as the *individualized education program*, or IEP. Either an IEP or its early childhood equivalent, the *individualized family service plan* (IFSP), must be in place and operating for every child designated as eligible for services under the IDEA. The IEP has been, and will continue to be, both the cornerstone of the IDEA and the heart of American special education.

The statute says simply, but with powerful implications, that "[t]he term 'individualized education program' or 'IEP' means a written statement for each child with a disability that is developed, reviewed, and revised in accordance with this section" (Pub. L. No. 94-142, § 614(d)(1)(A)). The law then specifies (1) the required content of each child's IEP; (2) how parents will receive progress reports; (3) who must, and who may, be included in the IEP team; (4) considerations in the development of the IEP, including certain special factors; (5) the role of the regular education teacher; and (6) the requirements for review and revision of the IEP. The regulations repeat the law, while expanding and clarifying where necessary. Chapter 10 of this text is devoted to a comprehensive discussion of the IEP with practical implications and recommendations.

FREE AND APPROPRIATE PUBLIC EDUCATION

A fundamental, nondebatable presumption embodied in the IDEA is that no child can be denied a public education. This is popularly known as the principle of zero reject. Regardless of the severity of disability, each and every child has the right to a public education. In fact, the groundswell of citizen advocacy in the late 1960s and the early 1970s that led to the zero reject principle was known as the "right to education" movement. Further, the IDEA states that the educational program for eligible children cannot be just any program of public education. Instead, the statute says that the program must be special education appropriate for the individual child.

The law's definition of *free appropriate public education*, or FAPE, is lean in terms of words, but robust in terms of implications:

> The term "free appropriate public education" means special education and related services that (A) have been provided at public expense, under public supervision and direction, and without charge; (B) meet the standards of the State educational agency; (C) include an appropriate preschool, elementary, or secondary school education in the State involved; and (D) are provided in conformity with the individualized education program under section 614(d). (Pub. L. No. 94-142, § 602(9))

The statute guarantees a FAPE and the corresponding actual availability of a FAPE to an eligible child for as long as necessary from the child's third birthday through his or her twenty-first year—with certain qualifications such as matriculation with a regular high school diploma. Chapter 7 explores all facets of FAPE.

LEAST RESTRICTIVE ENVIRONMENT

Another nondebatable presumption at the core of the IDEA is *least restrictive environment*, or LRE. Put simply, LRE requires that children with disabilities be educated in the same place as all other children. Though various terms have enjoyed currency since the enactment of Public Law No. 94-142 in 1975—including *integration*, *mainstreaming*, *inclusion*, *full inclusion*, and *least restrictive environment*—none has precisely the same meaning. Regardless, each of the terms embodies the bedrock belief enshrined in the U.S. Supreme Court's ruling in *Brown v. Board of Education* (1954): namely, that *separate is unequal*, as well as the converse, that *together is inherently better*. Parenthetically, the term *least restrictive environment* has appeared in the regulations since they were first promulgated in 1977 and thus has the effect of law.

Although the IDEA states that children with disabilities must be educated with children who are nondisabled, it also includes a critical qualifier: "to the maximum extent appropriate." What does that mean? The law offers a specific answer: "That separate classes, separate schooling or other removal of children with disabilities from the regular educational environment occurs only if the nature or severity of the disability is such that education in regular classes with the use of supplementary aids and services cannot be achieved satisfactorily" (Pub. L. No. 94-142, § 612(a)(5)). One can describe this qualifier as a necessary—though often frustrating—tension between two desirable objectives for children with disabilities. On the one hand, maximum inclusion of the child is mandated; on the other hand, an educational program that meets the child's needs may require some degree of separation from the educational environment shared by all students.

So how is this tension resolved? The law leaves the resolution to the IEP team, which includes the parents. Once an agreement is reached, the placement for the child becomes, by definition, the least restrictive educational environment for that child. Therefore, pull-out periods in a resource room coupled with regular classroom placement may be the LRE for a particular child, while instruction in a separate class may be the LRE for another child.

Professionals must bear in mind that when the IEP is being developed, the presumed placement must be the regular classroom with full inclusion in all other school activities. To the extent that this is not what is agreed on in the final IEP, that document must include an explanation of what options were considered and why something less than full-time inclusion in the regular setting was chosen. A comprehensive treatment of LRE, including the continuum of placement options, is available in Chapter 8.

APPROPRIATE EVALUATION

The evaluation is the process through which a child is determined to have a disability requiring the support of special education and related services. The evaluation process also should help identify the child's actual special education and related service needs, though the evaluation precedes the development of the IEP. A team of qualified professionals and the child's parent(s) must make the final eligibility determination.

The IDEA sets out many critical requirements for conducting an evaluation. These requirements, designed to protect against misidentification, include the use of a variety of assessment tools and strategies, a prohibition against the use of any single procedure as a sole criterion, assessment of the relative contribution of cognitive and behavioral factors in addition to physical or developmental factors, and protections against evaluation instruments that may be racially or culturally discriminatory.

The issue of nondiscriminatory testing and evaluation was the central concern in the original evaluation component of Public Law No. 94-142, and given the ever-increasing number of immigrants to the United States from non-English-speaking countries since the law's original enactment, the concerns surrounding this issue have grown. Once again, the rule that is fundamental throughout the IDEA applies in evaluation: namely, evaluation must be appropriate for determining the needs and strengths of each child on an individual basis. A full discussion of evaluation and reevaluation is offered in Chapter 9.

PARENT AND TEACHER PARTICIPATION

Central to the design and functioning of the IDEA—indeed, central to the success of special education throughout its history—is the family–professional partnership. *Family*, of course, means the child and the child's parents, and *professional* means the teachers and other individuals who apply their expertise to the child's education. The activities that occur daily in schools when parents and professionals partner in the learning enterprise for individual children are reflected at a distance in national politics. Parents were indispensable in obtaining passage of Public Law No. 94-142, and they remain vigilant guardians of both the content and the implementation of the IDEA to this day.

The section of the law addressing procedural safeguards focuses primarily on protecting the educational rights of children and their parents. If the law seems to some critics too heavily weighted toward parents, supporters argue that the single family unit would be at a distinct disadvantage in relation to public authorities and public school systems without such a deliberate tilting of the scales. Beyond procedural safeguards, the law guarantees the right of consent to and participation in every aspect of the educational process, including evaluation and reevaluation, placement, the IEP, and the uses of public and private insurance. The same aspects of guaranteed participation apply—where deemed appropriate—to the student, with involvement in the development of the IEP being a prime example. As a matter of law, the schoolhouse door is open wide to parent involvement. The importance of parent involvement is addressed throughout this text.

PROCEDURAL SAFEGUARDS

The *right to procedural safeguards*, also known as the right to redress of grievance and the right to due process of law, has a very long history; it dates back to early medieval English common law and was eventually carried forward into the U.S. Constitution's Bill of Rights. The guarantee of procedural safeguards appeared early in the development of the nation's special education law because such guarantees were required first by the courts in two historic 1972 "right to an education" decrees. The pair of rulings—*Pennsylvania Association for Retarded Citizens v. Pennsylvania* (1972) and *Mills v. Board of Education of the District of Columbia* (1972)—greatly influenced both the creation and the content of the procedural safeguards section of Public Law No. 94-142.

The opening lines of the IDEA's procedural safeguards section make a frank statement of purpose: "to ensure that children with disabilities and their parents are guaranteed procedural safeguards with respect to the provision of free appropriate public education" (Pub. L. No. 94-142, § 615). The law lists a number of essential guarantees, including the right to examine all educational records, the right to have an impartial hearing and an impartial hearing officer, the right to receive certain prior notices, the right to be afforded mediation, the right to be accompanied by an attorney, and the right to have a state-level appeal if a hearing has been conducted by a local education agency. Relating to the highly charged issue of discipline infractions, this section of the IDEA also contains protections for all parties—parents, students with and without disabilities, and school personnel—in an effort to balance the critical need for school safety with the right of a particular child with a disability to a continuing educational program.

Although the IDEA's procedural safeguards are focused primarily on providing protections to children and their parents, the reader should understand that these safeguards also benefit school systems, teachers, and other school personnel because the essence of due process is the right of *all parties* to make their case in an impartial setting. An examination of the concepts and dimensions of procedural safeguards is found in Chapter 11.

CONFIDENTIALITY OF INFORMATION

Along with the six pillars of the IDEA, other issues merit attention, including the matter of strict confidentiality of personally identifiable information. In keeping with Sections 612(a)(8) and 617(c) of the IDEA, the implementing regulations make it clear that "[t]he State must have policies and procedures in effect to ensure that public agencies in the State comply with §§ 300.610 through 300.626 related to protecting the confidentiality of any personally identifiable information, collected, used, or maintained under Part B of the Act" (34 C.F.R. § 300.123).

The foundation of the confidentiality regulations of the IDEA is the Family Educational Rights and Privacy Act (FERPA). Enacted by Congress in 1974 (the year before enactment of Public Law No. 94-142) under the sponsorship of then U.S. Senator James Buckley, FERPA effectively mandates privacy protections for all of America's schoolchildren and their families. And like the IDEA, FERPA's basics remain the law to this day. Given the frequently sensitive and far-reaching information gathered about them, no group of children and their families is more in need of a strict code of privacy than students who are receiving or are being considered for eligibility to receive special education services and their parents. Upon close scrutiny, the confidentiality provisions are actually a delicate balance of two necessary protections—*access* and *confidentiality.*

Let's first turn to the issue of *right of access*. The regulations state:

> Each participating agency must permit parents to inspect and review any education records relating to their children that are collected, maintained, or used by the agency under this part. The agency must comply with a request without unnecessary delay and before any meeting regarding an IEP, or any hearing pursuant to § 300.507 [overall due process] or §§ 300.530 through 300.532 [discipline procedures], or resolution session pursuant to § 300.510, and in no case more than 45 days after the request has been made. (34 C.F.R § 300.613)

In support of parents' right to inspection and review, the agency must respond to reasonable parental requests for explanations and interpretations; provide copies of the records if failure to do so would, in effect, deny the right to inspect; and allow the parents or their representative to inspect and review the records.

What about the information itself? Every state education agency must have available to the public its policy regarding information gathered about students. This policy should include a description of the children on whom personally identifiable data are maintained; the types of information sought; the methods the state intends to use in gathering information, including the sources from whom information is gathered; and the uses to be made of the information. All of the local education agencies (school districts) in the state must adhere to this state policy. (See 34 C.F.R. § 300.612.) When considering personal information gathered for special education purposes, a good rule of thumb is this: *The only information gathered should be information needed to provide appropriate special education and related services to the child.*

Now we proceed to the matter of *confidentiality*. While parents and authorized personnel from the school district generally have access to student information, for all other persons and parties access is greatly restricted. As a general rule, *parental consent* must be obtained before personally identifiable information is shared with anyone other than authorized personnel and, importantly, before the information is used for any purpose other than those specified under the IDEA. Further, each agency must keep a careful record of any other party who is given access, including the individual's name, the date when access was authorized, and the purpose for which access was authorized.

An important, but too often overlooked, stipulation in the federal IDEA regulations addresses the destruction of information. Because of the critically precise wording, the regulation is quoted:

Destruction of information

(a) The public agency must inform parents when personally identifiable information collected, maintained, or used under this part *is no longer needed to provide educational services to the child.*

(b) The information *must be destroyed at the request of the parents.* However, a permanent record of a student's name, address, and phone number, his or her grades, attendance record, classes attended, grade level completed, and year completed may be maintained without time limitation. (emphasis added) (34 C.F.R. § 300.624)

Importantly, the confidentiality regulations include their own due process procedures. Here is the trigger: "A parent who believes that information in the education records collected, maintained, or used under this part is inaccurate or misleading or violates the privacy or other rights of the child may request the participating agency that maintains the information to amend the information." The agency may then agree to amend the information or refuse to do so. If the agency refuses, it must inform the parents and provide the opportunity for a hearing. If, after a hearing, the agency still refuses to amend the information, it must allow the parents to place in the child's records a "statement commenting on the information or setting forth any reasons for disagreeing with the decision of the agency." This parental statement must be maintained in the child's records and be made available if the record or the contested section is disclosed to any party (34 C.F.R. §§ 300.618–300.621). Ideally, full-blown due process concerning educational records should rarely be required because parents and schools can amicably amend the records. Nonetheless, the heightened attention to discipline infractions over the past 20 years suggests attention by all parties to protections and procedural safeguards for matters involving personally identifiable data.

When evaluating access to and privacy of information in a particular case or locale, the reader is cautioned to investigate the precise policy and practice of the specific state or school district due to the possibility of loopholes and insufficient monitoring. The complete provisions on confidentiality may be found in the IDEA regulations at 34 C.F.R. §§ 300.610–300.627.

TRANSITION SERVICES

The 1997 amendments to the IDEA added requirements for transitioning disabled students to life after school. Specifically, the IDEA states, as a goal, its intent "to ensure that all children with disabilities have available to them a free appropriate public education that emphasizes special education and related services designed to meet their unique *needs and prepare them for employment and independent living*" (emphasis added) (Pub. L. No. 105-17, § 601(d)). Although access to education is a means to an end under the law, the supreme goal of the IDEA and special education clearly is preparation for self-fulfillment in the adult years.

Accompanying the IDEA regulations, a Notice of Interpretation includes a statement borrowed from other legislation that is a powerful rendering of the postschool objective for students with disabilities:

> Section 701 of the Rehabilitation Act of 1973 describes the philosophy of independent living as including a philosophy of consumer control, peer support, self-help, self-determination, equal access, and individual and system advocacy, in order to maximize the leadership, empowerment, independence, and productivity of individuals with disabilities, and the integration and full inclusion of individuals with disabilities into the mainstream of American society. (IDEA regulations, Appendix A, IEPS, III)

In requiring that a student's IEP include a transition component, the IDEA stipulated, until 2004, a two-tiered approach: one commencing when the student turns 14 and the second when the student turns 16. However, the law stated that in both cases the program could begin at a younger age if the IEP team considered it appropriate. The requirement at age 14 emphasized transition services that focused on courses of study, such as participation in advanced-placement courses or a vocational education program. The requirement at age 16 was much more focused on practical outcomes and included the critical requirement that non-education agencies, where appropriate, be involved in the provision of services. State vocational rehabilitation agencies and state employment and training agencies are obvious examples of such agencies.

The movement to mandate full-blown transition services at age 14 acquired special urgency because of the still disturbingly high dropout rate among students receiving special education services. In fact, experts argued that starting transition services for students with disabilities at age 14 (or earlier) constituted sound policy for three pragmatic reasons:

1. "The sooner, the better" makes eminently good sense for all students who have special challenges that may last throughout their lifetime.
2. If these students should still drop out, hopefully they will leave with useful life skills gained at a relatively early time.
3. Because of meaningful, future-oriented transition services, these students are more likely to be motivated to complete their education, obviously a more highly desired outcome than the preceding item.

However, in a move broadly condemned as a giant step backward, the 2004 IDEA amendments moved the age for initiation of transition services to 16. This significant setback occurred during Senate and House negotiations to produce a final joint bill. Even though the House bill had included services at both 14 and 16 and the Senate bill had required the initiation of all transition services at 14, 14 was stricken and 16 was inserted in the final bill without comment or justification from the conferees.

The student's participation in the IEP meeting is not a parent or professional option when the IEP team is considering transition services. The regulations require that the student be invited, regardless of age. If the student does not attend the IEP meeting, the education agency "must take other steps to ensure that the child's preferences and interests are considered" (34 C.F.R. § 300.321(b)).

Having been developed and refined over two decades, the IDEA's definition of *transition services* offers a reliable and useful summary for the practitioner:

> The term "transition services'" means a coordinated set of activities for a student with a disability that—(a) is designed within an outcome-oriented process, which promotes movement from school to post-school activities, including post-secondary education, vocational training, integrated employment (including supported employment), continuing and adult education, adult services, independent living, or community participation; (b) is based upon the individual student's needs, taking into account the student's preferences and interests; and (c) includes instruction, related services, community experiences, the development of employment and other post-school adult living objectives, and, when appropriate, acquisition of daily living skills and functional vocational evaluation. (Pub. L. 105-17, § 602(34))

DISCIPLINE

Considerations of a student's behavior under the IDEA are most often associated with the controversial discipline procedures added to the due process section of the law in the 1997 reauthorization. Too frequently overlooked, however, is the addition of an important requirement making behavior a consideration in the development of IEPs for all children eligible for special education services. Under the heading of "Consideration of special factors," the law stipulates that the IEP team must, "[i]n the case of a child whose behavior impedes his or her learning or that of others, consider, if appropriate, strategies, including positive behavioral interventions, strategies, and supports to address that behavior" (Pub. L. No. 105-17, § 614(d)(3)(B)). Further, if the IEP team decides that strategies of the nature outlined in the law are necessary, a statement to that effect must be included in the IEP of the child.

Not only is behavioral intervention a crucial component of support for the child, but also it provides a potentially important protection for the other students in an inclusive learning environment. Early behavioral intervention may, in actuality, provide an "ounce of prevention" against future behavior problems. Another important reason for utilizing early behavioral interventions is the possibility that failing to do so may be a violation of FAPE. Overall, the behavioral intervention requirement is meant to promote the participation of the child in the regular educational environment as opposed to a more restrictive setting. That this stipulation is an important safeguard in the guarantee of LRE for the child is amply reinforced by another statutory mandate that regular education teachers participate in determining appropriate positive behavioral interventions and strategies as members of the IEP team. (Pub. L. No. 105-17, § 614(d)(3)(C)). Finally, including behavioral strategies—again, only if appropriate—may be an important protection for the child if there should be a later discipline infraction, resulting in the need to determine whether the behavior was a manifestation of the child's disability.

As a result of both growing concerns over school safety and improved research in behavioral interventions for special-needs children, two terms have permanently joined the lexicon of special education: *functional behavioral assessment (FBA)* and *behavioral intervention plan (BIP)*. Deferring to the expertise of the professionals, Congress and the administering agency have not defined these terms. Nonetheless, the law expects the states, as part of their ongoing professional development programs, to "enhance the ability of teachers and others to use strategies, such as behavioral interventions, to address the conduct of children with disabilities that impedes the learning of children with disabilities and others" (34 C.F.R. § 300.382(f)). Thus, as both a professional and a legal responsibility, special and general educators are expected to be conversant with what might be called the behavioral sequence. The behavioral sequence includes

1. determination that a BIP, which includes positive behavioral intervention strategies and supports, is needed;
2. development of the BIP, following an FBA; and
3. implementation of the BIP, with periodic review and modification, as needed.

ENFORCEMENT

Under the IDEA, the federal government holds each state responsible for full compliance by all parties within its jurisdiction; the law requires that states engage in active monitoring and enforcement in all of their school districts and other participating entities. States are required to keep a written record concerning their policies and procedures related to the IDEA. These policies, which must be available for public review, are most likely to be housed in the special education division of the state education agency. Many of these documents are available on state education agency websites.

Correspondingly, the U.S. Department of Education actively monitors the states for continuing compliance. This monitoring of state IDEA compliance is typically done by the agency's Office of Special Education Programs (OSEP), which is housed within the larger Office of Special Education and Rehabilitative

Services (OSERS). State monitoring typically occurs on a rotating basis; it involves on-site visits by federal personnel and often includes public hearings, which can be highly valuable in discovering compliance shortcomings. OSEP advises states of any gaps in compliance, and those states that are out of compliance are expected to design a corrective action plan with a timetable for state revisions and modifications. The law requires full transparency to the public in all aspects of this monitoring process, meaning that any document declared "classified" or any denial of access to information should be treated suspiciously.

SUMMARY

The IDEA's essential features have remained remarkably stable and unaltered in the 30 years since the original enactment of Public Law No. 94-142. Structured in four parts (A through D), the law combines a bill of rights for children with disabilities and their families with provisions for federal fiscal support. In addition, the IDEA provides educational and other management directives to all levels of school governance along with ongoing infrastructure support that is administered at the national level. The law delineates the characteristics of the eligible population of children to be served, as well as the nature of the services to be provided.

The law contains six elements that represent the pillars of the IDEA, as well as American special education as a whole. Beyond these six elements, other features such as the confidentiality, transition, and behavioral provisions warrant careful attention and study.

CRITICAL THINKING QUESTIONS

1. How does this review of the IDEA compare with your prior perceptions of the IDEA?
2. Does the law strike you as unduly complex and prescriptive? If so, why?
3. In your personal experience, are there requirements in the special education regulations at the state and local levels that are not the result of the IDEA, though you thought they were? What are they?
4. Would you change any of the fundamental features of the IDEA as we advance into the twenty-first century? If so, what would you change and why?
5. Would you change any features of the IDEA regulations that were presented in this chapter? If so, what would you change and why?
6. What do you think would be the effect if the IDEA were totally repealed tomorrow?

7. If you are a teacher or other professional working in public education, which requirements of the IDEA and its accompanying regulations do you find most helpful? Which are least helpful?
8. As a professional, what changes would you recommend in your own working environment to make the IDEA more effective for everyone?

REFERENCES

Brown v. Board of Education, 347 U.S. 483 (1954).

Individuals with Disabilities Education Act (Education for All Handicapped Children Act of 1975), Pub. L. No. 94-142, 89 Stat. 773.

Individuals with Disabilities Education Act Amendments of 1997, Pub. L. No. 105-17, 111 Stat. 37.

Mills v. Board of Education of the District of Columbia, 348 F. Supp. 866 (D.D.C. 1972).

Pennsylvania Association for Retarded Citizens v. Pennsylvania, 334 F. Supp. 1257 (E.D. Pa. 1972), 343 F. Supp. 279 (E.D. Pa. 1972).

4

Section 504 of the Rehabilitation Act of 1973

Facts at a GLANCE

- Section 504 of the Rehabilitation Act of 1973 is a civil rights law.
- President Nixon signed the Act into law on September 26, 1973.
- The Act is considered the first comprehensive, nationwide law to protect individuals with disabilities in public schools.
- Students receiving services and protected under Section 504 have the same legal right to a free appropriate public education (FAPE) as students receiving services under the Individuals with Disabilities Education Act (IDEA).
- Students receiving services and protected under Section 504 have the same legal right to be educated in the least restrictive environment (LRE) as students receiving services under the IDEA.
- Eligible students needing accommodations and modifications in order to receive a FAPE under Section 504 are provided with a Section 504 plan.
- Congress defined students eligible for protection and services under Section 504 as follows: "Any person who (i) has a physical or mental impairment which substantially limits one or more of such person's major life activities, (ii) has a record of such an impairment, or (iii) is regarded as having such an impairment" (29 U.S.C. § 706(7)(B)).
- Unlike the IDEA regulations, the Section 504 regulations do not mandate written notice to parents regarding the intent of the school to evaluate a child. A school may inform parents either verbally or in writing. In addition, unlike the IDEA, Section 504 does not mandate that the school obtain parental consent prior to evaluating a child.
- The continuum of placements is as important under Section 504 as it is under the IDEA.
- The enforcement of the Act is the responsibility of the Office for Civil Rights (OCR) in the U.S. Department of Education.
- Individuals claiming discrimination under Section 504 have 180 days from the alleged incident to file a complaint with OCR.

- Unlike the IDEA, Section 504 does not have a funding mechanism to support its implementation; therefore, states and school districts receive no funds for the appropriate implementation of the law.
- The most significant difference between the IDEA and Section 504 affects the student with a disability who is either suspended on a long-term basis or expelled; under Section 504, the student does not have the right to educational services, but under the IDEA, these services must be provided.
- Although Section 504 does not specifically mandate functional behavior assessments or behavior intervention plans, it does require the development of a behavior management plan to deal with a student's behavioral difficulties.

Section 504 of the Rehabilitation Act of 1973 is a civil rights law that protects individuals with disabilities from discrimination in the workplace, public schools, and any entity receiving federal funding. President Nixon signed the Act into law on September 26, 1973. The government agency responsible for developing the regulations at the time—the now nonexistent Department of Health, Education, and Welfare (HEW)—did not finalize and release regulations until 1977, however. In *Cherry v. Matthews* (1976), the U.S. District Court for the District of Columbia found HEW negligent in not developing regulations. Yell (2006) notes: "The Federal District Court of Washington, DC, held that the secretary of Health, Education, and Welfare (HEW) was required to issue the regulations implementing the act. In the opinion, the court sarcastically noted that Section 504 was certainly not intended to be self-executing" (p. 119). The delay in promulgating regulations has been attributed to confusion and disagreement over the intent of Congress, political wrangling, and poor execution by HEW.

Experts consider the Act the first comprehensive, nationwide law to protect individuals with disabilities in public schools. The law prohibits schools from discriminating against "otherwise qualified" students with disabilities. In addition, it protects parents with disabilities against discrimination. Specific accommodations must be made to provide parents with disabilities opportunities and access comparable to those provided to nondisabled parents. Section 504 mandates individualized plans for eligible students with disabilities who need accommodations or modifications in order to ensure a free and appropriate public education (FAPE). Next to the Individuals with Disabilities Education Act (IDEA), Section 504 has the greatest daily impact on K–12 public school districts and personnel in relation to providing accommodations and protection from discrimination for students with disabilities.

Interestingly, after the passage of the Education for All Handicapped Children Act (what is now the IDEA) in 1975, New Mexico was the only state to abstain from filing a state plan for implementation and funding. The New Mexico Board of Education elected not to meet the expansive requirements of the law and to instead forfeit the federal funding accompanying the IDEA. New Mexico did not want to take on the financial burden of implementing the many provisions of the law, often referred to as an "unfunded mandate." In the case *New Mexico Association for Retarded Citizens v. New Mexico* (1982), the association claimed the state was discriminating against children with disabilities under Section 504 by not providing them with an appropriate public education. The association won the case, and since New Mexico had to comply with Section 504 and provide appropriate services to children with disabilities anyway, it decided to submit a state plan for the implementation of the IDEA and accept the federal funding. Simply put, Section 504 served as the impetus for New Mexico—the final state—to comply with the IDEA.

Section 504, which prohibits discrimination against individuals with disabilities in any federally funded program, is codified at 29 U.S.C. § 794:

Nondiscrimination under Federal grants and programs

(a) Promulgation of nondiscriminatory rules and regulations

■ No otherwise qualified individual with a disability in the United States, as defined in Sec. 705(20) of this title, shall, solely by reason of her or his disability, be excluded from the participation in, be denied the benefits of, or be subjected to discrimination under any program or activity receiving Federal financial assistance or under any program or activity conducted by any Executive agency. . . .

DISCRIMINATION UNDER SECTION 504

The following federal regulations prohibit discriminatory actions under Section 504; specifically, they state that a recipient, in providing any aid, benefit, or service, may not, directly or through contractual or other arrangements, on the basis of disability,

■ Deny a qualified individual with a disability the opportunity to participate in or benefit from the aid, benefit, or service (34 C.F.R. § 104.4(b)(1)(i)).

■ Afford a qualified individual with a disability an opportunity to participate in or benefit from the aid, benefit, or service that is not equal to that afforded others (34 C.F.R. § 104.4(b)(1)(ii)).

■ Provide a qualified individual with a disability an aid, benefit, or service that is not as effective as that provided to others (34 C.F.R. § 104.4(b)(1)(iii)).

■ Provide different or separate aid, benefits, or services to individuals with disabilities or to any class of individuals with disabilities unless such action is necessary to provide a qualified individual with a disability with aid, benefits, or services that are as effective as those provided to others (34 C.F.R. § 104.4(b)(1)(iv)).

■ Aid or perpetuate discrimination against a qualified individual with a disability by providing significant assistance to an agency, organization, or person that discriminates on the basis of disability in providing any aid, benefit, or service to beneficiaries of the recipient's program (34 C.F.R. § 104.4(b)(1)(v)).

■ Deny a qualified individual with a disability the opportunity to participate as a member of planning or advisory boards (34 C.F.R. § 104.4(b)(1)(vi)).

■ Otherwise limit a qualified individual with a disability in the enjoyment of any right, privilege, advantage, or opportunity enjoyed by others receiving an aid, benefit, or service (34 C.F.R. § 104.4(b)(1)(vii)).

■ Directly or though contractual or other arrangements utilize criteria or methods of administration (i) that have the effect of subjecting qualified individuals with disabilities to discrimination on the basis of disability, (ii) that have the purpose or effect of defeating or substantially impairing accomplishment of the objectives of the recipient's program with respect to individuals with disabilities, or (iii) that perpetuate the discrimination of another recipient if both recipients are subject to common administrative control or are agencies of the same state (34 C.F.R. § 104.4(b)(4)).

FREE APPROPRIATE PUBLIC EDUCATION

Students receiving services and protected under Section 504 have the same legal right to a FAPE as students receiving services under the IDEA. As with the IDEA, Section 504 FAPE requirements fall under two main areas: substantive and procedural. The U.S. Court of Appeals for the Third Circuit noted in 1995: "There appear to be few differences, if any, between IDEA's affirmative duty [to provide FAPE] and § 504's negative prohibition [of discrimination]" (W.B. v. Matula, 1995).

In relation to FAPE and K–12 education, the regulations stipulate as follows: "A recipient that operates a public elementary or secondary education program shall provide a free appropriate public education to each qualified handicapped person who is in the recipient's jurisdiction, regardless of the nature or severity of the person's handicap" (34 C.F.R. § 104.33(a)). The U.S. Department of Education's Office for Civil Rights (OCR), which enforces Section 504 among recipients of department funds, has found districts negligent in providing students with FAPE under Section 504 in these major areas:

1. failing to properly evaluate the student;
2. failing to identify all the items in the complete range of educational services and specific supplemental aids and services that the student needs to receive FAPE; and

LEAST RESTRICTIVE ENVIRONMENT

Students receiving services and protected under Section 504 have the same legal right to be educated in the least restrictive environment (LRE) as students receiving services under the IDEA. Section 504 stipulates specific expectations in three distinct areas: (1) academic settings, (2) nonacademic settings, and (3) comparable facilities. In relation to FAPE and K–12 education, the regulations stipulate as follows:

Educational setting

(a) Academic settings. A recipient to which this subpart applies shall educate, or shall provide for the education of, each qualified handicapped person in its jurisdiction with persons who are not handicapped to the maximum extent appropriate to the needs of the handicapped person. A recipient shall place a handicapped person in the regular educational environment operated by the recipient unless it is demonstrated by the recipient that the education of the person in the regular environment with the use of supplementary aids and services cannot be achieved satisfactorily. Whenever a recipient places a person in a setting other than the regular educational environment pursuant to this paragraph, it shall take into account the proximity of the alternate setting to the person's home.

(b) Nonacademic settings. In providing or arranging for the provision of nonacademic and extracurricular services and activities, including meals, recess periods, and the services and activities set forth in Sec. 104.37(a)(2), a recipient shall ensure that handicapped persons participate with nonhandicapped persons in such activities and services to the maximum extent appropriate to the needs of the handicapped person in question.

(c) Comparable facilities. If a recipient, in compliance with paragraph (a) of this section, operates a facility that is identifiable as being for handicapped persons, the recipient shall ensure that the facility and the services and activities provided therein are comparable to the other facilities, services, and activities of the recipient. (34 C.F.R. § 104.34)

ACCOMMODATIONS

The Rehabilitation Act mandates that all school districts with 15 or more employees assign an individual to serve as the Section 504 coordinator. This individual is responsible for ensuring the district stays in compliance with the regulatory requirements of the Act. Schools must provide eligible students needing accommodations and modifications in order to receive a FAPE under Section 504 with a Section 504 plan. The Section 504 plan lists the specific details of the child's individual needs. Schools have a wide array of options and a great deal of latitude in utilizing and implementing strategies, accommodations, and modifications. In 1991, the U.S. Department of Education provided a list, albeit not exhaustive, of

FIGURE 4.1
Guideline for Accommodations for Children with Disabilities

Providing a structured learning environment

Repeating and simplifying instructions about in-class assignments

Repeating and simplifying instructions about homework assignments

Supplementing verbal instructions with visual instructions

Using behavioral management techniques

Modifying test delivery

Using tape recorders

Computer aided instruction

Other audio-visual equipment

Selecting modified textbooks

Selecting modified workbooks

Tailoring homework assignments

Consulting with special education

Reducing class size

Use of one-on-one tutorials

Use of classroom aides

Use of classroom note takers

Involvement of a services coordinator to oversee implementation of special programs and services

Possible modification of nonacademic time such as lunchroom

Possible modification of nonacademic time such as recess

Possible modification of nonacademic time such as physical education

appropriate accommodations and services for students eligible for services under Section 504 in a *Joint Policy Memorandum* (1991). The list in Figure 4.1 serves as a guideline for appropriate accommodations and adaptations to the learning environment to best meet the needs of children with disabilities.

ELIGIBILITY FOR SERVICES

In a 1974 amendment designed to strengthen the Rehabilitation Act's language, Congress defined individuals eligible for protection and services under Section 504 as follows: "Any person who (i) has a physical or mental impairment which substantially limits one or more of such person's major life activities, (ii) has a record of such an impairment, or (iii) is regarded as having such an impairment" (29 U.S.C. § 706(7)(B)).

The implementing regulations further define the terms used in the statutory definition:

"Physical or mental impairment"

1. "[A]ny physiological disorder or condition, cosmetic disfigurement, or anatomical loss affecting one or more of the following body systems: neurological; musculoskeletal; special sense organs; respiratory, including speech organs; cardiovascular; reproductive, digestive, genito-urinary; hemic and lymphatic; skin; and endocrine"; or
2. "[A]ny mental or psychological disorder, such as mental retardation, organic brain syndrome, emotional or mental illness, and specific learning disabilities." 34 C.F.R. § 104.3(j)(2)(i)

"Major life activity"

"Functions such as caring for one's self, performing manual tasks, walking, seeing, hearing, speaking, breathing, learning and working" 34 C.F.R. § 104.3(j)(2)(ii). It is important to note that Congress did not intend to limit the possible activities to the list provided, but rather used broad language under which other limiting factors might fall.

"Substantially limits"

This term is more difficult to define. Similar to the word "appropriate" in FAPE, "substantially" is a word that is subjective and must be analyzed carefully by Section 504 teams. OCR has determined that the phrase is to be defined by the local educational agency (Letter to McKethan, 1994).

It is important to note that a child with a medical diagnosis of an impairment is not automatically eligible for services under Section 504. For example, a common misunderstanding is that a child with a medical diagnosis of attention deficit hyperactivity disorder/attention deficit disorder (ADHD/ADD) is automatically eligible for services. In fact, the eligibility team must determine if the condition limits one or more life activities—namely, learning. Many students with ADHD/ADD perform adequately without accommodations or modifications. Although not mandated, experts recommend referring a child who is found not eligible for services under the IDEA for consideration for services under Section 504.

EVALUATION

Section 504 mandates that school districts inform students with disabilities and their parents of the districts' responsibility to evaluate potentially eligible students, as well as the districts' responsibility not to discriminate against these students. In response to this mandate, school districts commonly provide complete information about their responsibilities—including evaluation, antidiscrimination language, eligibility,

FIGURE 4.2

Assessment and Evaluation Under Section 504

Assessment and Evaluation

- Whether a team or an individual evaluates a child is up to the school district
- All assessments must be valid and administered by trained personnel
- Educational needs must be measured; IQ cannot be used as a sole criterion in any circumstance
- All areas of suspected disability do NOT have to be assessed
- Prior to any significant change in educational placement, a student must be reevaluated
- Following the evaluation process, placement decisions must be made by a knowledgeable team of people

---

grievance procedures, OCR contact information, and district contacts for Section 504 information—via the Internet, school-based postings, fact sheets available in the guidance office, and mailings. (See Figure 4.2.)

Unlike the IDEA regulations, the Section 504 regulations do not mandate written notice to parents regarding the intent of the school to evaluate a child. A school may inform parents either verbally or in writing. In addition, unlike the IDEA, Section 504 does not mandate that the school obtain parental consent prior to evaluating a child. Clearly, Congress left much more procedural discretion to school districts under Section 504. In an attempt to explain the difference in language between the IDEA and Section 504, Huefner (2000) contends: "Because some evaluations can be quite informal and are without implications for a change of status (i.e., from a regular to a special education student), the need to seek consent is not as serious a due process issue as it is under IDEA" (p. 65). To ensure communication with parents and protection of the student, this author highly recommends providing written notice prior to any evaluation, eligibility meeting, or placement. The courts and administrative agencies (i.e., OCR) have supported the utilization of the IDEA's procedures with Section 504 issues.

PLACEMENT

Consistent with the IDEA, a team of knowledgeable people must determine the appropriate placement for an eligible student. The range of placement options includes, but is not limited to, the regular classroom, which is preferred when possible; pull-out classes; self-contained programs within a comprehensive school; day schools; private facilities; residential programs; and hospitalization. The continuum of placements is as important under Section 504 as it is under the IDEA. The team must place the child in the regular education setting with his or her regular education peers as much as possible.

HEALTH AND MEDICAL ISSUES

Under Section 504, schools are responsible for providing the health services that are necessary for students with disabilities to attend school. If a student is suspected of having a medical condition that could be a disability, the school is required to arrange and pay for the medical assessment (34 C.F.R. § 104.35(a)–(b)). Once it is determined which health services must be provided during the day, the school is responsible for ensuring that those services are provided "by a qualified school nurse or other qualified person." A vast array of medical conditions may need attention during the school day, and there is currently no express limitation on the types of services that a school may be required to provide. As a general rule for practitioners, if a student must have the service, assessment, administration of medication, or aid related to his or her disability in order to attend school, the school is required to provide it. There are examples of medical conditions and related services that have been deemed necessary for schools to provide by OCR and courts of law:

- **Asthma.** Provide access to oxygen, nebulizers and inhalers.
- **Attention Deficit Disorder.** Administer medication at appropriate times during the school day.
- **Diabetes.** Monitoring of snack distribution and consumption; blood-sugar monitoring; and a qualified individual to administer insulin injections; providing snacks; and development for emergency procedures and protocols.
- **Multiple Chemical Sensitivity (MCS).** Monitoring by school nurse twice per day and the utilization of a process for oxygen availability.

ENFORCEMENT

As noted above, the enforcement of Section 504 in the context of education is the responsibility of the Office for Civil Rights (OCR) in the U.S. Department of Education. As such, OCR has jurisdiction to investigate claims of discrimination that allege violation of any aspect of Section 504 or the department's implementing regulations by entities that receive funding from the department. The law does not require that OCR investigate every complaint. Instead, OCR officials review each complaint and determine if it raises an inference of unlawful discrimination and therefore warrants further investigation. The *OCR Case Resolution and Investigation Manual,* developed in 1994 and updated periodically, provides criteria for OCR officials to use in order to determine whether or not a claim warrants further investigation.

COMPLAINT FILING TIMETABLE

Individuals claiming discrimination under Section 504 have 180 days from the alleged incident to file a complaint with OCR. OCR officials do, however, retain the power to grant extensions under certain circumstances (34 C.F.R. § 80.7(b)). When multiple allegations of discrimination are filed with OCR, the 180-day timeline begins with the date of the most recent infraction.

PRIVATE RIGHT TO ACTION

Section 504 does not discuss a private right of action. Basically, no language exists that prohibits or supports an individual's right to bring a suit to court under Section 504 in order to receive financial remuneration. Although the U.S. Supreme Court has not yet ruled specifically on this issue with regard to Section 504, in *Cort v. Ash* (1975) the Court did establish a four-part test for determining if a private right to action exists:

1. Is the claimant a member of the class to be benefited by the statute?
2. Is there an explicit or implicit legislative intent to indicate whether there should be a private right of action?
3. Is it consistent with legislative intent to allow a private right of action?
4. Is the cause of action one that should traditionally be brought under state law?

To date, the clear majority of the federal circuit courts of appeals have ruled in favor of a private right of action under Section 504 (Rothstein, 2000).

FUNDING

Unlike the IDEA, Section 504 does not have a funding mechanism to support its implementation; therefore, states and school districts receive no funds for the appropriate implementation of the law. The law, however, can have a tremendous impact on federal funding to states and localities. As explicitly mandated by Congress, any organization found to engage in discriminatory practices may have all federal funding revoked. For example, if one school is found in violation of Section 504 by OCR, the entire school district may lose all federal funding from the U.S. Department of Education. In 1984, the U.S. Supreme Court supported the assertion in *Grove City College v. Bell* that a violation of Section 504 in one program should not impact the federal funding of an entity's other programs. Congress then amended Section 504 through the Civil Rights Restoration Act of

1987, adding language to make it clear that a violation of Section 504 in one program or activity could impact all programs of the entity found to be discriminating. Therefore, the federal funding of the entire agency could be withheld for a violation in a single program. According to Huefner (2000), "Congress apparently did not want to subsidize any institution that was discriminating anywhere within the program." Thus, while Section 504 provides no funding for its implementation, it can impose severe financial sanctions on those organizations that are found guilty of discrimination.

DISCIPLINE

Students eligible for protection under Section 504 may not be suspended or expelled for more than ten days if the infraction is a manifestation of their disability. Similar to the IDEA, Section 504 provides separate procedures and requirements for long-term removals from school that would result in a change in placement. In *S-1 v. Turlington* (1981), the U.S. Court of Appeals for the Fifth Circuit held that special procedures apply when a student with a disability is suspended for more than ten days under the IDEA and Section 504.

The most significant difference between the IDEA and Section 504 affects the student with a disability who is either suspended on a long-term basis or expelled. The IDEA mandates "no cessation of services" for students with disabilities, even if they are expelled for an entire year. Under the IDEA, the school district must continue to provide educational services. Under Section 504, if the student is expelled and the behavior is not a manifestation of his or her disability, the school district is *not* obligated to provide educational services (OSEP Memorandum 95-16, 1995).

The 1997 amendments to the IDEA included the implementation of functional behavioral assessments (FBAs) and behavior intervention plans (BIPs) for students whose behavior is impacting their academic progress. Although Section 504 does not specifically mandate FBAs or BIPs, it does require the development of a behavior management plan to deal with a student's behavioral difficulties (Morgan v. Chris L., 1997). OCR provided further guidance in *Elk Grove Unified School District* (1997):

> When a student who is disabled within the meaning of Section 504 manifests repeated or serious misconduct such that modifying the child's negative behavior becomes a significant component of what actually takes place in the child's educational program, a district is required to develop an individual behavioral management plan. (p. 761)

It should be noted that behavior management plans often provide alternatives to the general code of conduct applied to all students in a school district. Schools must adhere to the behavior management strategies provided through the Section 504 plan. Neither the IDEA nor Section 504 provides specific guidelines for the development of behavior management plans or behavior intervention plans. (See Figure 4.3.) Schools must look to district or state guidelines for the specific requirements of these plans.

FIGURE 4.3

Comparative Analysis: The IDEA and Section 504

Topic	IDEA	Section 504
Accessibility	Must be provided to satisfy FAPE mandate	Prescriptive regulations stipulate accessibility to programs and facilities
Accommodations and modifications	Must be provided to ensure a FAPE	Must be provided to ensure a FAPE
Consent	Mandated prior to evaluation, placement, or change in placement	No consent requirement
Discipline	When expelled or long-term suspended, a student must still receive educational services "no cessation of services."	If a student is long-term suspended or expelled for conduct that was found to be a manifestation of his or her disability, no educational services are mandated if the disability was not a manifestation of the disability.
Eligibility	Must be identified under one of the major disability categories; the student's disability must significantly impact his academic progress	Must have a mental or physical impairment that affects one or more major life functions; very broad spectrum of disorders are included under 504; easier to be eligible for protection than under the IDEA
Employment	Not addressed	Non-discrimination guidelines are provided
Enforcement	OSEP	OCR

Evaluation	Extensive requirements: no single assessment; multiple tools that are valid must be employed and conducted by qualified professionals; tests must be administered in the child's native language; parental input is encouraged; cultural and racial bias must be avoided and cannot influence the evaluation process.	Although use of the same standards as IDEA is recommended by OCR, Section, 504 is not as prescriptive. It does require that all evaluators be qualified; that assessments be valid, and that multiple assessments must be used; no specific timeline is provided.
FAPE	Specific mandate to provide a FAPE	Different language, but the FAPE expectation is the same as in the IDEA
Funding	Has a funding mechanism	No funding
Grievance procedures	Prescriptive due process procedures	Due process hearings OCR complaint process
IEP	Mandatory	504 plan
LRE	Mandates involvement in regular education classes as much as possible with necessary supports and accommodations	Different language, but the LRE expectation is the same as in the IDEA
Notice	Written notice is required prior to evaluation and placement.	Required prior to identification, evaluation, and placement
Placement	The LRE among the continuum of placements must be considered in determining LRE (the regular classroom is preferred); the IEP team must justify to the extent to which the child is removed from regular education classes (severity of disability must warrant removal)	Same expectation; however, the Section 504 team, not the IEP team, must justify any placement or services outside of the regular education classroom
Procedural Safeguards	Prescriptive, voluminous set of procedural safeguards including— prior written notice, informed consent for evaluations, stay-put provision, hearings, mediation, state complaint process	Very limited procedural safeguards—due process hearing and OCR complaint process

(Continued)

FIGURE 4.3 (Continued)

Protected ages	Birth to 21	Entire life
Purpose	To provide prescriptive mandates and procedural safeguards to ensure a FAPE in the LRE; provide funding for the appropriate implementation of the Act	To prevent discrimination against individuals with disabilities; civil rights law; provides powerful financial sanctions to prevent discrimination among those groups receiving federal funding

SUMMARY

Signed into law on September 26, 1973, by President Nixon, Section 504 of the Rehabilitation Act of 1973 is a civil rights law. Its broad, antidiscrimination language protects "otherwise qualified" individuals with disabilities from discrimination in relation to participation in or access to activities, programs, or facilities that receive federal funding.

The law states that a student is eligible for protection under Section 504 when he or she "(i) has a physical or mental impairment which substantially limits one or more. . . . major life activities, (ii) has a record of such an impairment, or (iii) is regarded as having such an impairment." (29 U.S.C. § 706(7)(B)). Eligible students may or may not need special education services. In contrast to the specific disability categories of the IDEA, Section 504 allows for a broad spectrum of disabling conditions. Although specific disabling conditions are listed in the law, the list is by no means exhaustive or intended to be so.

A student needing accommodations or modifications is provided with a Section 504 plan, which includes specific details of the student's needs and services. Each school district with 15 or more employees must appoint a Section 504 coordinator. This person is responsible for ensuring the district is in compliance with the Act.

The Office for Civil Rights in the U.S. Department of Education is responsible for the enforcement of Section 504 among recipients of funds from the department. Individuals may file discrimination complaints with OCR. A complaint must be filed within 180 days of the alleged infraction, although OCR does reserve the right to grant extensions in extenuating circumstances. While no language in Section 504 specifically addressing a private right of action to seek financial remuneration, the majority of federal circuit courts of appeals have found in favor of such actions.

All programs within a local or state agency may lose federal funding if one program within the agency is found guilty of discrimination under Section 504. As a pure civil rights law, the Act provides no funding; however, its authorization to withhold federal funding has powerful financial implications.

As under the IDEA, a school may not suspend a student protected under Section 504 for more than ten days if the behavior is a manifestation of his or her disability. However, if the student's behavior is not a manifestation of his or her disability, the student may be disciplined as a regular education student would be. Unlike the IDEA, Section 504 does not include a "no cessation of services" clause.

Applying the Law in the Classroom

Eva Mios is a third-grade student who recently moved into the Mountain View School District and enrolled in Pilgrim Elementary School (PES). Eva has a condition called athetoid cerebral palsy (CP). CP is a neurological disorder that affects an individual's ability to control his or her muscles. Eva's specific type of CP—athetoid—makes it difficult for her to control her arms and legs. In addition, she has difficulty speaking, and thus, it is difficult to understand her. Due to the severity of her CP, Eva must use a motorized wheelchair to ambulate. She is very bright, although she needs modifications to function successfully in the regular school environment. Eva has been completely integrated into the regular education setting and neighborhood school since kindergarten.

Upon enrolling Eva in PES, her parents requested a meeting with school representatives to discuss her Section 504 plan from her previous school and to develop a new one for the upcoming academic year. Eva's mother provided the Section 504 team members with a copy of the plan to review prior to the meeting. Eva had thrived at her other school, and her parents were very pleased with the accommodations and modifications in that plan:

■ scheduling of all classes on the first floor of the school or appropriate access provisions provided;

■ modified physical education, which included two days per week of one-on-one instruction by a qualified individual to focus on fine and gross motor skills;

■ toileting support and maintenance of her catheter by the school nurse twice daily;

■ speech therapy three times per week; and

■ support with packing and unpacking her books and supplies (students and teachers helped with this accommodation in her old school—not an aide)

In addition, Mrs. Mios provided a copy of Eva's cumulative file with all of her medical information. The meeting was promptly scheduled for the next day at 2:00 P.M.

The Section 504 team met at 9:00 A.M. without the parents to discuss Eva's Section 504 plan. After reviewing Eva's plan from her previous school and her cumulative file, the team determined that the school was not equipped or qualified to provide certain accommodations.

Not anticipating any issues, Eva's parents arrived promptly at 2:00 P.M. ready to discuss and collaboratively develop Eva's new Section 504 plan. The meeting was chaired by the district psychologist—Dr. Ellen Evans. She opened by reviewing the contents of last year's plan and Eva's academic and medical records. Then, without asking Mr. and Mrs. Mios for their input, Dr. Evans informed them that the school would be unable to implement certain components of Eva's old Section 504 plan. She agreed that the school could adequately provide speech therapy, access, and support with books and supplies. However, Dr. Evans stated that it was not the school's responsibility to provide medical services such as catheter care and physical therapy (specialized physical education). She noted that given the severity of their daughter's disability and the extent of her medical needs, PES could not feasibly meet her needs in the regular education setting.

The team recommended Eva for placement in a program for students with severe physical and mental disabilities located in a nearby elementary school. Dr. Evans informed the parents it would be the responsibility of the new school (program) to develop her Section 504 plan.

Application Questions

1. If you were Mr. or Mrs. Mios, how would you respond to Dr. Evans and the team?
2. How could the school have conducted the meeting in a better way?
3. Does Eva have the right to LRE under Section 504?
4. Do you believe the school is proposing to place Eva in the LRE? Why or why not?
5. Does it sound like the school is meeting the requirements of FAPE?

6. Is the school correct in asserting that PES does not have the responsibility of providing medically related services?
7. Do you believe that Eva is potentially being discriminated against under Section 504? Why or why not?
8. What course of action might Mr. and Mrs. Mios take if they believe discrimination is taking place?
9. Why is Eva being served under Section 504 rather than the IDEA? Could Eva be served under the IDEA?

CRITICAL THINKING QUESTIONS

1. From both historical and civil rights standpoints, why was the passage of Section 504 of the Rehabilitation Act of 1973 important?
2. Why is the Rehabilitation Act of 1973 considered a civil rights law and the IDEA is not?
3. How did a lawsuit under Section 504 significantly affect New Mexico's decision to file a state plan under the IDEA? Why do you think a state might not want to abide by the requirements of the IDEA?
4. In your opinion, what are the most significant differences between Section 504 and the IDEA?
5. Section 504 has fewer regulatory requirements than the IDEA does. List possible pros and cons of leaving more discretion to school districts.

REFERENCES

Cherry v. Mathews, 419 F. Supp. 922 (D.D.C. 1976).

Cort v. Ash, 422 U.S. 66 (1975).

Elk Grove Unified School District, 25 IDELR 759, 761 (OCR 1997).

Gorn, S. (2000). *The answer book on Section 504.* Horsham, PA: LRP.

Grove City College v. Bell, 465 U.S. 555 (1984).

Huefner, D. S. (2000). *Getting comfortable with special education law.* Norwood, MA: Christopher-Gordon.

Joint Policy Memorandum (ADD), 18 IDELR 116 (OSERS 1991).

Letter to McKethan, 23 IDELR 504 (OCR 1994).

Morgan v. Chris L., 106 F.3d 401 (6th Cir. 1997).

New Mexico Association for Retarded Citizens v. New Mexico, 678 F.2d 847 (10th Cir. 1982).

OCR Case Resolution and Investigation Manual. (1994). Washington, DC: OCR.

OSEP Memorandum 95-16, 22 IDELR 531 (OSEP 1995).

Rehabilitation Act of 1973 § 504, 29 U.S.C. § 794.

Rothstein, L. (2000). *Special education law* (3rd ed.). New York: Addison Wesley Longman.

S-1 v. Turlington, 635 F.2d 342 (5th Cir. 1981).

W.B. v. Matula, 63 F.3d 484 (3rd Cir. 1995).

Yell, M. (2006. *The law and special education* (2d Ed.). Upper Saddle River, NJ: Merrill/Prentice Hall.

5

The Americans with Disabilities Act

- The Americans with Disabilities Act (ADA) (Pub. L. No. 101-336) is codified at 42 U.S.C. §§ 12101–12213.
- President George H. W. Bush signed the Act into law on July 26, 1990.
- The signing of the Act was witnessed by one of the largest audiences in White House history.
- The Act is a civil rights law modeled after the Civil Rights Act of 1964.
- The Act extends the reach of Section 504 in order to further protect individuals with disabilities from discrimination.
- The Act, along with Section 504, extends to private schools, whereas the IDEA does not.
- The Act uses the same language as Section 504 to define protected individuals with disabilities.
- The Act comprises five titles, covering (1) employment, (2) public services, (3) public accommodations and services operated by private entities, (4) telecommunications, and (5) miscellaneous provisions.
- The three titles that most directly affect educators are Titles I (Employment), II (Public Services), and III (Public Accommodations).
- The Act protects individuals with HIV and tuberculosis.
- The ADA does not extend substantive or procedural rights beyond those provided by the IDEA and Section 504.
- In most education-related issues, ADA complaints and compliance issues are investigated by the Office for Civil Rights—as are Section 504 complaints and compliance issues.
- Case law involving K–12 education and the ADA is limited.
- In general, courts have analyzed ADA education cases consistently with those decided under Section 504.

The Americans with Disabilities Act (ADA) (Pub. L. No. 101-336) was signed into law on July 26, 1990, by President George H. W. Bush. The ADA is a civil rights law intended to expand the protection of individuals with disabilities from discrimination. In practical K–12 education terms, the ADA serves as an extension of Section 504 of the Rehabilitation Act of 1973. Whereas Section 504 is limited to regulating entities receiving federal funding, however, the antidiscrimination prohibitions of the ADA extend into the private sector without regard to funding. Although the ADA is a very important piece of civil rights legislation, it is necessary to put the various laws discussed in this text into perspective. In relation to the other major pieces of federal legislation that impact students with disabilities in K–12 education—No Child Left Behind, the Individuals with Disabilities Education Act (IDEA), and Section 504—the ADA has the least amount of daily impact on practitioners.

With strong legislation specifically addressing the education of children with disabilities and with no specific language in the ADA exceeding the substantive and procedural rights guaranteed by the IDEA and Section 504, the ADA does not provide additional rights (Wenkart, 1993). A limited body of case law exists regarding K–12 education and the ADA, and a review of these decisions indicates the courts have generally opined that ADA cases should be interpreted in a fashion consistent with Section 504 (Yell, 2006). In a nutshell, the courts have found that the ADA does not provide or extend any substantive or procedural rights to students with disabilities in K–12 settings beyond those provided by the IDEA or Section 504.

With that understanding, the practitioner may question why it is important to study and understand the ADA. One of the most important reasons is that the ADA extends to private schools. The ADA addresses major school-based issues related to facility accessibility and nondiscriminatory treatment of employees. Third, and possibly most important, it is essential for students with disabilities who are exiting high school to be aware of all their rights and protections in the workplace and community. More detailed discussion will follow with the analysis of the five titles that make up the ADA. This chapter will serve as a general overview of the structure, intent, requirements, enforcement, and implications of the law.

PURPOSE OF THE ACT

The purpose of the ADA is to protect the civil rights of individuals with disabilities. In a clear and concise manner, the lawmakers in the 101st session of Congress stated the purpose of the Act:

(b) Purpose.—It is the purpose of this chapter—
■ to provide a clear and comprehensive national mandate for the elimination of discrimination against individuals with disabilities;
■ to provide clear, strong, consistent, enforceable standards addressing discrimination against individuals with disabilities;

- to ensure that the Federal Government plays a central role in enforcing the standards established in this chapter on behalf of individuals with disabilities; and
- to invoke the sweep of congressional authority, including the power to enforce the fourteenth amendment and to regulate commerce, in order to address the major areas of discrimination faced. (42 U.S.C. § 12101(b))

Developed in the same spirit as and modeled after the Civil Rights Act of 1964, the ADA prohibits discrimination in employment, services rendered by state and local governments, places of public accommodation, transportation, and telecommunications. Congress noted in the ADA's "Findings" that

> (1) some 43,000,000 Americans have one or more physical or mental disabilities, and this number is increasing as the population as a whole is growing older; (2) historically, society has tended to isolate and segregate individuals with disabilities, and, despite some improvements, such forms of discrimination against individuals with disabilities continue to be a serious and pervasive social problem. . . . (42 U.S.C. § 12101(a)(1)–(2))

The second half of the twentieth century witnessed the greatest legislative strides in addressing discrimination against all Americans through civil rights acts. The support and need for the ADA are a testament to the long and expansive history of discrimination against individuals with disabilities. Furthermore, the Act demonstrates the extensive amount of regulatory protection and enforcement needed to ensure the civil rights of all individuals with disabilities.

DEFINITION OF A DISABILITY

Congress adopted the same criteria to define those individuals with disabilities protected under the ADA as it did for the Rehabilitation Act of 1973:

- a physical or mental impairment that substantially limits one or more of the major life activities of such individual;
- a record of such an impairment; or
- being regarded as having such an impairment. (42 U.S.C. § 12102(2))

STRUCTURE OF THE ACT

The ADA comprises five titles, specifically addressing the areas of (1) employment, (2) public services, (3) public accommodations and services operated by private entities, (4) telecommunications, and (5) miscellaneous provisions. As noted earlier, the Act as a whole has limited impact on daily K–12 education. The three titles most directly affecting educators are Titles I (Employment), II (Public Services), and III (Public Accommodations).

EFFECTIVE DATES

The ADA established different time lines for compliance within the myriad mandates of Titles I–V:

1. Employers with 25 or more employees: July 26, 1992.
2. Employers with 15 or more employees: July 26, 1994.
3. Public accommodations: July 26, 1992.
4. State and local government programs and activities: January 26, 1992.
5. Transportation: The most expansive range is found here. Accessibility requirements extend from 30 days to 30 years. Existing "key stations" in rapid rail, commuter rail, and light rail systems must be made accessible by July 26, 1993, unless an extension of up to 20 years is granted (30 years, in some cases, rapid and light rail).
6. Telecommunications: Three years following the effective date of the Act: July 26, 1992.

TITLE I, EMPLOYMENT

Title I of the ADA prohibits discrimination by "covered entities" against "qualified" individuals with disabilities in the workplace. Employers, including religious organizations, with 15 or more employees must provide the same levels of access and opportunity to qualified individuals with disabilities as they do to those without disabilities. Employers may not use discriminatory practices in recruitment, hiring, wage setting, promotion, training, or any other component of the employment process. According to Yell (2006), "Employers, employment agencies, labor organizations, and labor-management committees are referred to in the law as 'covered entities.' ... Neither the U.S. Government nor private membership clubs [are] covered by Title 1" (p. 161). Section 504 of the Rehabilitation Act already protects qualified school employees (e.g., teachers) from disability discrimination (Huefner, 2000). In order to ensure nondiscriminatory practices, this title (1) prohibits certain questions pertaining to disabilities and (2) mandates that reasonable accommodations be made for otherwise qualified individuals with mental or physical disabilities.

The U.S. Equal Employment Opportunity Commission (EEOC) is responsible for the enforcement of Title I. Complaints must be made to the EEOC within 180 days of the alleged incident or within 300 days if the complaint must be filed first with a designated state or local fair employment practices agency. Individuals may file a private lawsuit in federal court; however, they must first obtain a "right to sue" letter through the EEOC.

TITLE II, PUBLIC SERVICES

Title II prohibits all state and local governments, irrespective of size or public funding, from discriminating against individuals with disabilities. Every practitioner should understand that this title protects qualified individuals with disabilities in public schools. The list of services in which Title II specifically prohibits discrimination against protected individuals with disabilities includes, but is not limited to, public transportation, social services, recreational facilities, courts, schools, and health care (note that the federal government is not included).

Unlike Section 504, Title II covers those entities that do not receive federal funding. State and local governments are mandated to provide reasonable modifications to otherwise qualified individuals with disabilities so they can benefit from and engage in government-supported activities (Huefner, 2000). Under this title, state and local government agencies are responsible for adhering to the architectural standards for new and existing facilities covered in Title III. Agencies also are required to accommodate the communication needs of individuals with speech, hearing, and related communication disabilities.

Enforcement of Title II is the responsibility of the U.S. Department of Justice (DOJ). Complaints of discrimination must be filed within 180 days of the alleged infraction. After receiving the complaint, DOJ may choose to refer the case to a mediator or bring suit against the defendant.

TITLE III, PUBLIC ACCOMMODATIONS

Title III expressly prohibits discrimination against individuals with disabilities by commercial entities, nonprofit organizations, and privately owned businesses that provide services and accommodations to the public. Commercial groups include those entities that engage in any form of intrastate, interstate, or international commerce (i.e., communications, transportation, trade, and various forms of travel). Specifically, this title prohibits discrimination against individuals with disabilities by businesses or organizations that own, lease, or rent, including, but not limited to, public transportation; amusement parks; museums; private schools (nursery through postgraduate); private agencies and secondary or postsecondary programs offering licensing, credentialing, or certification for trade or professional use (e.g., teacher, electrical, and cosmetology licenses); hospitals; retail stores (e.g., shops in a mall); athletic venues (stadiums or arenas); day care providers; homeless shelters; funeral homes; and health clubs. This list is by no means exhaustive; however, it does provide examples of specific entities included in the broad categories covered by this title (42 U.S.C. § 12181(7)).

It is also vital to understand which organizations are not covered by Title III. With such a broad category as public accommodations, it would be easy to assume that certain organizations are prohibited from discriminating by Title III. However, critical groups including churches and religious organizations, public and parochial schools, and public entities in general are exempt from the requirements of this title.

Title III mandates that facilities of public accommodation—both existing and new—be accessible to individuals with disabilities. All new facilities fall under the specific regulations of this title, which provide prescriptive guidance regarding accessibility and architectural barriers. Existing facilities must remove architectural barriers if this can be done reasonably and without extensive expense. Congress did not intend to place unreasonable expectations and financial burdens on public accommodations. The term "readily achievable," used in this title to describe the responsibility of public accommodations to remove architectural barriers in already existing facilities, is subjective and intended to be applied on a case-by-case basis.

Enforcement of Title III is, like that of Title II, the responsibility of DOJ. After receiving a complaint, DOJ may choose to refer the case to a mediator or bring suit against the defendant. In addition, an individual has the right to bring a private suit without contacting DOJ.

TITLE IV, TELECOMMUNICATIONS

Title IV addresses access to television and telephone services for individuals with hearing and speech disabilities. The ADA requires telephone companies and "commercial carriers" to provide intrastate and interstate telecommunication relay service (TRS) 24 hours per day, 7 days per week. The TRS provides opportunities for individuals with hearing and speech disabilities to communicate through a third party. In addition, this title mandates that all federally funded televised public service announcements be provided with closed captioning—that is, all spoken language must be typed at the bottom of the screen for the hearing impaired. The Federal Communications Commission, which is responsible for the enforcement of this title, has established standards for the appropriate implementation of the TRS.

TITLE V, MISCELLANEOUS PROVISIONS

Title V is a "grab bag" of provisions that address a wide range of issues, including the ADA's relationship to other state and federal statutes, namely, the Rehabilitation Act of 1973; insurance; mediation and dispute resolution; technical assistance; and Congress as a covered entity. In brief summary, Title V

- specifically prohibits any type of constraints, intimidations, or threats against any individuals who exercises their rights under the ADA.
- ensures that the ADA cannot apply lesser standards than those established by the Rehabilitation Act of 1973.
- guarantees that the ADA will not place any limitations on any federal or state law that provides equal or greater protection.
- mandates that the ADA will have no effect on current state laws and policies overseeing insurance and will not limit valid underwriting procedures based on risk classification.

- does not protect conditions solely related to sexual identity rather than a disability.
- does not protect active drug users, but does not discriminate against those who are former drug users, with records that show they have participated in rehabilitation programs, or are mistakenly regarded as users.

EVALUATION

The ADA mandates that all school districts employing 50 or more individuals conduct an internal evaluation (self-evaluation). The evaluation must be kept on record for three years. If a district has already completed a Section 504 evaluation, only those policies and practices not yet reviewed must be considered in order to comply with the ADA evaluation requirement (28 C.F.R. § 35.105(d)). The district should invite all interested parties to engage in the evaluation by providing written input. In relation to the content of the evaluation, Yell (2006) notes: "The description of the self-evaluation should include the names of interested persons consulted, a description of problems identified, and modifications to correct these problem areas" (p. 171). As with all evaluations, the results should be used to improve the overall practices and procedures of the district.

SUMMARY

The Americans with Disabilities Act (ADA) is a piece of civil rights legislation. President George H. W. Bush signed the Act into law on July 26, 1990, in front of one of the largest audiences to witness the signing of a law at the White House. The purpose of the ADA is to ensure that each individual, regardless of disability, is free from discrimination and, therefore, has the access to, rights to, and opportunities for employment, public services, public accommodations, and telecommunications that nondisabled persons have.

The ADA comprises five titles, covering (1) employment, (2) public services, (3) public accommodations and services operated by private entities, (4) telecommunications, and (5) miscellaneous provisions. The enforcement of the ADA is the responsibility of the following federal agencies: the Equal Employment Opportunity Commission, the Department of Justice, and the Federal Communications Commission. Each school district employing 50 or more individuals must complete a self-evaluation. This evaluation must then be kept on file for at least three years. Although the ADA does not provide substantive or procedural protections beyond the IDEA or Section 504, it is critical the students with disabilities learn what their individual rights are under the ADA before they leave high school.

Applying the Law in the Classroom

Chandler is a 15-year-old tenth grader who has just enrolled in The Elite School—a private school without religious affiliation that employs 50 people. He has congenital muscular dystrophy and uses a motorized wheelchair. Chandler also is diagnosed as having attention deficit hyperactivity disorder (ADHD) and takes medication to help moderate his impulsivity. Chandler transferred to Elite after his ninth-grade year at Chesterfield High School—a local public school. While at Chesterfield, Chandler received accommodations through a Section 504 plan. Because his disability had rendered him very weak, Chandler was unable to take out his books, open doors, or use the bathroom without assistance. Therefore, his Section 504 plan at Chesterfield provided him with a one-to-one aide to help him with the opening of doors, basic transitions, and daily management of his academic and personal needs. Chesterfield also provided him with preferential seating in the front of each class.

Upon enrolling in The Elite School, Chandler's parents provided his new guidance counselor with a copy of his Section 504 plan. The counselor informed the parents that The Elite School was not legally bound to comply with the requirements of Section 504 because it did not receive federal funding. The counselor further noted that the parents would need to hire an aide to help Chandler throughout the day and that he would not be able to attend the advanced science or mathematics courses because these classes were taught on the second floor and the school did not have an elevator. The parents asked if the courses could be offered on the first floor, and the counselor said, "No, if students are not able, for whatever reason, to meet the standards of our school, then they should probably go back to the public schools." Chandler and his parents were discouraged by their meeting with the counselor; however, they were determined to ensure Chandler had equal opportunity for and access to the same education as all other children.

Application Questions

1. Is Chandler protected under the ADA at The Elite School?
2. Is The Elite School required to follow any component of Chandler's Section 504 plan from Chesterfield High School?
3. If The Elite School were affiliated with a religion (that is, a parochial school), would it affect whether or not the school is subject to the ADA? Why or why not?
4. Which title of the ADA addresses the protection of individuals with disabilities in private schools? What does the title require?

5. Is The Elite School required to provide Chandler access to the two advanced classes? If so, what is the school required to do?
6. Does Chandler have any protections under the IDEA or Section 504? If so, what are they?
7. If Chandler's parents believe that he is being discriminated against under the ADA, what steps should they take to bring a complaint? How much time do they have, and to which agency do they submit the complaint?
8. In your opinion, is a child with a disability that requires considerable services and accommodations more likely to receive better support and services in a private or a public school? Why? What variables must be taken into account when answering this question?

CRITICAL THINKING QUESTIONS

1. In what ways is the ADA significantly different from the other major education-related federal statutes?
2. In relation to K–12 education, what do you consider to be the most important contributions of the ADA?
3. How does the ADA extend the protections under Section 504?
4. Why do you think Congress used the same three-pronged definition of disability for the ADA as it did for Section 504?
5. Why is it essential for students with disabilities to understand the protections of the ADA prior to graduating from high school?
6. Do you think businesses and public accommodations have been successful in meeting the architectural requirements (removal of barriers, etc.) of the ADA?
7. Briefly describe each title that affects either public or private K–12 education. Which title do you think is most important and why?

REFERENCES

Americans with Disabilities Act of 1990, 42 U.S.C. §§ 12101–12213.

Huefner, D. S. (2000). *Getting comfortable with special education law*. Norwood, MA: Christopher-Gordon.

Wenkart, R. D. (1993). The Americans with Disabilities Act and its impact on public education. *Education Law Reporter, 82,* 291–302.

Yell, M. (2006). *The law and special education* (2nd ed.). Upper Saddle River, NJ: Merrill/Prentice Hall.

6

IDEA 2004 Meets No Child Left Behind

- The No Child Left Behind Act of 2001 (NCLB) is the most recent reauthorization of the Elementary and Secondary Education Act (ESEA) of 1965.
- The stated goal of NCLB is to "level the playing field" in education between the haves and the have-nots.
- NCLB requires that schools disaggregate the annual progress of individual subgroups of students, including all racial and ethnic groups, as well as students with disabilities and English language learners.
- Schools that fail to make adequate yearly progress (AYP) toward full proficiency for the school and all subgroups face an increasingly prescriptive list of sanctions for their failure to do so.
- The law stresses the importance of using "scientifically based research" in designing educational programs and activities, especially in the Reading First and Early Reading First programs.
- NCLB requires that all state education agencies (SEAs) and local educational agencies (LEAs) provide a proposal for annually boosting the percentage of teachers of core content areas who are deemed "highly qualified" under the law.
- The highly objective uniform state standard of evaluation (HOUSSE) was first introduced in the ESEA as an alternative means for veteran teachers to prove competency in subject areas.
- NCLB sets minimum standards for paraprofessionals, including those who assist students with special needs.
- States are required to develop their own academic standards and submit plans to the U.S. Department of Education describing how they will annually close the achievement gap and move all children to proficiency with respect to those standards by the close of the 2013–2014 school year.

■ After a school fails to reach its AYP threshold for two years and is identified for improvement, the district must offer all students—including those with disabilities—the option to transfer to a high-performing public school in the district.

■ Schools that fail to meet their AYP marks for three consecutive years must offer their low-income students supplemental educational services.

■ Each year NCLB requires that a minimum of 95 percent of all students in all subgroups—including students with disabilities—participate in grade-level testing.

■ Rules finalized by the U.S. Department of Education in April 2007 (34 C.F.R. § 200.1) expanded testing exemptions to include 2 percent of disabled students who may be assessed against "modified achievement standards."

The 2004 amendments to the Individuals with Disabilities Education Act (IDEA) marked a confluence of the two largest pieces of federal education legislation in the history of the nation, melding the broad accountability of the No Child Left Behind Act of 2001 (NCLB) with the singular focus on children with disabilities of the IDEA. Not since the federal government initially entered the public school arena in the 1960s with the enactment of the Elementary and Secondary Education Act (ESEA) of 1965 has there been such a singular attempt to ensure the best possible education for all students—whether disabled or from a disadvantaged background. When President George W. Bush signed the Individuals with Disabilities Education Improvement Act (Pub. L. No. 108-446) into law on December 3, 2004, he not only preserved the rights guaranteed in the IDEA, but also tied the reforms in that law to the massive restructuring of federal K–12 involvement that evolved with NCLB.

NCLB—the first major piece of domestic legislation that President Bush signed after taking office and the most recent incarnation of the Elementary and Secondary Education Act of 1965—signaled a major shift in the role the federal government would play in education. The Bush administration and Congress crafted the law with the intent of closing the achievement gap between minority and low-income students and their more affluent white peers; the stated goal of the statute was to "level the playing field" in education between the haves and the have-nots. No longer was the federal government content to simply pump billions of dollars into the American public education system; instead, lawmakers expected to see results—and to demonstrate those results, they expected states and schools to measure the progress of *all* students. Therefore, the law mandated that states develop and implement accountability systems and standards for reading and mathematics.

As a condition of receiving formula grants, the statute requires that schools test all students annually in grades 3–8 and once in high school in reading and mathematics, with a goal of having all students reach proficiency in both subjects by the close of the 2013–2014 school year. Moreover, NCLB requires that schools disaggregate the annual progress of individual subgroups of students, including all racial and ethnic groups, as well as students with disabilities and English language learners. Schools that fail to make *adequate yearly progress (AYP)* toward full proficiency for the school and all subgroups face an increasingly prescriptive list of sanctions for their failure to do so. For instance, schools that do not meet their AYP targets for two or more years may be required to offer low-income parents the option to transfer their children to a high-achieving public school or to receive tutoring at the district's expense.

NCLB also emphasizes the need for schools to adopt proven programs and have them implemented by competent teachers. The law stresses the importance of using "scientifically based research" in designing educational programs and activities, especially in the Reading First and Early Reading First programs. And to ensure that the instruction matches the academic rigor of the programs, NCLB establishes minimum qualifications for teachers and paraprofessionals. The statute requires that states develop plans to ensure that all those who teach core academic subjects are deemed "highly qualified" by the end of the 2005–2006 school year.

Congress made it clear from the start of the IDEA reauthorization process that two of its main goals were reducing administrative paperwork and addressing the overidentification of minority students as disabled. However, lawmakers also touted the concept of instituting a more results-based system that would be closely aligned with NCLB. Congress had realized that it would be revamping the IDEA close on the heels of NCLB and left many of the specifics with regard to students with disabilities until consideration of the IDEA legislation. After several years of work, federal lawmakers and President Bush hailed NCLB as a success; ultimately, they claimed the IDEA amendments were another important step in ensuring that no child in America is left behind.

So how successful was Congress in aligning the IDEA with NCLB? Certainly, it will be years before the education community can evaluate the full implication of the IDEA's most recent overhaul, but an early evaluation indicates that the IDEA successfully clarifies many of the gray areas in NCLB related to students with disabilities. The IDEA 2004 adopts NCLB language in a handful of definitions—most notably, the definition of "highly qualified" teacher—and it clarifies some specifics as to how students with disabilities are expected to participate in state accountability systems. The language used in Section 602 of the IDEA 2004 (Pub. L. No. 108-446) directly links to 20 U.S.C. § 7801(23) of NCLB, although it makes modifications in how it applies to special education teachers. The IDEA 2004 also cross-references NCLB's definitions of "core academic subjects" (Pub. L. No. 108-446, § 602(4)) and "limited English proficient" (Pub. L. No. 108-446, § 602(18)).

HIGHLY QUALIFIED TEACHERS

A fundamental component of NCLB is its emphasis on rigorous training and core content expertise of teachers. It requires that all state education agencies (SEAs) and local education agencies (LEAs) include a proposal for annually boosting the percentage of teachers of core content areas who are deemed "highly qualified" under the law until the end of the 2005–2006 school year, when all teachers of "core academic subjects" must be highly qualified (20 U.S.C. § 6319(2)–(3)). The NCLB implementing regulations also require school districts to inform parents when students have been taught for four or more consecutive weeks by a teacher who is not "highly qualified" in a core academic subject area (34 C.F.R. § 200.61(a)(2)). NCLB defines "core academic subjects" to include English, reading, or language arts; mathematics; science; foreign languages; civics and government; economics; arts; history; and geography (20 U.S.C. § 7801(11)). To be highly qualified under NCLB (20 U.S.C. § 7801(23)), a teacher must

- hold at least a bachelor's degree;
- be fully certified by the state (including through "alternative" routes) or pass a state teacher-licensing examination (teachers will not be deemed highly qualified if they have had their certification requirements waived on an emergency, provisional, or temporary basis, however); and
- demonstrate subject-matter competency in each of the core academic subjects that he or she teaches.

Elementary teachers who are new to the classroom can demonstrate competency by passing a rigorous state test of subject-matter knowledge and teaching skills in reading, writing, mathematics, and other areas that are part of the basic elementary curriculum (20 U.S.C. § 7801(23)(B)(i)). New middle and high school teachers may prove competency in core subject areas through a variety of methods, including the provision of documentation showing that they hold a major in the subject they teach, earned credits equivalent to a major in the subject, passed a state-developed test, possess an advanced certification from the state, or hold a graduate degree (20 U.S.C. § 7801(23)(B)(ii)). Veteran teachers can show competency by using any of the above methods or by meeting a highly objective uniform state standard of evaluation, or HOUSSE, as determined by the state. The HOUSSE was first introduced in the ESEA as an alternative means for veteran teachers to prove competency in subject areas (20 U.S.C. § 7801(23)(C)(ii); 34 C.F.R. § 200.56(c)).

The ESEA charged each state with developing its own HOUSSE process, which must be approved by the U.S. Department of Education. Some states have devised a HOUSSE for individual subject areas and grades, while others have created a more comprehensive evaluation that encapsulates multiple grades and subjects. A typical HOUSSE process consists of a competency rubric, with most states basing their evaluation on a 100-point scale. Under this process, teachers earn points for certification, additional coursework in core subjects, experience, ongoing professional development activities, service awards and presentations, and work on various task forces, among other things. Under the law, a valid HOUSSE must

- be set by the state for both grade-appropriate academic subject-matter knowledge and teaching skills;
- be aligned with challenging state academic content and student academic achievement standards and developed in consultation with core content specialists, teachers, principals, and school administrators;
- provide objective, coherent information about the teacher's attainment of core content knowledge in the academic subjects in which he or she teaches;
- be applied uniformly to all teachers in the same academic subject and the same grade level throughout the state;
- take into consideration, but not be based primarily on, the time the teacher has been teaching the academic subject;
- be made available to the public upon request; and
- consider multiple objective measures of teacher competency (optional).

The IDEA 2004 did not amend NCLB's definition of "highly qualified," but it provided additional options for special-needs instructors looking to meet the requirement in a multitude of different settings (see Figure 6.1) (Pub. L. No. 108-446, § 602(10)). The IDEA 2004 requires that *all* special education teachers meet state licensing requirements for special education (§ 602(10)(B)). In addition, special-needs instructors teaching in core content areas must meet the highly qualified requirements in that subject. The IDEA 2004 offers flexibility for teachers instructing in multiple subject areas, however, such as allowing *new* special-needs instructors to use a HOUSSE to demonstrate competency in specific instances. Comments from the IDEA 2004 House–Senate Conference Committee note that states can employ a HOUSSE for all teachers or create a separate process for special education teachers, including a single measure that would cover multiple subjects (House Report No. 108-779, 2004). The following is a breakdown of the flexibility offered for special education teachers to become highly qualified in two situations:

- **Special education teachers who are teaching to alternative standards.** Both new and veteran special education teachers who teach core content solely to students with the most severe disabilities who are assessed against alternative standards under NCLB can meet the highly qualified standard in one of two ways: (1) by meeting all applicable standards under NCLB for new or not new

FIGURE 6.1

Summary of Requirements to Be a Highly Qualified Special Education Teacher

Category of Special Education Teachers	Requirements Under Public Law No. 108-446
All special education teachers	Must hold at least a B.A. Must obtain full state special education certification or equivalent licensure Cannot hold an emergency or temporary certificate
New or veteran elementary school teachers teaching one or more academic subjects only to students with disabilities held to alternative achievement standards (students who are the most severely cognitively disabled)	In addition to the general requirements above, may demonstrate academic subject competence through a highly objective uniform state standard of evaluation (the HOUSSE process)
New or veteran middle or high school teachers teaching one or more core academic subjects only to students with disabilities held to alternative achievement standards (students who are the most severely cognitively disabled)	In addition to the general requirements above, may demonstrate "subject matter knowledge appropriate to the level of instruction being provided, as determined by the State, needed to effectively teach to those standards"
New teachers of two or more academic subjects who are highly qualified in mathematics, language arts, or science	In addition to the general requirements above, have a two-year window in which to become highly qualified in other core academic subjects and may do this through the HOUSSE process
Veteran teachers of two or more academic subjects only to children with disabilities	In addition to the general requirements above, may demonstrate academic subject competence through the HOUSSE process (including a single evaluation for all core academic subjects)
Consultative teachers and other special education teachers who do not teach core academic subjects	Must meet only the general requirements above
Other special education teachers teaching core academic subjects	In addition to the general requirements above, must meet relevant NCLB requirements for new elementary school teachers, new middle/high school teachers, or veteran teachers

Source: From *Individuals with Disabilities Education Act (IDEA): Analysis of Changes Made by P.L. 108-446*, by Congressional Research Service, 2005.

elementary, middle, or high school teachers or (2) by adequately completing a HOUSSE process (for elementary-level teachers) or by possessing "subject matter knowledge appropriate to the level of instruction...as determined by the [s]tate, needed to effectively teach to those standards" (Pub. L. No. 108-446, § 602(10)(C)(ii)).

■ **Special education teachers who are teaching two or more core subjects.** Special education teachers who teach two or more core academic areas exclusively to students with disabilities may meet the highly qualified standard through multiple methods, depending on their experience. All special education teachers of multiple subjects can qualify by meeting all applicable requirements in NCLB for new or veteran teachers at the appropriate grade level. Veteran special-needs teachers who teach multiple subjects may complete their state's HOUSSE process, which may include a single evaluation that covers multiple core subjects (Pub. L. No. 108-446, § 602(10)(D)(ii)). And new special education teachers instructing in more than one core academic area who are already highly qualified in mathematics, language, or language arts have two years from their hire date to demonstrate competency in other core subjects through their state's HOUSSE system (§ 602(10)(D)(iii)). This is the only exception to the school year 2005–2006 deadline NCLB sets for all teachers to be highly qualified.

The actual implementation of the "highly" qualified provision has proved difficult for many states, however, with no state actually having 100 percent of its teachers satisfying the requirements. In the spring of 2006, U.S. Education Secretary Margaret Spellings offered states an additional year to move all teachers to highly qualified status, provided they submitted an acceptable plan to do so. But one year later the U.S. Department of Education had no assurance that any state had satisfied the 100 percent requirement, although a number were close, according to state-reported figures. The department revised its monitoring protocol and evaluated states' progress on their plans for meeting the legislative requirement in the fall of 2007.

Further, the U.S. Department of Education has stated that it expects most—if not all—states to end the use of the HOUSSE process by the end of the 2006–2007 school year. Department officials reason that all veteran educators should have completed the HOUSSE process by that time, with any newly hired teachers able to be evaluated through the state's traditional route.

A majority of special-needs teachers work in "consultation" with the general education teachers who provide core content expertise, however, rather than providing direct instruction in a core academic subject, according to the Council for Exceptional Children (CEC). In this scenario, special and general educators collaborate to ensure that students have access to the general education curriculum. Congress recognized the importance of this integral relationship and granted some leeway to special education teachers who consult with the core content teachers in a general education environment.

The conference report that accompanied the IDEA 2004 legislation clarified that the intent of Congress was that a special-needs instructor who provides only "consultative services" to a teacher already deemed highly qualified need only have a degree in special education and an appropriate form of state licensure to be highly qualified under NCLB. Prior to the amendments of the IDEA 2004, NCLB required that any special-needs teacher teaching core content areas be highly qualified in special education and the core academic subject. The legislative conferees noted, however, that

> consultative services do not include instruction in core academic subjects, but may include adjustments to the learning environment, modifications of instructional methods, adaptation of curricula, the use of positive behavioral supports and interventions, or the design, use or implementation of appropriate accommodations to meet the needs of individual children. (House Report No. 108-779, 2004)

The IDEA 2004 also attempted to help states faced with a shortage of fully certified special education teachers; in 2004, nearly 60,000 special educators across the nation were uncertified or operating on temporary or provisional certifications. The law reiterates the NCLB provision that allows individuals to be considered highly qualified the day they enroll in an "alternative education program" (Pub. L. No. 108-446, § 602(10)(A)) and also allows states to create a licensing examination for special education teachers, which could simply be a written exam.

These provisions proved controversial with at least one advocacy group, however. The CEC took umbrage at the concept that an instructor could be deemed "highly qualified" in special education without learning the necessary pedagogy that comes from time spent in the classroom. Following the passage of the IDEA 2004 legislation, the CEC said that "special education skills must be assessed through multiple performance evaluations, not a single paper and pencil test. If individuals are permitted to become 'highly qualified' based simply on a test score, it will trivialize the term 'highly qualified'" (CEC, 2004).

Interestingly, Congress added a protection for states and school systems that— due to a shortage of qualified candidates—are unable to fill all available slots with highly qualified teachers and paraprofessionals. Lawmakers inserted a rule of construction that clearly states that schools are not liable under the IDEA if a student is not taught by a highly qualified teacher:

> (E) Rule of Construction.—Notwithstanding any other individual right of action that a parent or student may maintain under this part, nothing in this section or part shall be construed to create a right of action on behalf of an individual student or class of students for the failure of a particular State educational agency or local educational agency employee to be highly qualified. (Pub. L. No. 108-446, § 602(10))

It should be noted that this does not bar parents from filing due process proceedings against the district or state because their child is being taught by a non-highly qualified teacher; the law—as it is written—simply says that they have no "right of action" to do so.

NCLB also set minimum standards for paraprofessionals, including those who assist students with special needs, and the IDEA 2004 did not alter those requirements. The NCLB regulations define a *paraprofessional* as an employee of a school district who provides "instructional support" in a program that is supported in part by a Title I grant, including those paraprofessionals who work in schoolwide improvement programs and those who work in conjunction with an educator providing equitable services to eligible private school students (34 C.F.R. § 200.58(a)(2)). It is important to note that the federal requirements do not apply to special education paraprofessionals except when they are funded via Title I schoolwide programs. (See Figure 6.1.) Likewise, they do not apply to paraprofessionals with unique assignments, such as "one-on-one" behavioral assistants and healthcare assistants.

Paraprofessionals are not allowed under NCLB to provide any instructional assistance to a student unless they are working "under the direct supervision of a teacher" (34 C.F.R. § 200.59(c)). The law requires that new paraprofessionals complete at least two years of higher education, obtain at least an associate's degree, or demonstrate competency on a state evaluation (20 U.S.C. § 6319(c)). The law granted existing paraprofessionals until the end of 2006 to, at the very minimum, earn an associate's degree (20 U.S.C. § 6319(d)). To date, this requirement has not been achieved.

ACCOUNTABILITY

The central pillar of NCLB is its requirement that states, districts, and schools bolster their accountability for the children they educate. States are required to develop their own academic standards and submit plans to the U.S. Department of Education describing how they will annually close the achievement gap and move all children to proficiency with respect to those standards by the close of the 2013–2014 school year. Each state defines what it takes to be "proficient" in a subject area. As part of their individual plans, states must then design a statewide accountability system that annually measures the progress districts and schools are making toward academic proficiency. To measure that annual progress, states are required to define what it takes for districts and schools to make adequate yearly progress, or AYP, toward proficiency. In other words, states set annual AYP targets that districts and schools are expected to reach for the entire student body and for individual subgroups. Schools that do not reach their AYP marks in two or more consecutive years are labeled "in need of improvement"—a status that carries escalating penalties.

NCLB requires that AYP be based on the application of uniform high standards to all public school students in the state; be statistically valid and reliable; result in continuous academic improvement for all students; measure the progress of students based on yearly assessments; include separate annual objectives for all students and a variety of subgroups, including low-income children and those with disabilities; include valid and reliable data on graduation rates; and contain other academic indicators such as retention and attendance rates (20 U.S.C. § 6311(b)(2)(C)). States and districts are required to annually produce and disseminate "report cards," which offer parents and the public information on the progress students are making toward proficiency.

The IDEA 2004 clearly reiterates the NCLB accountability mandates by requiring that each state—as a condition of receiving IDEA funding—establish performance goals and indicators for students with disabilities that incorporate AYP measures (Pub. L. No. 108-446, § 612(a)(15)). A state's goals and performance indicators under the law must

- promote the purposes of the IDEA 2004 set forth in Section 601(d);
- match the state's definition of AYP, including its objectives for progress by children with disabilities described in the state's definition of AYP under Section 6311(b)(2)(c) of NCLB;
- address graduation and dropout rates, as well as other factors determined by the state; and
- stay consistent, to the maximum extent possible, with any other goals and standards for children established by the state.

The IDEA 2004 mandates that states annually report to the U.S. Department of Education and the public on the progress their schools have made toward meeting the goals and indicators they have established for students with disabilities (Pub. L. No. 108-446, § 612(a)(15)(C)). These reports may include elements of the reports required under 20 U.S.C. § 6311(h).

So what are the penalties under NCLB for not reaching AYP thresholds? They vary greatly; the harshest punishments involve "corrective action" or the "restructuring" of a school, but the most common sanctions involve public school choice and supplemental educational services.

PUBLIC SCHOOL CHOICE

After a school fails to reach its AYP threshold for two years and is identified for improvement, the district must offer all students—including those with disabilities—the option to transfer to a high-performing public school in the district, including public charter schools. Students are not allowed to move to a school that has missed its AYP targets or has been labeled as "persistently dangerous" under NCLB's unsafe school choice option (20 U.S.C. § 7912). The LEA must notify parents that they have the option to transfer their children no later than the first day of the academic year following the school year in which the school is marked for improvement—but the U.S. Department of Education has made it clear that the earlier parents are given options, the better (34 C.F.R. § 200.44(a)(2)).

The priority for transfers goes to the lowest-achieving students from the most disadvantaged families (34 C.F.R. § 200.44(e)), and if a student elects to move to another public school, the district is responsible for providing transportation to the new site (34 C.F.R. § 200.44(i)). The district's obligation to pay for transportation ends if the school from which the student transferred is removed from the "in need of improvement" list, although the student is still free to attend the new school. If all schools in the district are "in need of improvement," and therefore unable to receive additional students under NCLB, the district should seek cooperative agreements with neighboring public school districts that will allow their schools to accept students from the district that is "in need of improvement" (34 C.F.R. § 200.44(f)). It should be noted that the U.S. Department of Education has made it clear that a lack of capacity is no excuse for a school to turn away potential transfers from a public school that is "in need of improvement."

But what does this mean for students with disabilities? NCLB requires that students with disabilities covered under the IDEA or Section 504 of the Rehabilitation Act of 1973 continue to receive a free appropriate public education (FAPE) if they elect to transfer to a new school (34 C.F.R. § 200.44(j)). Receiving schools have several options as to how handle FAPE, however. Nonregulatory guidance released by the U.S. Department of Education gives receiving schools the option of implementing the individualized education program (IEP) developed at the student's previous school or convening an IEP team meeting to develop a new program in consultation with the parents. The guidance also says that the district should weigh the child's special needs when looking for a school to transfer him or her to and pay particular attention to a school's ability to provide that student FAPE. Also, it is important to understand that the transfer of a student under the public school choice program does not necessarily represent a "change of placement" under the IDEA; procedural safeguards are triggered only if the receiving school proposes revising the IEP.

SUPPLEMENTAL EDUCATIONAL SERVICES

Schools that fail to meet their AYP marks for three consecutive years must offer their low-income students supplemental educational services, paid for by the district. NCLB defines supplemental educational services, which most commonly involve tutoring, as being

- in addition to normal daily instruction,
- specifically designed to boost students' learning in areas covered by annual state assessments and push them toward proficiency with respect to state academic standards, and
- high quality and research-based. (34 C.F.R. § 200.45(a)(2))

Unlike the public school choice option, only students from low-income families are given the option to receive supplemental educational services (34 C.F.R.

§ 200.45(b)). The district must offer students the opportunity to continue supplemental services throughout the school year (34 C.F.R. § 200.45(c)(3)). School districts that do not have sufficient funding to offer supplemental services to all eligible children must give priority to the lowest-achieving students (34 C.F.R. § 200.45(d)).

While parents are given the option to select the supplemental educational services provider of their choice, the SEA is responsible for identifying, approving, and monitoring the providers from which parents may select (34 C.F.R. § 200.47). The regulations give states wide latitude in the types of organizations that can act as supplemental educational service providers, saying that *provider* "means a non-profit entity, a for-profit entity, an LEA, an educational service agency, a public school, including a public charter school, or a private school" (34 C.F.R. § 200.47(b)(1)). Providers must have a demonstrated record of effectiveness in bolstering student achievement, use high-quality research-based instruction, and be financially sound. A public school district, school, or charter school that has been identified as "in need of improvement" under NCLB cannot act as a service provider, however (34 C.F.R. § 200.47(b)(1)(iv)).

Districts are responsible, among other things, for annually providing parents of eligible students notice of the availability of supplemental educational services for their children (34 C.F.R. § 200.46(a)) and offering parents assistance in selecting a provider, if so asked. In addition, local school systems must ensure that eligible students with disabilities covered under the IDEA and Section 504 receive appropriate tutoring services and accommodations (34 C.F.R. § 200.46(a)(4)). NCLB requires that the district enter into an agreement with each provider selected; this agreement includes a statement, made in consultation with the parents, that

■ establishes specific achievement goals for the student,
■ offers a description of how the student's progress will be measured, and
■ creates a time line for improving achievement. (34 C.F.R. § 200.46(b)(1))

However, nonregulatory guidance issued by the U.S. Department of Education in 2003 offers additional options for LEAs that are unable to reach an agreement with a viable service provider, even if that school district is designated as "in need of improvement." The guidance says that an LEA "in need of improvement" that cannot reach an agreement with a provider can provide supplemental educational services, but only

after completing an exhaustive review of the providers on the State's approved list. It is possible, for instance, that nearby providers (that is, providers located close to but not within the geographic jurisdiction of the LEA) or those that offer distance learning services will be able to provide services to those two populations, even if no provider located within the area served by the LEA can do so. (U.S. Department of Education, *Supplemental Educational* Services, 2003) Districts are responsible, among other things, for annually providing parents of eligible students notice of the availability of supplemental educational services for their children (34 C.F.R.

§ 200.46(a)) and offering parents assistance in selecting a provider, if so asked. In addition, local school systems must ensure that eligible students with disabilities covered under the IDEA and Section 504 receive appropriate tutoring services and accommodations (34 C.F.R. § 200.46(a)(4)).

NCLB charges districts with ensuring that students receive supplemental educational services through the end of the school year in which the services were first received (20 U.S.C. § 6316(e)(8)), but a 2005 ruling from the U.S. Department of Education allowed the School District of Philadelphia to set a deadline by which the bulk of supplemental services must be completed. The decision allows the school district to continue its "80/90 policy," which requires service providers to conduct 80 percent of their work with 90 percent of enrolled students by the time the state assessments are administered in late March (U.S. Department of Education, 2005). The law does grant a district the power to terminate an agreement with a provider if that provider's services are not meeting the student's academic goals or the time line for meeting those goals (34 C.F.R. § 200.46(b)(2)(iii)).

In the case of a student with a disability covered under the IDEA or Section 504, NCLB mandates that the provisions of the agreement with the service provider be consistent with the student's IEP or individualized services under Section 504 (34 C.F.R. § 200.46(b)(3)). And more specifically, nonregulatory guidance establishes the obligations of SEAs and LEAs in providing supplemental educational services to students with disabilities:

> An SEA and each LEA that arranges for supplemental educational services must ensure that eligible students with disabilities and students covered under Section 504 may participate. Furthermore, the supplemental educational services program within each LEA and within the State may not discriminate against these students. Consistent with this duty, an LEA may not, through contractual or other arrangements with a private provider, discriminate against an eligible student with a disability or an eligible student covered under Section 504 by failing to provide for appropriate supplemental educational services with necessary accommodations. Such services and necessary accommodations must be available, but not necessarily from each provider. Rather, SEAs and LEAs are responsible for ensuring that the supplemental educational service providers made available to parents include some providers that can serve students with disabilities and students covered under Section 504 with any necessary accommodations, with or without the assistance of the SEA or LEA. If no provider is able to make the services with necessary accommodations available to an eligible student with a disability, the LEA would need to provide these services, with necessary accommodations, either directly or through a contract.
>
> Supplemental educational services must be consistent with a student's individualized education program under Section 614 of the Individuals with Disabilities Education Act (IDEA) or a student's individualized services under Section 504. However, these services are in addition to, and not a substitute for, the instruction and services required under the IDEA and Section

504 and should not be written into individualized education programs under IDEA or into any Section 504 plans. In addition, parents of students with disabilities (like other parents) should have the opportunity to select a provider that best meets the needs of their child. (U.S. Department of Education, *Supplemental Educational* Services, 2003)

Finally, the IDEA 2004 authorizes additional funding for state-level activities: States can use their IDEA state-level reserve to provide technical assistance and professional development to LEAs or schools that have missed AYP for two or more years solely on the basis of the scores of their subgroup of students with disabilities (Pub. L. No. 108-446, § 611(e)(2)(C)(xi)).

ASSESSMENTS

Assessments are the fuel that drives NCLB's accountability system; they provide a standardized method for measuring student progress toward proficiency. Each year NCLB requires that a minimum of 95 percent of all students in all subgroups—including students with disabilities—participate in grade-level testing (34 C.F.R. § 202(b)(3)). The law does give some leeway in this regard, however, allowing three-year averages for participation rates. Each state is charged with developing a system of tests in reading and mathematics to be given annually to all students in grades 3–8 and at least once in grades 10–12 (20 U.S.C. § 6311(b)(3)(C)(vii). And by the 2007–2008 school year, states are required to assess students in science at least once in grades 3–5, 6–9, and 10–12 (20 U.S.C. § 6311(b)(3)(C)(v)(II). According to the regulations (34 C.F.R. § 200.2(b)), the assessments must

- be the same assessments used to measure the achievement of all students;
- be designed to be valid and accessible for use by the greatest range of students possible, including students with disabilities and English language learners;
- be aligned with the state's standards;
- be valid and reliable;
- be supported by evidence from test publishers;
- be administered according to the time line prescribed in the law;
- involve multiple measures of student academic achievement, including measures that gauge higher-order thinking and understanding of challenging content;
- objectively measure academic achievement, knowledge, and skills without assessing personal information;
- provide for the participation of all students in all grades being assessed;
- produce reports that disaggregate data on student subgroups, including students with disabilities; and
- enable itemized score analyses to be produced and reported to districts and schools.

The 2004 amendments to the IDEA altered the previous version's assessment participation requirements to better align them with NCLB. The IDEA 2004 requires that *all* students with disabilities be included in *all* state- and districtwide assessments, including those mandated under NCLB, with accommodations or alternative assessment only where stipulated in a child's IEP (Pub. L. No. 108-446, § 612(a)(16)(A)). Although the law is silent on what "appropriate accommodations" are, nonregulatory guidance issued by the U.S. Department of Education defines them as "changes in testing materials or procedures that ensure that an assessment measures the student's knowledge and skills rather than the student's disabilities" (U.S. Department of Education, *Standards and Assessments*, 2003). Alternate assessments are to be aligned with the state achievement standards developed under NCLB, as well as the alternate standards that are developed for students with disabilities (§ 612(a)(16)(C)(ii)).

Students with disabilities who are unable to participate in the regular state assessment process, even with the assistance of accommodations, may take alternate assessments (34 C.F.R. § 200.6(a)(2)). Alternate assessments may range from teacher observations to a portfolio of a student's work to an evaluation of student performance in an on-demand setting. The alternate assessments must yield results for the grade in which the student is enrolled in reading and mathematics—and science beginning in school year 2007–2008—with the exception of students with the "most significant cognitive disabilities" (34 C.F.R. § 200.6(a)(2)(B)).

Students with the most significant cognitive disabilities may take alternate assessments based on alternate achievement standards. If a child's IEP team determines that he or she cannot participate in a general state assessment and instead recommends an alternate assessment, the IEP team must include a statement describing the reason the child cannot participate in the general assessment and justifying the choice of alternate assessment as appropriate (Pub. L. No. 108-446, § 614(d)(1)(A)(i)(VI)(bb)). The U.S. Department of Education's nonregulatory guidance makes it clear, however, that the "vast majority" of students should be able to participate in the general state assessment process, using appropriate accommodations when needed (U.S. Department of Education, *Standards and Assessments*, 2003).

NCLB allows states to develop their own definition of "alternate achievement standards," but requires that those standards be aligned with the state's general content standards, promote access to the general curriculum, and reflect "professional judgment of the highest standards possible" (34 C.F.R. § 200.1(d)). An alternate achievement standard is, defined in its simplest term, an expectation of student performance that differs in complexity from a grade-level achievement standard.

After much internal debate, the U.S. Department of Education updated the NCLB regulations in 2003 and offered states and districts relief in the testing of the "most severely cognitively disabled" students (IDEA 2004 adopted "most severely cognitively disabled" to describe the same group of students). The so-called 1 percent rule gives states the flexibility to count the "proficient" and "advanced" scores of students with the most significant cognitive disabilities who take alternate assessments based on alternate achievement standards in their AYP calculations—provided the number of those "proficient" and "advanced" scores does not exceed 1 percent of all students in the grades tested. Without this flexibility, those scores would have to be assessed against grade-level standards and would be considered "not proficient." Any "proficient" and "advanced" scores based on alternate achievement standards above the 1 percent cap must be counted as "not proficient" relative to grade-level standards. The 1 percent cap applies to the number of "proficient" and "advanced" scores that may be included in AYP determinations; it does not limit the number of students that can take an assessment based on alternate achievement standards.

No scores may be excluded from AYP calculations, however. For an alternate assessment based on grade-level achievement standards, states must count all "proficient" and "advanced" scores in AYP calculations. The 1 percent rule came under significant fire in some education arenas by the time Congress finalized its work on the IDEA reauthorization in December 2004. Many schools and districts throughout the nation failed to reach their AYP targets solely because of the results of their subgroup of students with disabilities, prompting calls for additional flexibility. National civil rights advocates and parents' groups opposed any expansion of the 1 percent rule, and Congress resisted making any modifications to NCLB, but a change in leadership at the U.S. Department of Education led to even greater flexibility in the number of disabled students that can be assessed by alternate standards. In a move that indicated a philosophical shift from her predecessor, Roderick Paige, U.S. Education Secretary Margaret Spellings announced in April 2005 that the department was expanding alternate testing to "gap kids"— those students who are not severely disabled, but who will never achieve proficiency on state assessments.

New rules finalized by the department in April 2007 (34 C.F.R. § 200.1) expanded testing exemptions to include 2 percent of students with disabilities who may be assessed against "modified achievement standards." These modified standards represent less-rigorous expectations than do grade-level standards, although the regulations make it clear that the modified standards must be *based* on standards that are appropriate for the student's grade level. Modified standards also must (1) be aligned with the state's academic content standards, (2) specify three levels of progress (proficient, basic, and below basic), (3) include descriptions of the competencies expected for each achievement level, and (4) provide cut scores for each achievement level.

As it did with students with the most significant cognitive difficulties, the U.S. Department of Education refrained from specifically defining the new category, instead leaving that to the states. IEP teams ultimately will decide, based on the state's definition, whether a student should be assessed against modified achievement standards. The move raised the overall cap on students who could be assessed against alternate ("1 percent rule") or modified ("2 percent rule") standards to 3 percent of the total school-age population, or roughly one-third of all students with disabilities. In making the announcement of the policy change on April 7, 2005, Secretary Spellings said:

> Under this policy, students with academic disabilities will be allowed to take tests that are specifically geared toward their abilities, as long as the state is working to best serve those students by providing rigorous research-based training for teachers, improving assessments, and organizing collaboration between special education and classroom teachers. If you stand up for the kids and provide better instruction and assessment, we will stand by you. This policy builds on current regulations, which allow states to give students with the most significant cognitive disabilities—up to 1 percent of them—alternate tests based on alternate achievement standards. This new approach recognizes that children should not all be treated alike. (Spellings, 2005)

New research indicating that the student with academic difficulties can make progress toward grade-level standards when given high-quality instruction and modified tests prompted the change in policy. The 2 percent rule permits states to develop achievement standards that are aligned with grade-level content standards, but modified so as to reflect reduced breadth or depth of grade-level content (and assessments that measure achievement based on those standards) (34 C.F.R. § 200.1). States and LEAs may include the "proficient" and "advanced" scores from assessments based on modified achievement standards in AYP—although the total amount is subject to a 2 percent cap at the district and state levels (34 C.F.R. § 200.13(c)(2)).

In creating alternate assessments based on modified standards, states have the option of either modifying their existing tests or creating entirely new ones. A state electing to adapt an existing assessment may, for instance, modify a multiple-choice question by removing one of the incorrect answers, that is, a "distracter." The U.S. Department of Education also released new guidance in conjunction with the final 2 percent regulation that is intended to help states develop modified achievement standards and alternate assessments (U.S. Department of Education, 2007).

Ultimately, according to U.S. Department of Education officials, the goal of the new regulations is to

- ensure that states hold this population of students with disabilities to challenging, though modified, achievement standards that enable them to approach, and even meet, grade-level standards;
- ensure access to the general curriculum so that students are taught to the same high standards;
- measure progress with high-quality alternate assessments so parents are confident that their students are learning and achieving;
- provide guidance and training to IEP teams to identify these students properly; and
- provide professional development to regular and special education teachers who teach this population of students with disabilities.

Finally, both NCLB and the IDEA 2004 require states to report on the participation of students with disabilities in state assessments (Pub. L. No. 108-446, § 612(a)(16)(D)). Specifically, the IDEA 2004 mandates that states report the number of students with disabilities that participate in regular assessments, participate in regular assessments using accommodations, participate in alternate assessments, participate in alternate assessments that are based on alternate achievement standards, and participate in modified assessments based on modified standards. The IDEA 2004 also requires that states report the performance of children with disabilities on regular and alternate assessments compared with the achievement of all children, including students with disabilities, on those examinations.

SUMMARY

The 2004 amendments to the IDEA marked a confluence of the two largest pieces of education legislation in the history of the nation, melding the broad accountability of NCLB with the singular focus on the special needs of individual children in the IDEA. NCLB mandated that states develop and implement accountability systems and standards for reading and mathematics. The statute requires, as a condition of receiving formula grants, that schools test all students annually in grades 3–8 and once in high school in reading and mathematics, with a goal of having all students reach proficiency in both subjects by the close of the 2013–2014 school year. Moreover, NCLB requires that schools disaggregate the annual progress of individual subgroups of students, including all racial and ethnic groups, as well as students with disabilities and English language learners.

Schools that fail to make adequate yearly progress—or AYP—toward full proficiency for the school and all subgroups face an increasingly prescriptive list of sanctions for their failure to do so, including provisions for public school choice and supplemental educational services for students. The IDEA 2004 clearly reiterates the NCLB accountability requirements by requiring that each state—as a condition of receiving IDEA funding—establish performance goals and indicators for students with disabilities that incorporate AYP measures.

Assessments are the fuel that drives NCLB's accountability system; they provide a standardized method for measuring student progress toward proficiency. Each year NCLB requires that a minimum of 95 percent of all students in all subgroups—including students with disabilities—participate in grade-level testing. The IDEA 2004 now requires that *all* students with disabilities be included in *all* state- and districtwide assessments, including those mandated under NCLB, with accommodations or alternative assessment where stipulated in a child's IEP.

Students with disabilities who are unable to participate in the regular state assessment process, even with the assistance of accommodations, may take alternate assessments—ranging from teacher observations to a portfolio of a student's work to an evaluation of student performance in an on-demand setting. Federal regulations also have carved out exceptions for students with the "most significant cognitive disabilities" and "gap kids." These provisions enable up to 3 percent of all students to be counted as "proficient" for accountability purposes under NCLB. Further, the IDEA 2004 mandates that states report the number of students with disabilities that participate in regular assessments, participate in regular assessments using accommodations, participate in alternate assessments, participate in alternate assessments that are based on alternate achievement standards, and participate in modified assessments based on modified standards.

And to ensure that the instruction matches the academic rigor of the programs, NCLB establishes the minimum qualifications for teachers and paraprofessionals. The statute requires that states develop plans to ensure that all teachers of core academic subjects are deemed "highly qualified" by the end of the 2005–2006 school year. The law also requires school districts to inform parents when students have been taught for four or more consecutive weeks by a teacher who is not "highly qualified" in a core academic subject area (34 C.F.R. § 200.61(a)(2)). The IDEA 2004 did not amend NCLB's definition of "highly qualified," but it provided additional options for special-needs teachers looking to meet the requirement in a multitude of different settings. The actual implementation of the "highly qualified" provision has proved difficult for many states, however, with no state actually having 100 percent of its teachers satisfying the requirements as of the summer of 2007.

CRITICAL THINKING QUESTIONS

1. Did Congress better align the IDEA and NCLB, and if so, did it do so for the betterment of children with disabilities? What have your experiences been thus far?
2. If there was one thing you could change about NCLB with regard to students with disabilities, what would it be, and why?
3. Was the 2 percent expansion in the testing cap for "students with persistent academic difficulties" fair? Why or why not?
4. What should Congress focus on when it looks to reauthorize NCLB?
5. What portions at the intersection of these laws seem most prescriptive? Which provide enough flexibility to allow school districts to meet the individual needs of their students?
6. Is it fair to expect the vast majority of students with disabilities to be proficient in reading/language arts and mathematics by the 2013–2014 school year? Why or why not?

References

Council for Exceptional Children. (2004). *The new IDEA: CEC's summary of significant issues*. Arlington, VA: Author.

House Report No. 108-779, (2004).

Individuals with Disabilities Education Improvement Act of 2004 (IDEA 2004), Pub. L. No. 108–446, 118 Stat. 2652.

No Child Left Behind Act of 2001 (NCLB), 20 U.S.C. §§ 6301–7941.

Spellings, M. (2005, April 7)NPR. Spellings: flexibility on 'No Child Left Behind' by Michele Norris. http://www.npr.org/templates/story/story.php?storyId =4580692.

U.S. Department of Education. (2003, March 10). *Standards and assessments: Nonregulatory guidance*. Washington, DC: Author.

U.S. Department of Education. (2003, August 22). *Supplemental educational services: Nonregulatory guidance*. Washington, DC: Author.

U.S. Department of Education. (2005, January 28). Letter of finding.

U.S. Department of Education. (2007, April 4). *Modified academic achievement standards: Nonregulatory guidance*. Washington, DC: Author.

7

Free and Appropriate Public Education

Facts at a GLANCE

- The Individuals with Disabilities Education Act (IDEA) does not mandate that a student achieve his or her expected level of academic progress or potential (*Board of Education of Hendrick Hudson Central School District v. Rowley*, 1982). However, the school has to make a "good-faith effort" toward helping the child achieve his or her individualized education program (IEP) goals.
- The Americans with Disabilities Act (1990) and Section 504 of the Rehabilitation Act of 1973 have a *free appropriate public education* (FAPE) clause that is consistent with the IDEA.
- In relation to FAPE and students with disabilities, judicial precedents have held that "free" does not apply to the basic costs all students must pay (locker fees, instrument rental, etc.). The IDEA does not specifically address these fees, but Section 504 does specifically note that parents of students with disabilities are not exempt from such fees (34 C.F.R. § 104.33(c)).
- There is no specific definition of "appropriate." As a result, the subjective nature of the term has led to significant amounts of litigation. The most important U.S. Supreme Court ruling related to "appropriate" is *Board of Education of the Hendrick Hudson Central School District v. Rowley* (1982).
- The *Rowley* case established that schools do not have to provide "maximum benefit" to students with disabilities; rather, they are responsible only for providing a "basic floor of opportunity." In lay terms, schools do not have to provide the best program services available. The IEP must be "reasonably calculated" for the child to make progress toward achieving his or her goals and objectives and receive "some educational benefit."
- Placement and program development cannot be done unilaterally. No single person can decide the program for students with disabilities. The IEP team is responsible for ensuring a FAPE is developed and provided.

■ Schools and teachers bear the responsibility for determining the service delivery models, methodology, and strategies utilized for students with disabilities. Parents may not mandate that schools employ specific programs or methodologies (*Board of Education of Hendrick Hudson Central School District v. Rowley*, 1982; *Barnett v. Fairfax County School Board*, 1991).

■ The IDEA mandates extended school year (ESY) services if a student is likely to regress significantly without such services. ESY services must be considered on a case-by-case basis and cannot be tied to a category of disability. The IDEA does not provide a formula for eligibility for ESY services; it leaves the establishment of such standards to the states.

■ Students who are unilaterally placed in private schools by their parents do not have a legal right to FAPE or ESY.

■ The IDEA mandates that transition services be addressed beginning at age 16; Section 504 does not mandate transition services.

■ Schools must provide a continuum of services for students with disabilities. The regular education setting is not necessarily the least restrictive environment for all students; however, the regular education setting must be considered first.

■ Financial considerations may be a factor when determining placements when an undue burden on the school district might be created.

■ Although passing grades and promotion to the next grade can be reasonable factors in determining if a student is receiving a FAPE, they do not automatically indicate a school is providing FAPE. The *Rowley* decision indicated that several factors must be weighed on an individual basis to ascertain if FAPE is being achieved.

Although a seemingly simple principle and term to understand, *free appropriate public education* (FAPE) is one of the more difficult components of the Individuals with Disabilities Education Act (IDEA) to operationally define and consistently implement. As one of the essential pillars of the law, the assurance of FAPE for all children protected under the IDEA is paramount. In order to comply with the legal requirements of FAPE, every child with a disability between the ages of 3 and 21 must be found, evaluated, and provided with an appropriate individualized education program (IEP). The zero reject policy mandates that no child between these ages is to be excluded from appropriate public educational services regardless of the severity of the child's disabling condition.

The inclusion of FAPE in the IDEA (Pub. L. No. 94-142) when it was enacted in 1975 was one of the most important and prominent areas of language in the statute. (See Figure 7.1.) Congress explicitly addressed the overwhelming number of children completely denied access to a FAPE (1 million) and those inappropriately placed and served (8 million) in the law's Findings (§ 3). In fact, one may safely say that mandating and ensuring a FAPE for all children with disabilities was the driving force behind the passage of the Act.

FIGURE 7.1

2004 Amendments to the IDEA

The Findings at 20 U.S.C 1400(c) reflect the concerns and issues in regard to U.S. children with disabilities which drive substantive and procedural components of IDEA. The 2004 Amendments reflect considerable demographic changes, concerns over mislabeling and dropout rates of minority students, transition to post-secondary education, personnel preparation, and concern for students whose primary language is not English. It is essential to note the additional language in the Findings in order to understand the current status of and issues facing the field of special education. The recognition of the growing diversity and the need to meet new challenges in providing FAPE for all students with disabilities is the overriding theme of the four new subsections at 20 U.S.C. § 1400(c) (11) through 20 U.S.C. § 1400(c) (14).

(11) (A)   The limited English proficient population is the fastest growing in our Nation, and the growth is occurring in many parts of our Nation.

    (B)   Studies have documented apparent discrepancies in the levels of referral and placement of limited English proficient children in special education.

    (C)   Such discrepancies pose a special challenge for special education in the referral of, assessment of, and provision of services for, our Nation's students from non–English language backgrounds.

(12) (A)   Greater efforts are needed to prevent the intensification of problems connected with mislabeling and high dropout rates among minority children with disabilities.

    (B)   More minority children continue to be served in special education than would be expected from the percentage of minority students in the general school population.

    (C)   African-American children are identified as having mental retardation and emotional disturbance at rates greater than their White counterparts.

    (D)   In the 1998–1999 school year, African-American children represented just 14.8 percent of the population aged 6–21, but comprised 20.2 percent of all children with disabilities.

    (E)   Studies have found that schools with predominately White students and teachers have placed disproportionately high numbers of their minority students into special education.

(13) (A)   As the number of minority students in special education increases, the number of minority teachers and related services produced in colleges and universities continues to decrease.

    (B)   The opportunity for full participation by minority individuals, minority organizations, and Historically Black Colleges and Universities in awards for grants and contracts, boards of organizations receiving assistance under this title, peer review panels, and training of professionals in the area of special education is essential to obtain greater success in the education of minority children with disabilities.

(14)   As the graduation rates for children with disabilities continue to climb, providing effective transition services to promote successful post-school employment or education is an important measure of accountability for children with disabilities.

The IDEA mandates that schools individualize each child's educational program. Because each child's program differs, Congress did not define specifically what is "appropriate." As this chapter will demonstrate, the courts—in the absence of explicit statutory language—have shouldered the burden of determining congressional intent with regard to individual districts' responsibility to provide FAPE.

The FAPE provision affects IEP teams, parents, and teachers on a daily basis. FAPE is problematic in its actual implementation, however, due to the nebulous and subjective nature of what constitutes an "appropriate" education. Part of the problem arises from the different views of the parties involved: What a parent considers appropriate may be vastly different from what the school finds to be appropriate. Unfortunately, the law offers no single, definitive answer to the question of what constitutes the most appropriate education for a child with a disability. Regardless, school districts must provide specific services designed to meet the particular educational needs of each student with a disability. Although the IDEA mandates a continuum of services, the law does not stipulate a prescriptive or specific list of services based on disabling conditions. The law simply charges the IEP team with determining what is most appropriate for the child based on his or her needs.

FEDERAL REQUIREMENTS

The federal regulations implementing the IDEA define FAPE as:

special education and related services that—

(a) Are provided at public expense, under public supervision and direction, and without charge;

(b) Meet the standards of the SEA [state education agency], including the requirements of this part;

(c) Include an appropriate preschool, elementary school, or secondary school education in the State involved; and

(d) Are provided in conformity with an individualized education program (IEP) that meets the requirements of Sections 300.320–300.324. (34 C.F.R. § 300.17)

UNDERSTANDING FAPE

To better comprehend FAPE and, therefore, implement it correctly, readers should understand each word in the term. The National Information Center for Children and Youth with Disabilities (NICHCY) has effectively dissected the term (Figure 7.2). Since the IDEA was enacted, the U.S. Supreme Court and myriad federal courts have issued decisions defining *free* and *appropriate*; nevertheless, both terms will continue to be argued over and addressed on individual bases through the courts.

FIGURE 7.2

The NICHCY Definition of FAPE

Looking at each of the words alone can be a useful way of understanding what FAPE is. "Free" is a vital part of the law's requirement, for the education of each child with a disability must be 'provided at public expense . . . and without charge' to the child or the child's parents. The law, in its definition of special education, uses the phrase 'at no cost to the parents.' The existing regulations define the meaning of this phrase, as follows:

> At no cost means that all specially designed instruction is provided without charge, but does not preclude incidental fees that are normally charged to nondisabled students or their parents as a part of the regular education program. (34 CFR §300.17)

What is an "appropriate" education differs for each child with a disability. Yet each child with a disability is entitled to an education that is 'appropriate' for his or her needs. The law requires this and specifies in some detail how the school and parents are to plan the education that each child receives so that it is appropriate. For example, evaluations are conducted to identify as closely as possible what the child's individual needs are. These evaluations are expected to inform the decision making process, so that the school and parents can design an education that responds to the child's needs. Together, the school and parents specify what this education will be and put it down in writing in the Individualized Education Program (IEP). The IEP must be reviewed and, as appropriate, revised each year, to ensure that the education being delivered remains appropriate to the child's needs.

'Public' generally refers to our public school systems. Children with disabilities have the right to attend public school just as other children do, regardless of the nature or severity of their disabilities. The public school system must serve students with disabilities, respond to their individual needs, and help them plan for their futures.

"Education" is what the law is all about. IDEA is, among its credits, an education act. It guarantees that a free appropriate public education is available to eligible children with disabilities and that this free appropriate public education consists of 'special education and related services . . . provided in conformity with an IEP' that meets requirements specified within the law and is based upon the child's individual needs [34 CFR §300.8]. FAPE is an exciting and important principle of the law. While in practice FAPE differs for each child, in principle for each child it is the same: a guarantee of access to a free appropriate public education that indeed opens the doors of opportunity and learning.

Source: Provided by NICHCY copyright free.

THE *ROWLEY* DECISION

In 1982, the U.S. Supreme Court decided a case involving how far schools must go to provide FAPE. This decision set the precedent for all courts and schools in the nation when considering and determining FAPE. In *Board of Education of Hendrick Hudson Central School District v. Rowley* (1982), the High Court established a *"basic floor of responsibility."* (See Figure 7.3.) This term reflects the Supreme Court's

FIGURE 7.3

The *Rowley* Two-Part Test

In order to provide lower courts with a standard to determine if the FAPE mandate of the Act has been satisfied, the Supreme Court developed a two-part test:

1. Has the school complied with the procedures of IDEA?
2. Is the IEP, developed through the procedures of the Act, reasonably calculated to enable the child to receive educational benefit? (Rowley, 206–207)

If the two questions can be answered yes, then the school has met the FAPE mandate and is in compliance with IDEA.

belief that a school is not responsible for providing the maximum level of services possible to meet the goals of a child's IEP. The High Court noted that the IDEA mandates that school districts provide not the "optimal level of services," but rather a "basic floor of opportunity" and "some educational benefit" (*Rowley*, 1982, pp. 189, 201). The parents of Amy Rowley had contended that the school was required by law to provide a full-time sign language interpreter for their hearing-impaired daughter. The school argued that Amy made reasonable academic progress without the assistance of a sign language interpreter. The Rowleys acknowledged their daughter's lip-reading skills, but argued that she was not able to comprehend approximately 40 percent of spoken language. As a result, the Rowleys claimed, Amy required the services of a sign language interpreter in school. The district argued that Amy could sufficiently read lips and, with the addition of other accommodations, had received a FAPE. In the end, the school district successfully demonstrated—through Amy's grades and progress in relation to her peers—that the IEP team had reasonably calculated for her to receive a FAPE.

In this landmark decision, the Supreme Court established that schools were not responsible for providing maximum educational services; rather, they were responsible for meeting the basic needs of the child in order to provide a FAPE. Prior to this ruling, mixed opinions existed as to whether schools had to maximize student potential when providing services to students with disabilities.

POST-*ROWLEY* DECISIONS

Following *Rowley*, families raised a number of FAPE-related claims; however, these challenges necessitated that the lower courts analyze and incorporate the precedents set by the Supreme Court. As a result, many of the legal scenarios surrounding FAPE have been constructed through the lower courts' interpretations of the

Rowley decision. In 1984, the U.S. Court of Appeals for the First Circuit interpreted the broad language of "some educational benefit" to mean that Congress intended for students under the IDEA to demonstrate measurable progress that yields "effective results" (*Burlington School Committee v. Massachusetts Department of Education*, 1984).

In similar fashion, the U.S. Court of Appeals for the Third Circuit, in *Polk v. Central Susquehanna Intermediate Unit 16* (1988), interpreted the meaning of the term "some educational benefit." The case involved a 14-year-old boy suffering from encephalopathy, which resulted in severe mental and physical limitations. The school district refused to provide physical therapy, and the parents claimed the district's decision denied their son a FAPE. Considered the most significant case interpreting "some educational benefit," the court in *Polk* stated that de minimis progress is not acceptable and concluded that the program should include physical therapy. In its decision, the Third Circuit noted that "the question of how much benefit is sufficient to be 'meaningful' is inescapable" (p. 173.).

In 1999, the Third Circuit decided a similar case regarding FAPE, *Ridgewood Board of Education v. N.E* (1999). The appellate court overturned the ruling of the lower court, which had asserted that the IDEA required that the child's IEP merely provide "more than a trivial educational benefit." The Third Circuit asserted that measurable gains are necessary in order to demonstrate "meaningful benefit" and "significant learning." Numerous circuit courts have issued similar FAPE decisions, including *Roland M. v. Concord School Committee* (1990), *Doe v. Smith* (1989), and *Fort Zumwalt School District v. Clynes* (1997).

PROCEDURAL ERRORS

Courts generally find that unless the procedural error has a serious impact on the child's ability to receive a FAPE, the error will not be sufficient to support a determination that a FAPE has been denied. In *Kingsmore ex rel. Lutz v. District of Columbia* (2006), the U.S. Court of Appeals for the District of Columbia Circuit determined that the school district's procedural error, failing to provide a full transcript or recording of the student's due process hearing, did not violate the disabled student's substantive right to a FAPE under the IDEA. The student's claim was viable only if the failure to meet that procedural requirement had affected the student's substantive rights. In a similar ruling related to a procedural error, the U.S. Court of Appeals for the Eighth Circuit, in *School Board of Independent School District No. 11 v. Renollett* (2006), ruled that the school district's failure to develop a behavioral intervention plan did not deny the student a FAPE, since district staff responded to the student's behavioral incidents with set procedures.

In *Adam J. v. Keller Independent School District* (2003), the U.S. Court of Appeals for the Fifth Circuit ruled in favor of the district. The court agreed that the IEP was appropriate and the procedural violations did not produce substantive harm. The court noted that in order for procedural violations to be an issue, they must result in the child experiencing a loss of educational benefit and, thus, being denied a FAPE.

The IDEA contains stringent procedural safeguards to ensure substantive rights are not denied to parents and students. The following case represents how the procedural error must be linked to a substantive right in order for a FAPE to be denied. In *Amanda J. ex rel. Annette J. v. Clark County School District* (2001), procedural error did result in a denial of a FAPE. The school district violated procedural requirements when it failed to disclose the student's records to her parents in a timely manner. The records contained information that indicated the student possibly suffered from autism and suggested that further psychiatric evaluation was needed. With the parents being denied the knowledge that their child might be suffering from autism, an appropriate IEP could not be created, and thus, the child was denied a FAPE.

SERVICE DELIVERY MODELS

The judicial system has generally stayed away from ruling on behalf of the parents in cases where specific service delivery models or methodological approaches are in dispute. If the courts were to begin micromanaging and determining how schools provide services and designating specific strategies, not only would the judicial system be inundated with a landslide of litigation, but also the rulings would undermine the professional decision-making of educators. Only on a limited basis—and under mitigating circumstances— have post-*Rowley* courts have accepted and ruled on FAPE cases involving methodological issues.

In *Grim v. Rhinebeck Central School District* (2003), the U.S. Court of Appeals for the Second Circuit determined that the district court inappropriately imposed its preference for a specific methodological approach for a student with dyslexia. In its ruling, the Second Circuit asserted that it is not the responsibility or the role of the courts to determine methodological approaches.

The U.S. Court of Appeals for the Seventh Circuit, in *Lachman v. Illinois State Board of Education* (1988), demonstrated the general trend of the courts staying out of methodological issues. Whereas the parents wanted cued-speech instruction at the neighborhood school, the school district offered a different method (total communication) outside of the neighborhood school. Because the case involved a difference of opinion regarding methodological approaches, the court found in favor of the district and noted that methodological decisions should be made by the schools. In keeping with the principle that methodological decisions fall under the authority of the school, the U.S. Court of Appeals for the Fourth Circuit asserted, in *Barnett v. Fairfax County School Board* (1991), that that specific methodology used to best meet the needs of a child with a disability is the decision of the school.

Importantly, the IDEA requires parents to inform the school district of their intentions prior to placing their child in a private placement if they wish to pursue remuneration. If the parents do not and prevail in due process, they may receive partial reimbursement or none. In *Rafferty v. Cranston Public School Committee* (2002), the U.S. Court of Appeals for the First Circuit upheld the lower court's decision. The appellate court found in favor of the school division regarding the nonreimbursement of private school tuition for two reasons: (1) The private placement was inappropriate, and (2) the parents did not provide ten days' notice of the change to the school.

AUTISM

As noted above, only under mitigating circumstances will the courts accept and rule on cases involving methodological issues. Courts have considered methodical issues only when the questions of "appropriateness" and the denial of FAPE are related to a methodological approach. In relation to autism, the courts have become increasingly more involved in methodological issues. Autism-related litigation has shown a sustained increase since the 1990s. The central issue involving methodology tends to revolve around applied behavioral analysis (ABA)/Lovaas therapy. Lovaas therapy, an intensive program designed mainly for preschool-aged autistic children, involves up to 40 hours per week of intensive one-on-one work. The program is expensive and involves considerable training.

In *Deal v. Hamilton County Board of Education* (2004), the U.S. Court of Appeals for the Sixth Circuit found that the school system's predetermination not to offer a student with autism intensive ABA amounted to a procedural violation under the IDEA. Further, because predetermination of placement effectively deprived the student's parents of meaningful participation in the IEP process, it caused substantive harm and, therefore, deprived the student of FAPE.

In *Board of Education of the City School District of the City of New York* (2000), the parents of a six-year-old child with autism invoked due process in order to seek reimbursement for ABA services not provided by the school district. The state hearing officer agreed with the parents and ordered the district to reimburse the parents. The officer found that the methodology proposed by the school did not meet the child's needs and that the ABA services were appropriate, since the child's communication skills were improving under the therapy.

In *Delaware County Intermediate Unit No. 25 v. Martin K. & Melinda K.* (1993), the U.S. District Court for the Eastern District of Pennsylvania addressed a methodological dispute between the district and the parents of an autistic child. The court found that the TEACCH program used by the district was not meeting the needs of the child—citing minimal progress in reading and mathematics over a two-year period. The court sided with the parents and mandated that the district utilize the Lovaas program. The court ruled that the TEACCH program was not providing an "appropriate" education.

After an extensive review of administrative and judicial decisions, Gorn (1999) identified three major trends in autism-related cases where methodological appropriateness was a primary issue:

> **Educational Methodology:** In some instances, the parents claim that the school district's program is not reasonably calculated to provide an educational benefit, but the district contends that the dispute is merely about selection of educational methodology.
>
> **Quantum of Benefit:** Parents naturally advocate for programming to provide the maximum potential educational benefit even in those states that follow the lesser "meaningful benefit" standard of the IDEA.
>
> **Generalization:** A student's ability to generalize what is taught in school to the same situations in the home environment is a critical concern for parents. But the obligation of a school district to provide services that will allow a student to transfer classroom progress to other settings is an open issue. (p. 3:8)

Many educators see this trend of imposing methodologies in autism-related cases as disturbing. Nevertheless, although several courts and hearing officers have opted to impose methodological approaches on schools, many courts and hearing officers have steadfastly stayed away from stepping over the methodological line in relation to autism. In *Gill ex rel. Gill v. Columbia 93 School District* (2000), the parents filed for reimbursement for private Lovaas services for their seven-year-old child with autism. The U.S. Court of Appeals for the Eighth Circuit denied the family reimbursement, finding the methodology provided by the district was appropriate. The court deferred to the professional decision-making of the school district. Under similar circumstances, the U.S. District Court for the Southern District of Indiana, in *J.P. by Popson v. West Clark Community Schools* (2002), refused to impose a particular methodology. The court did not believe that ABA was the only appropriate method for educating a four-year-old child with autism and, therefore, found the IEP to be appropriate.

FINANCIAL CONSIDERATIONS

Contrary to common belief, financial considerations can be a factor when determining educational placements. As a by-product of the *Rowley* decision, courts have found in favor of school districts that deny placements that would place an undue burden on the district—provided an appropriate, less expensive alternative has been offered. The key principle is that cost is not the only factor to consider in making the placement decision. In *Doe v. Tullahoma City School District* (1993), the U.S. Court of Appeals for the Sixth Circuit provided a now famous metaphor: "The Act requires that the [school district] provide the educational equivalent of a serviceable Chevrolet to every handicapped student... [T]he [school district] is not required to provide a Cadillac..." (pp. 459–460).

In *Cheltenham School District v. Joel P.* (1996), the U.S. District Court for the Eastern District of Pennsylvania held that the potential fiscal burden on the school district could be a factor in the placement decision. The parents of a child with mental retardation wanted a special life-skills program within the neighborhood school. To provide this placement, the school district would have had to build a special classroom and hire additional employees. The school district argued that placing the child in a neighboring district with a preexisting program would meet the needs of the child. The court also did a cost-benefit analysis and concluded that because the program would support only four children, it did not justify the exorbitant cost.

In relation to services and accommodations, in *Sherman v. Mamaroneck Union Free School District* (2003), the U.S. Court of Appeals for the Second Circuit determined, as had the impartial hearing officer and the state review officer, that the school district's denial of the use of an advanced calculator in the student's mathematics course for students with learning disabilities did not deprive the student of a FAPE. Even though the student was failing mathematics, the evidence demonstrated the student was capable of passing the class with the assistance of a less advanced calculator in a manner consistent with the education goals of the class's curriculum. It was determined the student's lack of effort contributed to the failing grade.

SCHOOL-BASED MEASURES TO DETERMINE IF FAPE IS ACHIEVED

When schools and parents debate the appropriateness of a placement, the central argument involves whether the current placement is meeting the individual needs of the child. To determine the appropriateness of the placement, IEP teams, hearing officers, and courts use multiple criteria to evaluate whether a child is making reasonable progress under the current educational program. Pitasky (2002) lists the following as three of the most commonly used factors in determining the appropriateness of an educational program (p. 5:5).

STUDENT GRADES AND PROMOTION

Grades are commonly used by IEP teams to determine if a child is making reasonable progress in school. While grades and promotion from grade to grade are common indicators of progress, they do not automatically render a child's educational program appropriate (*Walczak v. Florida Union Free School District*, 1998). According to the *Rowley* decision, each case must be analyzed individually. Therefore, student grades and grade promotion are subject to scrutiny as measures of progress. For example, a student may be promoted for social reasons, and promotion under this circumstance would not be a meaningful measure of progress.

PROGRESS ON IEP GOALS

The focal point of educational progress is embedded in the goals and, if appropriate, the objectives of the child's IEP. The IDEA requires special education teachers to track and measure student progress on annual goals and short-term objectives. Making progress or mastering measurable, appropriate goals that are linked to the present level of performance is a common indicator of an appropriate education. But if a student fails to make progress on his or her IEP goals, it does not automatically mean the education program is inappropriate (*Houston Independent School District v. Caius R.*, 1998; Gill *v. Columbia 93 School District*, 1999).

STANDARDIZED TEST SCORES

IEP teams often use standardized test scores to demonstrate educational progress (*Hall v. Vance County Board of Education*, 1985). For example, during an annual or triennial review, a team may compare the grades, age equivalents, and standard scores from prior testing and newer testing. The team will generally interpret improved scores as an indication of educational progress. Using standardized test scores can be problematic, however. The scores are nationally normed and may not accurately measure or assess the student's progress. Teacher-developed curriculum-based measures might provide a more accurate picture of the student's progress in the school's curriculum.

SUMMARY

Every child eligible for special education services has a right to a FAPE, one of the pillars of the IDEA. Thus, it is essential that schools do everything in their power to ensure that every eligible child receives a *free* and *appropriate* education. Since the initial implementation of the IDEA, the FAPE requirement has proven problematic.

The broad and nebulous term *appropriate* has generated significant debate and litigation as it pertains to FAPE. In the case of *Board of Education of the Hendrick Hudson Central School District v. Rowley* (1982), the U.S. Supreme Court set the precedent for FAPE. The High Court stipulated that the "optimal level of services" is not necessary or mandated to provide a FAPE. Rather, the Court ruled that every student with a disability must be provided a "basic floor of opportunity" and must receive "some educational benefit" through his or her IEP.

Applying the Law in the Classroom

Samir is a ninth-grade student at Heritage High School (HHS). Samir attended the public elementary and middle schools that feed into HHS, with the exception of his eighth-grade year. Samir's parents, Mr. and Mrs. Soid, pulled him from the local public middle school and placed him in The Noble School, a small private school for children with learning disabilities. Samir has been a solid "C+" student his entire academic career. However, his parents feel strongly that he is capable of much more and that his learning disability is impeding his ability to reach his full potential. They are highly involved parents who are very concerned about their son's learning difficulties. Mr. Soid is a personal injury lawyer in a small, local firm. Mrs. Soid is a teacher at an elementary school in a neighboring school district.

On Tuesday, September 7, the first day of school, Samir's parents came to the high school, but he did not. They requested in person and in writing that an IEP meeting be held and that an official from the central office be present. The Soids agreed verbally to a meeting the following Monday, September 13, at 9:00 A.M. and were provided with a letter of prior notice from Mrs. Smoot, the HHS chair of special education. Although it was in Samir's records, the IEP team was not aware Mr. Soid was an attorney. The school arranged for the full IEP team to meet, along with a central office representative who was authorized to commit the district's resources in order to provide a full continuum of services.

Both Mr. and Mrs. Soid arrived promptly at 9 A.M. They presented the IEP team with copies of a recent independent educational evaluation (IIE), conducted by The Noble School. In addition, they requested to tape-record the meeting. The IEP team reviewed the IEE and then began to discuss the IEP. After the school presented a potential program for Samir, the parents expressed their concern that their son would not benefit from any educational program provided by HHS. They noted that their son needed a small setting that would address his specific needs. Members of the IEP team from HHS noted that the self-contained classes ranged in size from 4 to 12 students and that the school employed fully licensed special educators trained to educate students with specific learning disabilities. The parents did not agree with the members of the IEP team and requested homebound instruction.

Although many of the team members did not consider the homebound placement appropriate or the least restrictive environment, the team agreed to the placement for a two-month period. In doing so, the team followed the lead of the central office representative, who stated his support for the placement. A member of the team noted that the teacher would not be a special educator and that the child would receive limited support. The parents felt the severity of Samir's school-based anxiety superseded any educational benefit he would receive at HHS. The IEP team signed off on an IEP that placed Samir in homebound instruction until November 8.

A month later, on October 16, the parents requested another IEP meeting. The meeting was scheduled on October 19, at 10 A.M. The parents requested again to record the meeting. They presented a letter from a local psychiatrist, which the team then reviewed. The letter noted that Samir would receive the greatest educational benefit in a small school setting at The Noble School. The parents then stated that the homebound placement was not meeting the needs of their son. Mrs. Smoot presented documentation that demonstrated Samir had met with the teacher only three times over the month period. She further noted that the teacher had attempted several times to arrange appointments and that the parents were unable to schedule times to meet with the teacher. The parents rebutted by saying that they, too, had made several attempts to schedule times and that the teacher was unable to accommodate their schedule.

Mr. Soid stated his intention to place his child at The Noble School, effective immediately, and said he expected reimbursement from the school district for tuition. A member of the team asked if they intended to withdraw their child from HHS, and the parents said they did not because it could compromise their ability to seek reimbursement. Mrs. Smoot acknowledged Mr. and Mrs. Soid's intentions and began to present a proposed IEP. The parents refused to sign the IEP and noted that they would be sending a letter of rebuttal shortly.

A week following the last IEP meeting, the HHS registrar informed Mrs. Smoot that Samir was still enrolled. Mrs. Smoot contacted the Soids and requested an explanation, in writing, as to why they had not disenrolled their child. As of November 8, the Soids had not corresponded with the school. Mrs. Smoot contacted the school district's homebound services department to check the status of Samir's services. The director of homebound services reported that the teacher assigned to Samir had stopped corresponding with the family following the last session on September 28. When Mrs. Smoot asked why services and contact had been ceased, the director was at a loss for an answer. Mrs. Smoot strongly urged the director to reestablish contact and document attempts to provide the services in the IEP signed on September 13.

Application Questions

1. Based on what you have learned about appropriate placements, which placement do feel is the least restrictive for Samir?
2. Apply the *Rowley* two-part test to determine whether or not the regular school environment is appropriate.
3. When the parents requested to tape-record the meeting, why should this have been a major "red flag" to the IEP team?
4. Do the parents have an automatic right to reimbursement if they unilaterally place their child in a private placement?
5. Why might the school district be in a difficult position when staff did not continue to provide homebound instruction (or document regular communication)?
6. By getting the district to approve an IEP place the child in homebound instruction, how did the parents make it easier to argue that a private placement was necessary (think about the continuum of services and whether or not homebound is likely to meet Samir's needs)?
7. If a parent is an attorney by trade, why should the IEP team have legal counsel?

CRITICAL THINKING QUESTIONS

1. Why has the word *appropriate* led to an extensive amount of litigation in relation to FAPE?
2. Why are the Findings of the IDEA noted in this chapter important in relation to FAPE?
3. Explain the importance of the *Rowley* case and its impact on FAPE and the field of special education as a whole.
4. What important distinction did the Supreme Court draw in the *Rowley* case?
5. How did post-*Rowley* lower courts further define the FAPE mandate?
6. In relation to FAPE, how have the courts tended to view methodological disputes? When ruling in favor of parents, what factors have the courts taken into account?

REFERENCES

Adam J. v. Keller Independent School District, 328 F.3d 804 (5th Cir. 2003).
Amanda J. ex rel. Annette J. v. Clark County School District, 267 F.3d 877 (9th Cir. 2001).

Barnett v. Fairfax County School Board, 721 F. Supp. 755, 757 (E.D. Va. 1989), aff'd, 927 F.2d 146 (4th Cir. 1991).

Board of Education of the City School District of the City of New York, 33 IDELR 58 (SEA N.Y. 2000).

Board of Education of the Hendrick Hudson Central School District v. Rowley, 458 U.S. 176 (1982).

Burlington School Committee v. Massachusetts Department of Education, 736 F.2d 773 (1st Cir. 1985).

Cheltenham School District v. Joel P., 949 F. Supp. 346 (E.D. Pa. 1996).

Deal v. Hamilton County Board of Education, 392 F.3d 840 (6th Cir. 2004).

Delaware County Intermediate Unit No. 25 v. Martin K. and Melinda K., 831 F. Supp. 1206 (E.D. Pa. 1993).

Doe v. Smith, 879 F.2d 1340 (6th Cir. 1989).

Doe v. Tullahoma City Schools, 9 F.3d 455 (6th Cir. 1993).

Gill v. Columbia 93 School District, 31 IDELR 29 (W.D. Mo. 1999).

Gill ex rel. Gill v. Columbia 93 School District, 217 F.3d 1027 (8th Cir. 2000).

Gorn, S. (1999). *The answer book on special education law.* Horsham, PA: LRP.

Grim v. Rhinebeck Central School District, 346 F.3d 377 (2d Cir. 2003).

Hall v. Vance County Board of Education, 774 F.2d 629 (4th Cir. 1985).

Houston Independent School District v. Caius R., 30 IDELR 578, (TX, 1998).

Huefner, D. S. (2000). *Getting comfortable with special education law.* Norwood, MA: Christopher-Gordon.

Individuals with Disabilities Education Act (Education for All Handicapped Children Act of 1975), Pub. L. No. 94-142, 89 Stat. 773.

J.P. by Popson v. West Clark Community Schools, 230 F. Supp. 2d 910 (S.D. Ind. 2002).

Kingsmore ex rel. Lutz v. District of Columbia, 466 F.3d 118 (D.C. Cir. 2006).

Lachman v. Illinois State Board of Education, 852 F.2d 290 (7th Cir. 1988).

The National Center for Children and Youth with Disabilities, nichcy.org.

Pitasky, V.M. (2002). *The answer book on placement under the IDEA and Section 504.* Horsham, PA: LRP.

Polk v. Central Susquehanna Intermediate Unit 16, 853 F.2d 171 (3d Cir. 1988).

Rafferty v. Cranston Public School Committee, 315 F.3d 21 (1st Cir. 2002).

Ridgewood Board of Education v. N.E., 172 F.3d 238 (3d Cir. 1999).

Roland M. v. Concord School Committee, 910 F.2d 983 (1st Cir. 1990).

School Board of Independent School District No. 11 v. Renollett, 440 F.3d 1007 (8th Cir. 2006).

Sherman v. Mamaroneck Union Free School District, 340 F.3d 87 (2d Cir. 2003).

Walczak v. Florida Union Free School District, 142 F.3d 119 (2d Cir. 1998).

Fort Zumwalt School District v. Clynes, 119 F.3d 607 (8th Cir. 1991).

8

Least Restrictive Environment

- Students should be removed from the regular education setting only when the nature and severity of their disabilities warrant such a removal and when they are included with their nondisabled peers to the maximum extent appropriate.
- The least restrictive environment (LRE) provision is intended to protect children with disabilities from discriminatory practices and ensure access to education with their nondisabled peers.
- *Pennsylvania Association for Retarded Citizens v. Pennsylvania* (1972) and *Mills v. Board of Education of the District of Columbia* (1972) decreed that students with disabilities—no matter the severity of their disabilities—had a constitutional right to public education.
- The regular classroom is the least restrict placement along the continuum; however, it certainly may not be the least restrictive learning environment for every child.
- *Mainstreaming* refers to the involvement of students with disabilities in the regular education setting as appropriate.
- Educators now widely use the term and philosophy of *inclusion* as a successor term to *integration* and *mainstreaming*.
- The IDEA mandate of *zero reject* is as simple and direct as the term: No child between the ages of 3 and 21 may be excluded from public education.
- The LRE is determined on a case-by-case basis by the individualized education program (IEP) team.
- No individual may unilaterally determine the placement or educational program for a child.
- The U.S. Courts of Appeals for the Fourth, Fifth, Sixth, and Ninth Circuits have rendered decisions impacting the LRE mandate.
- Although different language is used, the LRE mandate of the IDEA is virtually identical to the legal requirements of Section 504 of the Rehabilitation Act of 1973.

As one of the essential components of the Individuals with Disabilities Education Act (IDEA), the least restrictive environment (LRE) mandate is the legal linchpin that ensures educators and families continually strive to include all students with disabilities—no matter the severity of their disabilities—in the regular education setting and with their age-peers to the maximum extent appropriate. "One of the primary principles of the IDEA is the concept of educating children with disabilities along with children who are not disabled to the maximum extent appropriate, ideally in the regular classroom" (Rothstein, 2000, p. 125). Although the LRE for all students with disabilities is not the regular education setting, the mandate is that the regular education setting must be the first to be considered.

Prompted by decades of segregation and isolation of students with disabilities, Congress found in 1975 that at that time "one million of the handicapped children in the United States are excluded entirely from the public school system and will not go through the educational process with their peers" (Pub. L. No. 94-142, § 3(b)(4)). According to Pitasky (2002),

> In the early history of public school education, many students with disabilities were automatically warehoused in institutional facilities without regard to the severity of their disabilities or special education needs. To guard against this reoccurring, a key component of the IDEA is its guarantee that initial consideration will be given to the least restrictive environment for all students with disabilities. (p. 6:1)

Although no specific formula or program can be prescribed for specific disabilities—and in fact, it is illegal to predetermine placements based on disability—the continuous goal is to find the most beneficial and appropriate setting for each child with a disability.

FEDERAL DEFINITION OF LRE

> In General.—To the maximum extent appropriate, children with disabilities, including children in public or private institutions or other care facilities, are educated with children who are not disabled, and special classes, separate schooling, or other removal of children with disabilities from the regular educational environment occurs only when the nature or severity of the disability of a child is such that education in regular classes with the use of supplementary aids and services cannot be achieved satisfactorily. (20 U.S.C. § 1412(a)(5)(A))

The critical points in this definition—which every school district and individualized education program (IEP) team must remember—are that students should be removed from the regular education setting only when the nature and severity of their disabilities warrant such a removal and when they are included with their nondisabled peers to the maximum extent appropriate. Prior to the removal, supplementary aids and services also must be considered. "Basically, LRE refers to the educational setting closest to the regular classroom in which FAPE can be delivered to a special education student" (Huefner, 2000, p. 241). Many school districts and IEP teams are guilty of placing students in more restrictive environments prior to exhausting legitimate and reasonable supplementary aids, services, and placements—all of which would keep these students in the regular education setting.

INTENT AND PURPOSE OF THE LRE REQUIREMENT

The LRE provision is intended to protect children with disabilities from discriminatory practices and ensure access to education with their nondisabled peers. Advocates fighting for the involvement of students with disabilities in the mainstream culture of American education prior to the passage of the IDEA argued that segregating these students is inherently wrong and unjust. Using *Brown v. Board of Education* (1954) as a precedent for equal access and protection under the law for all students, advocates successfully articulated the adverse impacts of excluding students with disabilities from regular interaction with their "normal" age-peers. In addition, advocates successfully highlighted both the social and the academic benefits of affording students with disabilities nondiscriminatory treatment and placement in the regular education setting as much as possible and appropriate.

In the early 1970s, two pivotal legal decisions reinforced the *Brown* decision and set powerful precedents for the free appropriate public education (FAPE) and LRE mandates. *Pennsylvania Association for Retired Citizens v. Pennsylvania* (1972) and *Mills v. Board of Education of the District of Columbia* (1972) decreed that students with disabilities—no matter the severity of their disabilities—had a constitutional right to public education. In these decisions, each court demonstrated a preference for the placement of students with disabilities with their regular education age-peers to the greatest extent practicable. In fact, these cases provided the foundation for many critical components of Public Law No. 94-142. Readers should be aware, however, that the parents and organizations involved in these cases were predominately parents of students with severe disabilities. Parents of the children with the most severe and profound disabilities should be credited with much of the early progress made through the judicial process, even though children with the most severe and profound disabilities make up the smallest percentage of students with disabilities.

A commonly misunderstood tenet of the LRE mandate is the notion that the regular education classroom *is* the least restrictive environment. The regular education classroom is the least restrict placement along the continuum; however, it certainly may not be the least restrictive learning environment for every child.

In many circumstances, in order for a student's needs to be met, the student may need an array of services and potential placements that pull him or her out of the regular classroom. In *L.E. v. Ramsey Board of Education* (2006), the U.S. Court of Appeals for the Third Circuit found sufficient evidence supporting the administrative law judge's determination that the student could not receive a FAPE under the IDEA in a regular classroom with supplemental services. The appellate court supported the school board's determination that the placement of the student in a school for students with disabilities the least restrictive environment for that student. During testimony, school officials and educators argued successfully that the school for students with disabilities was the most inclusive environment in which the student could receive an appropriate education and that the school board had considered a full range of options for the student. It is critical for the practitioner to note that, whenever a student is placed outside of the regular education classroom, the IEP team *must* document its consideration of the full continuum of options and placements (see Figure 8.1).

In *Beth B. v. Van Clay* (2002), the school district recommended that a student with severe mental and physical disabilities be placed in a special education classroom with mainstreaming opportunities. The parents argued that by not placing the child in the regular classroom full-time, the school district was violating the LRE mandate. The U.S. Court of Appeals for the Seventh Circuit concluded that

---

Listed below are some of the many special education service models. The names and the methods of implementation may vary from district to district.

- **Regular class only:** regular teacher meets all the needs of the student
- **Special educator consultative:** regular teacher meets the needs of the students with occasional help from the special education teacher
- **Co-teaching or collaborative teaching:** general education and special education teacher work together to meet the student's in the general education classroom. Students are seldom removed from the general education classroom
- **Resource:** Students attend a regular class most of the day but go to a special education class several hours or for a block of time
- **Self-contained:** special education classes are attended most of the day and is included in regular education activities minimally
- **Hospital or home bound:** instruction provided in the hospital or home until student is able to return to regular school from which they are temporarily or totally withdrawn
- **Special day school:** instruction provided in a separate school
- **Residential placement:** students receive their services in a full-time living environment

FIGURE 8.1

Special Education Service Models

the IEP recommended by the school district met the FAPE and LRE requirements of the IDEA and was, thus, appropriate.

Traditionally, issues and cases surrounding placement and the LRE mandate have involved parents advocating for their child's right to be educated with nondisabled peers. However, it is not uncommon for contemporary LRE cases to involve parents advocating for students to be placed in segregated, private schools. For example, in *A.B. ex rel. D.B. v. Lawson* (2004), the parents of a student with a disability who had difficulty in reading and writing, but who was otherwise of above-average intelligence, brought suit against the school district, claiming the student was not receiving a FAPE because the student was inappropriately placed in the neighborhood school. The student was mainstreamed with other regular education students, but the parents wanted the student placed full-time in a private school for students with disabilities. The U.S. Court of Appeals for the Fourth Circuit found in favor of the school district, asserting that the IEP was appropriate and that the child was properly placed in the neighborhood school with regular education peers.

In *McLaughlin v. Holt Public Schools Board of Education* (2003), the U.S. Court of Appeals for the Sixth Circuit determined that the student's placement in her neighborhood school was not the least restrictive environment (see Figure 8.2). The appellate court found that due to the extent of the student's specific needs, the private school placement that the parents requested was the least restrictive environment—even though the private school was not in close proximity to their home.

The federal regulations provide a framework for schools to follow in order to best ensure that each individual educational program is appropriate for a child with a disability receiving special education services. According to 34 C.F.R. § 300.552, the following criteria must be followed when determining appropriate placements:

- Must be made in conformity with the least restrictive environment provisions of the regulations;
- Must be determined at least annually;
- Must be based on the child's IEP;
- Must be as close as possible to the child's home;
- Unless the IEP of a child with a disability requires some other arrangement, the child must be educated in the school that he or she would attend if nondisabled;
- In selecting the LRE, consideration must be given to any potential harmful effect on the child or on the quality of services that he or she needs.
- A child with a disability must not be removed from education in age-appropriate regular classrooms solely because of needed modifications in the general curriculum.

FIGURE 8.2

Federal Regulations and Criteria for Determining Appropriate Placement

TERMINOLOGY

Too often, the terms *LRE*, *mainstreaming*, and *inclusion* are used synonymously and, thus, incorrectly. Each term is different and must be accurately understood. "Over the years the term *LRE* has been joined by the terms *mainstreaming* and *inclusion*, all of which are used, sometimes indiscriminately, with respect to placement preferences. Treating these three terms as synonyms represents a misunderstanding of the legal meaning of LRE" (Huefner, 2000, p. 240). As discussed previously, the LRE is a legal mandate referring to the involvement of children in the regular education setting to the maximum extent appropriate, with supplemental aids and services where needed. The LRE is a broad mandate that encompasses the appropriate placement of and program development for children with disabilities.

Mainstreaming, however, refers to the involvement of students with disabilities in the regular education setting as appropriate. Individual students can be mainstreamed into the regular education setting for vastly different amounts of time. Two different children might be considered mainstreamed; however, one might spend all day in regular education classes, while the other might spend 40 percent of the day in self-contained classrooms. Mainstreaming students into the regular education setting may take several different instructional forms and methodologies. Hallahan and Kauffman (1998) report that authorities in the field recommend eight strategies for mainstreaming: (1) prereferral teams, (2) peer collaboration, (3) collaborative consultation, (4) cooperative teaching, (5) cooperative learning, (6) peer tutoring, (7) partial participation, and (8) curriculum materials designed to change attitudes (p. 66).

Educators now widely use the term and philosophy of *inclusion* as a successor term to *integration* and *mainstreaming*. Yell (2006) notes: "Inclusion generally connotes more comprehensive programming than the somewhat dated term mainstreaming" (p. 310). However, a small, but vocal group of advocates has fought over the years for *full inclusion* of all children, full-time in the regular education classroom, no matter the nature or severity of their disabilities. These advocates, generally parents of students with severe and profound disabilities, are reacting to decades of complete segregation from public education. Huefner (2000) states: "Prior to the 1975 enactment of Public Law 94-142, many school districts denied public school admission to many children with disabilities, especially those with mental retardation, physical disabilities, and behavioral disorders" (p. 239). Proponents of full inclusion do not support a continuum of placements because they believe the LRE for a student with a disability is the regular education setting for the entire school day. In any event, *full inclusion* is not a legal term, and it should be approached with caution when discussing the determination of the LRE. When applied in this manner, full inclusion can violate the mandates for a continuum of placements and LRE.

ZERO REJECT

The IDEA mandate of *zero reject* is as simple and direct as the term: No child between the ages of 3 and 21 may be excluded from public education. Boyle and Weishaar (2001) note:

> *Zero reject* means that local school districts cannot exclude students with disabilities from public schools due to the nature or degree of their disabilities. All students ages 3 to 21 must be located, evaluated, and provided with appropriate education programs. States are also required to locate and evaluate children with disabilities between birth and 3 years of age. (p. 3)

This mandate guarantees that all children have appropriate, publicly funded educational services from birth through age 21.

The zero reject principle is a fundamental component of the IDEA. As noted earlier, 1 million students with disabilities were excluded from the educational process prior to the passage of the IDEA. The zero reject principle ensures that all students—no matter the nature or severity of their disabilities—will benefit from FAPE in the LRE.

DETERMINING THE LRE

The regulations provide prescriptive legal requirements as to how school districts should ensure that children with disabilities are included in the regular education setting with supplementary aids and services as appropriate. The regulations, however, do not and cannot provide school districts with guidance regarding the voluminous and subjective information that must be considered when working to achieve the LRE for each child. The LRE must be determined on a case-by-case basis by the IEP team. No individual may unilaterally determine the placement or educational program for a child. There is no exact science or formula for determining the perfect program. Therefore, IEP teams always must work diligently to look at as many factors and options as necessary in order to include all children with disabilities with regular education students to the maximum extent possible.

Yell (1998) provides a helpful and legally sound checklist for educators to consider when determining the LRE for students with disabilities. (See Figure 8.3.) Although this list is not exhaustive, it is a solid foundation from which educators should work to establish the LRE. Yell's five-pronged approach is shown in Figure 8.3.

FIGURE 8.3

Checklist for Educators when Determining LRE for Students with Disabilities

1. Has the school taken steps to maintain the child in the general education classroom?
   - What supplementary aids and services were used?
   - What interventions were attempted?
   - How many interventions were attempted?
2. Benefits of placement in general education with supplementary aids and services versus special education.
   - Academic benefits
   - Nonacademic benefits (e.g., social, communication)
3. Effects on the education of other students.
   - If the student is disruptive, is the education of other students adversely affected?
   - Does the student require an inordinate amount of attention from the teacher, thereby adversely affecting the education of others?
4. If a student is being educated in a setting other than the general education classroom, are there integrated experiences with nondisabled peers to the maximum extent appropriate?
   - In what academic settings is the student integrated with nondisabled peers?
   - In what nonacademic settings is the child integrated with nondisabled peers?
5. Is the entire continuum of alternative services available from which to choose an appropriate placement.(p. 260)

Source: Yell, M. (2006 and 1998). *The law and special education* Merrill Publishing. Upper Saddle, New Jersey.

LITIGATION

Since 1975, only four of the federal appellate courts—the U.S. Courts of Appeals for the Fourth, Fifth, Sixth, and Ninth Circuits—have issued decisions that set out substantive criteria and tests for determining the LRE. As Yell (2006) notes:

> Although a number of LRE cases have been heard by the U.S. Courts of Appeals, there exist only four acknowledged tests for determining placement in the LRE. . . . Of these tests, the *Daniel Test* [developed by the Fifth Circuit] has proven the most persuasive, subsequently being adopted by the U.S. Courts of Appeals for the Third and Eleventh Circuits. (p. 324)

Over half of the country falls under the four circuits referenced above, and six more states and the Virgin Islands are included in the Third and Eleventh Circuits (refer to Figure 1.6 for a map of the federal circuits).

RONCKER V. WALTER (1983)

Roncker v. Walter (1983) involved the placement of Neil Roncker, a nine-year-old child with moderate mental retardation. The IEP team placed him in a school specifically for students with disabilities, and thus, regular education students did not attend this school. Neil's parents invoked due process, arguing that the district had violated FAPE and LRE because their son was not being educated with nondisabled peers to the maximum extent appropriate.

The U.S. District Court for the Southern District of Ohio supported the school district in its decision. The district court contended that the school district had broad authority and discretion regarding the placement of students with disabilities. Upon review, however, the Sixth Circuit overturned the lower court's holding and found in favor of the parents. The appellate court ruled that the intent of Congress was to integrate students with disabilities to the maximum extent appropriate and that the school district had failed to comply with the mainstreaming provision and the LRE mandate.

Through this decision, the Sixth Circuit developed the *Roncker portability test.* The two-part test evaluates the following: (1) Is it possible for the services provided in the segregated placement to be reasonably provided in an integrated placement? (2) If the answer to question 1 is no, then the more restrictive placement is appropriate. If the answer is yes, then the segregated placement is not the LRE and is inappropriate.

DANIEL R.R. V. STATE BOARD OF EDUCATION (1989)

Considered one of the most important cases regarding LRE, *Daniel R.R. v. State Board of Education* (1989) involved a six-year-old student with Down syndrome. The student attended a school in the El Paso (Texas) Independent School District. His IEP team placed him for one half of the day in a regular prekindergarten program and for the other half in an early childhood special education class. Daniel's teacher reported he was not making progress in the regular education setting. Further, she noted that he was still unable to accomplish basic tasks and objectives even with one-on-one, intensive support from her and the aide. Daniel's IEP team decided to pull him out of the regular education class and keep him in the special education class. The team allowed him to attend recess and lunch with his regular education peers.

Daniel's parents appealed the decision. The Fifth Circuit held that it was the intent of Congress to allow educators at the local district level to make instructional and placement decisions. In its decision, the Fifth Circuit held that placement in the least restrictive, most appropriate setting supersedes placement in the regular education setting. In general, local school districts must make decisions regarding teaching methodology and placement, utilizing the full continuum of placements to provide children with FAPE in the LRE.

Like the Sixth Circuit, the Fifth Circuit developed a two-part test for lower courts to use when determining if a school has complied with the LRE mandate: (1) Can the child receive a satisfactory education in the regular education class with supplemental aids and services? If the school has not made reasonable accommodations for the child, then the school is in violation of the LRE mandate and the test is over. If the school has satisfied the first part by providing supplemental aids and services, however, then the court considers the second prong. (2) Has the school integrated the child into the mainstream to the maximum extent appropriate?

After applying the two-part test, the Fifth Circuit determined that the school district had satisfactorily complied with both parts, thus complying with the LRE mandate. As noted above, this case proved to be very significant, establishing a precedent in the Fifth Circuit and being adopted by the Third Circuit in *Oberti v. Board of Education of the Borough of Clementon School District* (1993) and by the Eleventh Circuit in *Greer v. Rome City School District* (1991).

SACRAMENTO CITY UNIFIED SCHOOL DISTRICT V. RACHEL H. BY HOLLAND (1994)

Rachel Holland, an 11-year-old student with moderate mental retardation, attended special education schools from the start of her academic career (1985). In 1989, her parents requested a more integrated, mainstreamed placement. The school offered to include her generally in electives, lunch, recess, and nonacademic courses and to place her in a self-contained special education setting for all academic classes. Rachel's parents rebuffed the school's placement and requested that she spend all day in regular education classes. The parents invoked their due process rights and requested a hearing. They also unilaterally placed Rachel in a private school during the due process proceedings.

The hearing officer supported the parents' position, noting that the school district had not met its responsibility to integrate Rachel with her regular education age-peers to the maximum extent appropriate. The school district appealed the decision to the district court, and like the hearing officer, the district court found in favor of the parents. In reaching its decision, the district court applied a four-pronged test now known as the *Rachel H. four-factor test*:

1. The first factor analyzes whether the more restrictive setting is significantly more beneficial than the general education setting with supplemental aids and services. The court determined that no evidence suggested the special education services were superior to or more beneficial than the regular education setting.

2. The second factor addresses the social and nonacademic needs of the child. The parents successfully argued that Rachel had benefited from interaction with regular education peers. They noted growth in her social, emotional, and communication development. The court agreed that the regular classroom would better meet her social/emotional needs.

3. The third factor examines whether the presence of the student with a disability adversely impacts the regular education teacher or class. The court determined that Rachel's presence in the regular education classroom did not compromise the

education of the other students in the classroom, nor did it place undue stress or demand on the teacher's time.

4. The fourth factor addresses whether or not the placement in the regular education classroom is exceedingly expensive. The school district did not provide evidence to convince the court that the school district would have to bear an exceedingly high financial burden.

After considering the four factors, the district court held that the LRE for Rachel was a full-time regular education setting with supplemental aids and services.

The school district appealed the ruling to the Ninth Circuit. Using the same four-factor test, the Ninth Circuit affirmed the lower court's decision. The school district then appealed to the U.S. Supreme Court, but the High Court declined to review the circuit court's holding.

The Ninth Circuit again applied the Rachel H. four-factor test in *Clyde K. v. Puyallup School District* (1994). The case involved a 15-year-old boy named Ryan who had been diagnosed with Tourette's syndrome and attention deficit hyperactivity disorder. Ryan was placed in the general education classroom and was pulled out for resource support. Ryan demonstrated highly disruptive behaviors in the regular classroom, including profanity, sexual harassment of female students, and insubordination. The Ninth Circuit determined it was appropriate for the child to be removed from the regular education classroom and into a more restrictive setting. The court noted that although the placement in the regular classroom was not inappropriate, the setting was not conducive to meeting his needs and was unsuccessful.

HARTMANN V. LOUDOUN COUNTY BOARD OF EDUCATION (1998)

Hartmann v. Loudoun County Board of Education (1998) involved the placement of Mark Hartmann, an 11-year-old child with autism, in a comprehensive school. The district provided Mark the following services via his IEP: a full-time aide, three hours per week of special education services, five hours per week of speech therapy, individualized training for his teacher and aide, and training for the entire staff of the school on working with children with autism. Mark's extensive supports, however, did not alleviate his difficulty in the regular education setting. Mark consistently demonstrated aggressive, dangerous, and highly disruptive behaviors. His IEP team determined that Mark was not making progress toward his IEP goals and recommended that his placement shift to a specialized program for students with autism inside a comprehensive elementary school. Mark's parents strongly disagreed with the decision and charged that the school district was violating the LRE mandate by not mainstreaming their son with his regular education age-peers.

The district court found in favor of the Hartmanns, holding that the school system did not do enough to include Mark in the mainstream. But the 4th Circuit overturned the lower court's ruling. The court applied the following criteria—originally used in an earlier decision—in determining when placement in regular education classes is not appropriate: (1) Regular education courses will not provide educational benefit; (2) a more restrictive placement significantly outweighs the benefits of mainstreaming; and (3) due to disruptive behavior, the child compromises the education of other students in the classroom. The Fourth Circuit stated that social benefits of mainstreaming are secondary in importance to academic needs.

LRE AND SECTION 504 OF THE REHABILITATION ACT OF 1973

Although different language is used, the LRE mandate of the IDEA is virtually identical to the legal requirements of Section 504 of the Rehabilitation Act. The regulations for Section 504 define the requirement as follows:

> Academic setting. A recipient to which this subpart applies shall educate, or shall provide for the education of, each qualified handicapped person in its jurisdiction with persons who are not handicapped to the maximum extent appropriate to meet the needs of the handicapped person. A recipient shall place a handicapped person in the regular educational environment operated by the recipient unless it is demonstrated by the recipient that the education of the person in the regular education environment with the use of supplementary aids and services cannot be achieved satisfactorily. Whenever a recipient places a person in a setting other than the regular educational environment pursuant to this paragraph, it shall take into account the proximity of the alternative setting to the person's home. (34 C.F.R. § 104.34(a))

As a result, students served under a Section 504 plan have the same rights to LRE as students under the IDEA. Although outdated, the language of the 1973 statute and regulations is of historical interest. Today the term *handicapped* has been replaced by *disabled*, and the child always precedes the disability (child first language). These changes in language were intentional to emphasize the individual before the disability and to more appropriately define an individual with a disability. Today it is clear that the presence of a disability does not necessitate a handicapping condition.

SUMMARY

The LRE mandate is one of the essential components of the IDEA. With 1 million children with disabilities completely excluded from public education and 8 million not placed and served appropriately prior to 1975, Congress found it necessary to mandate that every child with a disability be educated with regular education students to the maximum extent appropriate with related services and supplementary aides. Congress recognized that every child's LRE is not full-time placement in the mainstream; the IEP team must consider the continuum of services, beginning with the regular education setting and then moving to more restrictive placements.

Pennsylvania Association for Retired Citizens v. Pennsylvania (1972) and *Mills v. Board of Education of the District of Columbia* (1972) are considered two of the most critical, pre-IDEA precedent-setting cases addressing the right of all students—regardless of the severity of their disabilities—to public education. The cases provided the foundation for many critical components of Public Law No. 94-142. The zero reject principle in the IDEA affirms the courts' findings by mandating that no child, no matter how severe the disabling condition, be excluded from a FAPE.

Understanding the terminology of the mandate is essential for appropriate implementation. Often misunderstood, the LRE is not the regular education classroom. The regular education classroom is the least restrictive placement along the continuum of options and the first to be considered. Congress intended for all children to be educated to the maximum extent possible in the regular education classroom; however, certain circumstances and disabling conditions may necessitate services or a placement outside the regular classroom. Although the goal is the maximum involvement of students with disabilities with their nondisabled peers, the LRE for one student with a disability may be markedly different than that of another student.

A significant body of case law exists regarding placement and the LRE mandate. Since no specific formula exists, the determination of what is the *least restrictive environment* is often as difficult to agree on as is the determination of what is *appropriate*. No specific LRE case has been heard by the U.S. Supreme Court. Four U.S. court of appeals cases—*Daniel R.R. v. State Board of Education* (1989), *Hartmann v. Loudoun County Board of Education* (1998), *Roncker v. Walter* (1983), and *Sacramento City Unified School District v. Rachel H. by Holland* (1994)—established substantive criteria and guidelines that are commonly used today to guide lower court decisions.

Applying the Law in the Classroom

In the early fall, Mike Smith transferred into Adams Middle School (AMS), a suburban school with a long-standing reputation for high academic achievement and strong parental involvement. Mike is a 12-year-old male who has just moved into his fifth foster home. He has been labeled seriously emotionally disturbed (SED) and has been placed in self-contained classrooms for his academic subjects; he is mainstreamed in his electives and physical education. Mike's new foster family is stable and loving, with two professional parents and two older siblings. Both parents are in their mid-forties and exploring the foster child experience for the first time.

To help with the transition, the foster organization brought Mike to school on his first day at AMS. During the principal's first meeting with the child, Mike lay on the ground, unresponsive, and refused to come into school. The principal understood, based on that first observation, that Mike was a child who would need significant services.

Mike's IEP and cumulative records indicated that he was provided with a personal, six-hour aide and had experienced relative success integrating into the previous comprehensive middle school (where he attended fifth grade). At first glance, the progress reports on the IEP seemed to discuss a different child. During the writing of his new IEP, the team determined that the school would provide Mike a personal aide; nonetheless, some time would pass before the paperwork and the personnel process would actually provide Mike with his aide. Since it was required by the IEP, the principal immediately pulled an existing aide and assigned her to Mike. As with his prior IEP, the IEP team placed Mike in self-contained academic courses and mainstreamed him into electives and physical education.

Mike's full-scale IQ is 120, and he has a high capacity to learn. However, the severity of his behavioral and social maladjustments mandate a high degree of support, troubleshooting, teamwork, and patience. His social background indicated that he was taken by social services when his alcoholic and abusive mother was declared unfit to care for him. He experienced a high degree of physical and mental abuse between birth and age six. The records further indicated that his emotional problems originally manifested in kindergarten through tantrums, aggressive acts toward staff and students, and complete withdrawal and insubordination at times. In kindergarten and first grade, Mike was served in a small, full-day program for children with pervasive developmental delays. The records were incomplete in relation to second through fourth grades, during which time he moved among three families and three schools.

In Mike's first month at AMS, he made an offhand comment to an administrator that he was going to kill her. As a result, the school suspended him for ten days. The district determined, however, that the behavior was a manifestation of his disability. Interestingly, it was determined not that the behavior was causally related to his disability, but that his IEP might not be appropriate. Primarily, the principal expressed concerns that Mike might not be placed in the least restrictive environment. The IEP team decided that it needed additional time to consider whether a more restrictive environment was necessary to serve Mike. In addition, the team members agreed that they needed more time to attempt further interventions, strategies, and classroom configurations. The team felt the behavior might be related to and compounded by the stress and difficulty of Mike's new home, school, and social environment.

Mike continued to have problems behaving appropriately in class throughout the first semester, although a significant improvement was observed when his new aide arrived in early November. A functional behavior assessment had been conducted and a behavior intervention plan (BIP) implemented just prior to the arrival of the new full-time aide. The BIP required the aide to remove Mike from class as soon as he was triggered or demonstrated anxiety. Two separate time-out rooms (which were not intended to be punitive) were established. During the time-outs, the aide worked with Mike on controlling his emotions and reacting appropriately. She diligently worked to teach him new ways of dealing with anxiety and emotions.

Mike often had not even attempted his work during the first semester, but he demonstrated considerable academic achievement during the second semester. With little effort, he did very well in his academic courses. Mike was scheduled to take drama during the second semester, but he refused to enter the classroom for two consecutive days. On the third day, he entered, but was removed quickly for demonstrating overt, bizarre behavior (making animal sounds, jumping up and down, etc.). The instructor apprised the principal, and he decided to place Mike in a seventh-grade electronics class with a teacher he suspected Mike would respect. Mike did exceptionally well in the class and developed a very close relationship with the teacher. Nonetheless, Mike continued to have a great deal of difficulty with gym class. The school switched teachers and developed an individualized physical education program for him. The program called for him to work independently with his aide, and over time, he would ease into full-class activities. This approach appeared to have worked well, with Mike participating half of the time with the class and the other half with the aide.

As the end of the year drew near, issues with teachers exacerbated Mike's disability. Due to the extent of Mike's disability and his BIP (which called for him to be pulled out of class when his behavior problems were escalating), he often was not disciplined in the same manner as other students. The teachers felt that a separate standard had been set for Mike; they blamed the principal. Because the aide always removed Mike from their classrooms, the teachers had not referred him to the principal, and he was therefore unaware of Mike's specific behaviors. The principal also had minimized discipline throughout the year due to his perception of Mike's disability. The teachers were accurate in their assessment that the principal had taken a special interest in Mike and was working with him more closely than with other children. The question was whether or not the principal had compromised Mike's discipline because of his close relationship with Mike.

The principal met with the IEP team during its May meeting to write Mike's program for the following year. The review indicated significant improvements in his ability to control his emotions and remain in class. The team also noted that although he had progressed considerably, Mike was still a significant distraction in the regular classroom at times. Since early in the first semester, team members had been asking whether Mike was in his LRE. The IEP team had to address whether or not Mike's behavior was compromising the education of other children. The team now had the task of developing his IEP and making his placement for the seventh-grade year.

Application Questions

1. Based on the information provided, do you believe Mike is placed in the LRE?
2. What different measures did the school take to try to meet the LRE mandate?
3. What should the IEP team do to ensure that the LRE mandate is achieved for the upcoming school year? Should the current placement be continued, or should it be changed? Why?
4. If the IEP team decides to place Mike in a special education school, his foster parents may decide to invoke due process to keep him in a comprehensive middle school with regular education interaction. Apply the Roncker portability test and the Rachel H. four-factor test to Mike's current placement as a court might do. Based on the tests, which placement is more appropriate—the current less-restrictive placement or the more-restrictive special education school placement?
5. How does an IEP team decide what behavior is too disruptive and what is acceptable? In answering this question, take into account that most students with behavioral disorders or emotional disturbances will have a behavior intervention plan and will have behavior goals as part of the IEP.

CRITICAL THINKING QUESTIONS

1. Why do you suppose a pure LRE case has not made it to the U.S. Supreme Court?
2. Why is the regular education classroom not always considered the least restrictive environment?
3. Why is the concept of LRE so open to interpretation and litigation?
4. Define *LRE* in your own operational terms.

5. Should the category of disability determine the LRE? Why or why not?
6. In relation to interpretation and ambiguity, how are FAPE and LRE similar?

REFERENCES

A.B. ex rel. D.B. v. Lawson, 354 F.3d 315 (4th Cir. 2004).

Beth B. v. Van Clay, 282 F.3d 493 (7th Cir. 2002).

Boyle, J., & Weishaar, M. (2001). *Special education law with cases*. Boston: Allyn & Bacon.

Brown v. Board of Education, 347 U.S. 483 (1954).

Clyde K. v. Puyallup School District, 35 F.3d 1396 (9th Cir. 1994).

Daniel R.R. v. State Board of Education, 874 F.2d 1036 (5th Cir. 1989).

Greer v. Rome City School District, 950 F.2d 688 (11th Cir. 1991).

Hallahan, D.P., & Kauffman, J.M. (1998). *Exceptional learner* (7th ed.). Boston: Allyn & Bacon.

Hartmann v. Loudoun County Board of Education, 118 F.3d 996 (4th Cir. 1998).

Huefner, D. S. (2000). *Getting comfortable with special education law*. Norwood, MA: Christopher-Gordon.

Individuals with Disabilities Education Act (Education for All Handicapped Children Act of 1975), Pub. L. No. 94-142, 89 Stat. 773.

L.E. v. Ramsey Board of Education, 435 F.3d 384 (3d Cir. 2006).

McLaughlin v. Holt Public Schools Board of Education, 320 F.3d 663 (6th Cir. 2003).

Mills v. Board of Education of the District of Columbia, 348 F. Supp. 866 (D.D.C. 1972).

Oberti v. Board of Education of the Borough of Clementon School District, 995 F.2d 1204 (3d Cir. 1993).

Pitasky, V. M. (2002). *The answer book on placement under the IDEA and Section 504*. Horsham, PA: LRP.

Pennsylvania Association for Retarded Citizens v. Pennsylvania, 334 F. Supp. 1257 (E.D. Pa. 1972), 343 F. Supp. 279 (E.D. Pa. 1972).

Roncker v. Walter, 700 F.2d 1058 (6th Cir. 1983).

Rothstein, L. (2000). *Special education law*. New York: Longman.

Sacramento City Unified School District v. Rachel H. by Holland, 14 F.3d 1398 (9th Cir. 1994).

Yell, M. (2006). *The law and special education* (2nd ed.). Upper Saddle River, NJ: Merrill.

9

Evaluation and Assessment

Facts at a GLANCE

- The IDEA requires that students be given a comprehensive initial individual evaluation before receiving any special education services.
- Before a school can conduct an eligibility evaluation, the parents of the child must provide informed consent by signing a form indicating that they understand and agree to specific assessment procedures.
- The IDEA requires that schools complete the full evaluation in order to determine the student's educational needs within 60 days of receiving parental consent for the initial individual evaluation.
- The individual evaluation is conducted to determine how the student's program can be designed to meet his or her educational needs.
- The IDEA requires that all assessments be nondiscriminatory and all procedures be nonbiased.
- The IDEA regulations require that the assessment instruments be technically or psychometrically sound.
- The IDEA originally envisioned the traditional assessment model, with its refer-test-place sequence. But the 2004 amendments to the IDEA incorporate an early intervention model whereby students receive intensive interventions prior to referral.
- When a parent requests that a student be independently evaluated, the school is responsible for the cost of that individual evaluation, as the court ruled in *Seals v. Loftis* (1985).
- *Response to intervention* is the model recommended for addressing the needs of at-risk learners and students with potential disabilities.
- The IDEA does not require that a discrepancy formula be used to determine eligibility for special education services as a result of learning disabilities.

For both general students and students with special needs, educators use evaluations to monitor progress, make educational decisions, measure achievement, and determine when a student may require additional support services such as those provided under the Individuals with Disabilities Education Act (IDEA) or Section 504 of the Rehabilitation Act of 1973. Since 1975, the IDEA has provided prescriptive procedural safeguards in relation to evaluation. In order to ensure appropriate assessment, determination of eligibility, and placement of students with disabilities, Congress instituted a stringent process for evaluating students. Many scholars argue over the terms *evaluation* and *assessment*. For purposes of consistency in this text, assessment refers to actual statewide, districtwide, and diagnostic tests (e.g., Woodcock-Johnson Achievement Test). Evaluation, on the other hand, refers to the full process from prereferral to triennial evaluation.

The passing of Public Law No. 94-142 provided a free appropriate public education (FAPE) for all students with disabilities. The concept of an appropriate education for each child with a disability via an individualized education program (IEP) means that every child must have a program specifically designed for him or her. In order to determine which children should receive such special education support and how that support should be offered, however, schools must evaluate each student suspected of having a disability.

Students struggling to maintain academic progress are referred for an initial individual evaluation. Before any student can receive special education services, the school must conduct the initial individual evaluation to determine if the student meets the criteria for any of the IDEA's 13 categories of disability. Following the initial evaluation, the IEP team members meet to determine if the student meets the criteria for any of the IDEA's special education categories. If the team members determine that the student requires special education services, they subsequently will design an IEP to meet the student's needs and identify an appropriate placement. This is the traditional model of assessment illustrated in Figure 9.1.

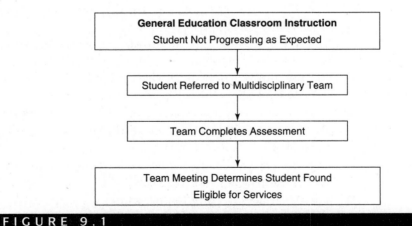

FIGURE 9.1

The Traditional Assessment Model

Source: Overton, T. (2006). *Assessing learners with special needs: an applied approach.* 5th edition. Pearson Merrill/Prentice Hall.

THE EVALUATION PROCESS

When a student exhibits academic or behavioral difficulties or significant developmental delays, the student's parents or teachers should refer the student for a comprehensive initial individual evaluation. The IDEA requires that the parents receive a copy of its procedural safeguards at the time of the initial referral. The IDEA further mandates that school officials obtain informed consent from the parents to conduct the evaluation. The informed consent provision requires that the school inform the parents about specifics related to the content of the various instruments that will be administered as part of the evaluation and the potential implications for their child. Then, before a school can administer these instruments, the parents of the child must indicate they are providing informed consent by signing a form stating that they understand and agree to specific assessment procedures. The IDEA includes provisions for obtaining consent for students who are wards of the state and students whose parents cannot be located.

The 2004 amendments to the IDEA mandate that the initial evaluation be completed within 60 days of receiving the parents' consent. Assessment personnel determine what types of data are needed and parent consent is obtained. This comprehensive evaluation is an opportunity to gather all the data needed to make instructional decisions and possibly determine that the student is eligible for special education support. The team members plan the evaluation in order to be certain that it includes techniques and instruments that will provide a comprehensive view of the child's current functioning. The team may consider and use existing data as part of the initial evaluation. These existing data may include the results of statewide accountability examinations, classroom work, and evaluations previously conducted by other agencies, as well as information provided by the parents.

In collecting the additional data that are needed, the team must use measures that assess all areas affected by a suspected disability. Assessments should be selected that will provide results that are relevant to instructional interventions. The assessments must provide information sufficient for the team to plan future instructional and behavioral strategies that will move the student toward general educational expectations. The purpose of the evaluation is to determine where the student is functioning academically, behaviorally, and developmentally.

Medical data, such as visual and auditory acuity screening results and developmental and health histories, also should be included in the overall evaluation. In *Shelby S ex rel. Kathleen T v. Conroe Independent School District* (2006), the U.S. Court of Appeals for the Fifth Circuit determined that despite a lack of parental consent, the school district could compel a medical examination of a special education student where it was necessary for IDEA-mandated reevaluation purposes. In this case, allowing a medical evaluation without consent did not violate the student's right to privacy because she had the option to decline services under the IDEA as an alternative to the medical evaluation. However, most legal analysts recommend that schools never evaluate students without parental consent—except in special and serious circumstances.

In the *Shelby* case, the school district prevailed only because the family had the right to decline services under the IDEA. However, in another decision, *Fitzgerald v. Camdenton R-III School District* (2006), the U.S. Court of Appeals for the Eighth Circuit held that the school district could not force a child to be evaluated under the IDEA to determine whether the child needed special services. In this case, the parents were homeschooling their child. They refused to consent to the testing and expressly waived all benefits and services under the IDEA, which was the critical factor in this case. The appellate court noted that the purpose of the IDEA is to make FAPE available to all children with disabilities, with parents retaining the right to waive a child's right to services.

The IDEA's implementing regulations offer specifics concerning how the evaluation must be conducted. For example, the law requires that the assessments be nondiscriminatory; in other words, the assessments must be fair to all students regardless of their ethnic, cultural, or linguistic background. In addition, the measures utilized must be fair for students regardless of their socioeconomic background or previous educational history. In *Larry P. v. Riles* (1986), the U.S. Court of Appeals for the Ninth Circuit affirmed the lower court's ruling banning the use of intelligence quotient (IQ) tests to determine whether an African-American child is mentally retarded because such tests are racially biased. Further, the Ninth Circuit expanded the ban for all special education purposes. The elimination of IQ testing was troublesome, however, because educators had difficulty finding African-American children eligible for services as a result of certain disabilities (e.g., learning disabilities). The Ninth Circuit reversed its decision in *Crawford v. Honig* (1994) and allowed IQ testing for students with learning disabilities. The court did not, however, lift the ban on using IQ tests to assess mental retardation in African-American students.

The IDEA mandates that schools assess students in the language and form that will provide the most accurate information about their current ability levels. This means that a student who is more proficient in Spanish should not be evaluated in English alone. In another example, educators should evaluate students requiring sign language or other nonverbal means of communication with this in mind. In addition, a student who responds via an electronic communication board should be allowed to communicate in this manner during the evaluation. In *Park ex rel. Park v. Anaheim Union High School District* (2006), the Ninth Circuit ruled that a school district did not violate the IDEA's procedural requirements by not assessing a child afflicted with 5p- syndrome in Korean—the child's native and primary language. The child's mother consented to the assessment plan, which specified that the speech and language assessment would be conducted in English. The occupational therapy, physical therapy, and vision assessments were nonverbal. In addition, the psychological assessment was largely nonverbal, and while a Korean interpreter was present during verbal portions of the assessment, direct verbal cues were not given in Korean because this would have adversely affected the validity of the test.

The IDEA's regulations also require that the assessment instruments be technically or psychometrically sound. The instruments must be reliable and valid for use in determining students' academic and behavioral functioning. Moreover, the instruments must be used for the purposes set forth by the test publishers. For example, a screening test developed to assess early reading skills for placement in a reading textbook series should not be used as a comprehensive diagnostic reading instrument to determine eligibility for special education services. Likewise, schools should not use a mathematics instrument that includes only basic addition facts to assess a student's total ability in mathematics.

The regulations further require that schools incorporate multiple methods of information collection during evaluations. The evaluation is meant to be comprehensive, and therefore, educators should use multiple evaluators using multiple methods. These methods may include the use of norm-referenced instruments, informal classroom methods and observations, questionnaires, interviews, and analyses of the student's work samples or permanent products. Figure 9.2 presents various types of assessment that are used in individual evaluations. During the deliberation on eligibility, no single measure should be the basis for the decision; instead, all of the information collected, including information provided by the student's parents, should be considered.

The IDEA requires that the appropriate professionals administer the instruments and implement the methods used in the evaluation. Individuals who are properly trained to perform these assessments and interpret the resulting data must administer these instruments. Appropriate assessment personnel might include school psychologists, speech clinicians, special education teachers, occupational therapists, and physical therapists. When assessing a student's cognitive ability or emotional functioning, for example, a school psychologist would be expected to complete the assessment. But when a student's speech and language skills are being evaluated, a speech clinician would assess the student. Further, the student's parents and other individuals close to the students should provide information about how the student functions within the home and community at large.

The U.S. Court of Appeals for the Third Circuit, in *Holmes v. Millcreek Township School District* (2000), held that a school psychologist's lack of fluency in American Sign Language (ASL) did not render the school district's evaluation of a deaf student inappropriate pursuant to the IDEA. The administrative review panel determined that the psychologist—a member of the student's multidisciplinary team (MDT)—appropriately evaluated the student. The court found that the psychologist provided valuable information concerning the student's need for increased interpreter services and that the district's determinations regarding the student were not based on the expertise of any one MDT member.

In addition to selecting instruments and methods that are nondiscriminatory and technically sound, the trained personnel administering these instruments must do so according to the directions provided by the publisher. This is most notably an issue when the instruments selected are standardized. Standardized instruments are

FIGURE 9.2

Types and Methods of Assessment

Informal assessment	Nonstandardized methods of assessment that may include teacher-made tests, curriculum-based measurement, classroom observations, or student work samples.
Norm-referenced tests	Instruments used to compare one student with a national sample of students the same age.
Standardized instruments	Instruments that must be administered in precisely the same manner every time to every student.
Curriculum-based measurement	Frequent measurement of student progress within the curriculum to compare the student's actual progress with the expected rate of progress.
Formative assessment	Ongoing assessment to monitor progress during the acquisition of a skill.
Summative assessment	Assessment that is completed at the conclusion of an instructional period to determine level of acquisition or mastery.
Achievement tests	Instruments used to assess what the student has retained from educational and environmental experiences.
Cognitive assessment	Testing the student's intellectual level or capacity.
High-stakes testing	Accountability assessment of state or district standards, which may be used for funding or accreditation decisions.
Alternative assessments	Assessment methods for certain students with disabilities, designed to measure progress in or toward the general education curriculum.

Source: Overton, T. (2006). *Assessing learners with special needs: an applied approach.* 5th edition. Pearson Merrill/Prentice Hall.

developed to be administered in exactly the same manner to each student. These instruments also are often norm-referenced. Norm-referenced tests typically are used to compare a specific student's ability with that of other students in the same age group. By administering the instrument in exactly the same manner every time, the reliability or consistency of the results and the validity of the prediction based on the results increase. For example, measures of intellectual ability are often timed. A young student may not be expected to complete the tasks as quickly as a more mature student. On the other hand, teachers might expect a student of superior intellectual ability to complete the tasks more quickly. The element of time is used to determine the efficiency of the skills being assessed. Therefore, the strict time requirements must be followed so that the results will accurately determine if the student is able to complete the task as quickly as expected for his or her age.

The 2004 amendments to the IDEA address the need to continue with the evaluation process in a timely manner when the child transfers from one school to another and from one district to another. The law states that the new school system should coordinate with the previous district so that the evaluation can be completed as quickly as possible. This level of coordination enables the team members to ensure that any required special education services are designed to meet the educational needs of the child and begin in the new school as soon as possible.

The IDEA requires that students receiving special education services be reevaluated every three years. Although districts are required to conduct a triennial appraisal of these students, the evaluation may not comprise all of the assessments conducted during the initial evaluation. The IDEA grants IEP teams discretion in relation to the data collected and the assessments administered. For example, if a student with a learning disability is demonstrating progress in his academic program and no problems are suspected, the IEP team does not have to conduct a new social history. The team may choose, however, to administer the Woodcock-Johnson Test of Academic Achievement and compare the student's scores to those from his or her last evaluation.

THE TRADITIONAL MODEL OF ASSESSMENT

The traditional model of assessment follows a referral-assessment-placement sequence in which a majority of the students referred are assessed and eventually found eligible for special education (Algozzine, Christenson, & Ysseldyke, 1982; Algozzine, Ysseldyke, & Christenson, 1983; Del'Homme, Kasari, Forness, & Bagley, 1996). The traditional assessment model historically has employed the use of norm-referenced tests, or tests that compare a student's performance with that of a national sample of students the same age. The literature indicates that, after several years of using this traditional assessment model, problematic patterns emerge. These patterns include issues with the referral process, bias in the referral and assessment processes, and overrepresentation of minorities in special education, specifically in the categories of mental retardation and emotional disturbance (Andrews, Wisnieswski, & Mulick, 1997; Del'Homme et al., 1996; Harvey, 1991; McIntyre, 1988; Soodak & Podell, 1993; Reschly, 1986). The U.S. Department of Education's *Twenty-Second Annual Report to Congress on the Individuals with Disabilities Education Act* (2000) included the percentages of ethnic groups in the various special education categories. These data provided additional evidence that minorities were and are overrepresented in special education. Assessment experts believe that inconsistencies in the referral and assessment processes contribute to the overrepresentation of minorities in special education.

THE CONTEMPORARY MODEL OF ASSESSMENT

Largely due to increasing concerns about the problems of bias and inconsistency in the referral and assessment processes, professionals in the field began implementing a different model of assessment. The main focus of this model shifted from assessment for the purpose of eligibility—determining whether or not a child will meet the IDEA eligibility criteria—to assessment as a component of a problem-solving process—determining what strategies can be implemented to move the child along in the general education curriculum. That assessment is only one stage in the problem-solving model is graphically displayed in Figure 9.3.

The contemporary model seeks to monitor the progress of students early and often so that educational or behavioral strategies can be implemented immediately after students show signs of struggling. In other words, if a child in kindergarten struggles with early reading readiness skills—such as phonemic awareness—that child would receive intervention prior to the development of a *significant* reading disability. In the same manner, a school would evaluate a young student exhibiting difficulties with behavioral or social skills to determine the appropriate strategy for promoting positive behaviors in the general classroom environment.

The first step in the contemporary model of assessment is the close monitoring of student progress. This assessment-for-progress monitoring is implemented for all students, not just those who are referred for special education. The monitoring includes measures typically used for all students, such as curriculum-based measurement, student work samples, teacher-made tests, end-of-chapter tests, and behavioral observations. This close monitoring of progress during the acquisition of new skills is called *formative assessment*. By monitoring all students during the learning or skill acquisition process, teachers can determine how they are progressing. This monitoring spotlights students who are not progressing at the same pace as their peers. The school can then provide additional intense interventions for the students identified during the monitoring.

Teachers also can identify students who are struggling by using summative evaluation. A *summative evaluation* is an assessment administered at the end of an educational unit or at the end of a particular period of time in which skills were taught—like the end of a reporting period. Students struggling during skill acquisition likely will perform poorly on summative assessments as well.

Schools must provide intense interventions to students who are performing below the level of their peers, having difficulty acquiring skills or knowledge at the same pace as their peers, or exhibiting behaviors that interfere with their educational achievement. The classroom teacher typically administers the first interventions. Should the student continue to struggle, however, the teacher

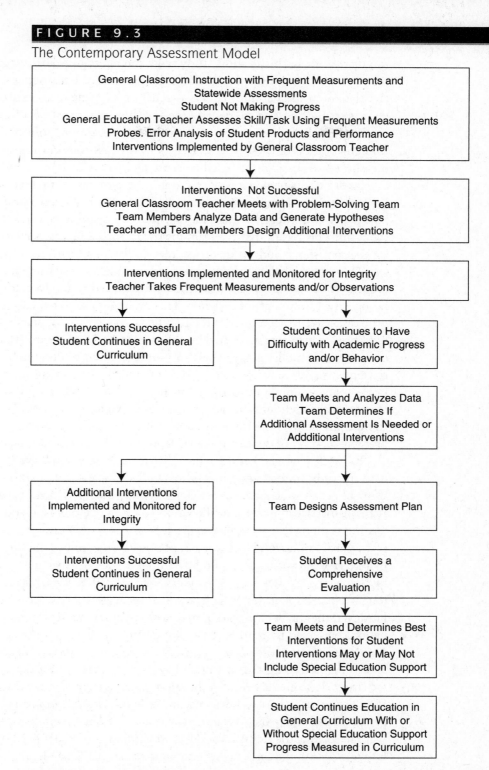

Source: Overton, T. (2006). *Assessing learners with special needs: an applied approach*. 5th edition. Pearson Merrill/Prentice Hall.

might consult with the child study team members to evaluate the overall implementation of these interventions. In this approach, the team members—including the classroom teacher and parents—generate hypotheses to explain why the student is struggling and to identify the variables that must be adjusted to promote academic or behavioral success. Team members should informally monitor the implementation of these new strategies in the classroom, using frequent informal measures like curriculum-based measurement and classroom observations.

In the traditional assessment model, the prereferral interventions and referral practices are problematic. In the contemporary model, all interventions are monitored for fidelity and integrity to ensure that they are being implemented as designed by the team. This means that the team members, including teachers and parents, evaluate the consistency and the quality of the implementation of the interventions.

The concept behind the contemporary model is that students unable to make progress following intense interventions might need to receive additional evaluation beyond the assessment for progress. This evaluation might involve assessments that were discussed earlier as part of the traditional model, such as standardized and norm-referenced assessments conducted by various members of the team. The difference in the contemporary model is that these measures are used to determine what additional strategies might be implemented to assist students in making progress. These additional strategies might or might not include special education support. In other words, the goal of the traditional model is to determine eligibility for special education services. In the contemporary model, on the other hand, the goal is to identify strategies that will promote success. Those strategies may require the use of special education services.

Regardless of whether the school district completes a full evaluation, the parents have the right to request an independent educational evaluation (IEE) at any time—using either the traditional or the contemporary model. When the parents request an IEE, the district must do the following: "(i) File a due process complaint to request a hearing to show that its evaluation is appropriate; or (ii) Ensure that an independent educational evaluation is provided at public expense, unless the agency demonstrates in a hearing pursuant to §§ 300.507 through 300.513 that the evaluation obtained by the parent did not meet agency criteria" (34 C.F.R. § 502(b)(2)). It is very clear that if a parent acquires an IEE, the IEP team must consider all the information. However, the threat of litigation may arise when the district is confident in the evaluation conducted by its staff. The U.S. Court of Appeals for the Seventh Circuit, in *Evanston Community Consolidated School District No. 65 v. Michael M.* (2004), upheld the lower court's finding that a school district did comply with the IDEA regulations requiring that parents be given the appropriate agency criteria when they request an IEE. The preponderance of evidence in the administrative record did not support the parents' claim; therefore, the parents were not entitled to reimbursement for the IEE.

The focus of the IDEA is to educate the child within the general education curriculum or to return the child to that curriculum as soon as possible. For students receiving special education support, educational personnel must continually monitor the progress of these students so that they can exit special education when possible. The goal of the implementation of special education interventions is to move the student toward the same expectations held for his or her peers within the general education curriculum.

RESPONSE TO INTERVENTION

Response to intervention or *responsiveness to intervention* (RTI) is a multitier process intended to identify, support, and monitor the progress of students struggling to meet age- or grade-appropriate learning expectations (at-risk learners). Students who consistently fail to respond appropriately to research-based interventions may be referred, and subsequently, found eligible for special education services. Bender and Shores (2007) contend "Response to intervention is, simply put, a process of implementing high-quality, scientifically validated instructional practices based on learner needs, monitoring students' progress, and adjusting instruction based on the student's response. When a student's response is dramatically inferior to that of his peers, the student may be determined to have a learning disability" (p.7).

The goal of the approach is to decrease the number of children needing special education services through early identification and the use of improved, research-based instruction and interventions. In addition to decreasing the number of students in need of special education, RTI is intended to improve school-wide instruction and bolster the approaches to addressing the needs of at-risk learners. The RTI process began to gain significant momentum and national exposure following the 2004 reauthorization of the IDEA. The 2004 amendments to the IDEA provide an alternative to the traditional discrepancy formula—significant discrepancy between intelligence quotient (IQ) and achievement—for determining if a student has a learning disability. Mellard and Johnson (2008) note, "Additionally, evaluation procedures for students with LDs resulted in a 'wait to fail' model, because of the need to demonstrate a discrepancy between aptitude and achievement. RTI addresses many of these shortcomings through its focus on alignment of general classroom instructions, progress monitoring, and evidence-based interventions. RTI can help schools work more efficiently and effectively in addressing the needs of all learners." (1). The data collected through the RTI process should be used in conjunction with other valid evaluation methods and data points.

The 2004 amendments to the IDEA state that

- a local education agency shall not be required to take into consideration whether a child has a severe discrepancy between achievement and intellectual ability in oral expression, listening comprehension, written expression, basic reading skill, reading comprehension, mathematical calculation, or mathematical reasoning.
- a local education agency may use a process that determines if the child responds to scientific, research-based intervention as a part of the evaluation procedures. (Pub. L. No. 108-446, § 614(b)(6))

Readers should note that there is no single, definitive method for implementing RTI. The following three-tier approach provides a basic framework for the RTI process.

TIER 1: UNIVERSAL SCREENING

School districts identify students struggling to meet grade-level expectations or make reasonable academic progress using data from a broad spectrum of assessments, including, but not limited to, universal screeners, curriculum-based measures, state tests, district assessments, norm-referenced tests, and teacher-made tests. Several RTI approaches recommend the collection of data on the entire school population three times per year; these data then act as baseline and benchmark data for the fall, winter, and spring. The intent at this initial tier is to cast a broad net to identify those students at risk for academic failure and in need of more support. The students identified in this group should begin to receive supplemental educational services and differentiated instruction in the regular classroom. The teachers should begin using these research-based interventions immediately and monitor the results closely to determine if the students are making significant progress. If a student does not make acceptable gains at tier 1, he or she progresses to tier 2.

TIER 2: TARGETED INTERVENTIONS

Students elevated to tier 2 receive more prescriptive, targeted interventions. Schools still provide differentiated instruction to address the students' specific deficits during regular instruction and, in addition, small-group instruction. It is critical that professionals utilize research-based interventions during all phases of RTI. As in tier 1, students' progress should be monitored closely, using reliable and valid assessment instruments. Curriculum-based measures have proven effective in monitoring student progress. Students' progress should be assessed at a minimum of once per month. If a student does not make acceptable gains at tier 2, he or she progresses to tier 3.

TIER 3: INTENSIVE INTERVENTIONS AND EVALUATION

Students in tier 3 are demonstrating significant weaknesses and deficits in critical academic areas. In this tier, students receive intensive, individualized instruction using targeted interventions. It is important to note that many scholars and professionals use the terms "special education" and "Tier 3" interchangeably. However, in many cases, students in Tier 3 may not have been found eligible for special education services. Therefore, student progress should be monitored at least biweekly, and students not responding adequately to these interventions should be considered for special education services. School personnel may refer a child for evaluation for special education services at any point during this process. One caution, however: If a child has not yet been referred, it is recommended that the child be considered for special education services when not responding to tier 3 services. The child study and/or IEP team should consider all of the data collected during the RTI process when making eligibility decisions. As noted earlier, RTI data should be used along with other valid and reliable assessment data (e.g., IQ and achievement data).

MONITORING PROGRESS AND ACCOUNTABILITY IN EDUCATION

The 1997 amendments to the IDEA required that all students receiving special education support services be assessed along with their nondisabled peers on statewide or districtwide assessments. These instruments—often called high-stakes assessments—are designed to promote the educational achievement of all students. To promote accountability for special education, the law required that schools administer the same tests to special education students that they administer to all other students. Historically, research found that students receiving special education support services did not achieve at the same level as their general education peers. Students in special education, in fact, lost ground compared with their peers. Subsequently, the dropout rate for students with special needs continued to rise, indicating that the services were ineffective. Additional research determined that disabled students unable to complete high school were generally underemployed as adults. Thus, former special education students most likely worked in jobs that were below their capability level after leaving school.

The movement for accountability in education was underscored by the No Child Left Behind Act of 2001 (NCLB). This law mandated that students make adequate yearly progress, or AYP, or their schools would face consequences. The 2004 amendments to the IDEA further aligned the law with NCLB. For these reasons, all students receiving special education support must now be assessed using statewide achievement measures. (See Figure 9.4.) Students receiving special education support are allowed to receive accommodations during the assessment that they require in their educational environment, as documented in their IEPs. In general, students receiving special education support are now expected to make adequate progress toward proficiency in the general education curriculum. For those students who are the most cognitively depressed, alternative assessments may be used.

ELIGIBLE CHILDREN

Though discussions have occurred over the years about how the definition of a child with a disability could be changed from a straight listing of diagnostic categories to a so-called functional definition without categories, Congress and special education stakeholders have thus far maintained the listing. As such, the law defines a child with a disability as

> a child with mental retardation, hearing impairments (including deafness), speech or language impairments, visual impairments (including blindness),

FIGURE 9.4

2004 IDEA Amendments (Pub. L. No. 108-446) Affecting State- and Districtwide Assessments

- **No Child Left Behind:** NCLB language mandates the inclusion of all students, regardless of disabling condition, in all state- and districtwide assessments. The assessments must be administered with appropriate accommodations, and alternate assessments must be provided when mandated by the IEP. (§ 612(a)(16)(A))
- **Alternate Assessments:** These must be aligned with the state's assessment program for all students. Where the state has developed alternate standards, children with disabilities taking alternate assessments must be assessed by those standards. (§ 612(a)(16)(C)(ii))
- **Reporting Requirements:** Both district and state educational agencies must report (1) the number of students with disabilities taking regular assessments with and without accommodations and (2) the number of students with disabilities taking alternative assessments. (§ 612(a)(16)(D)(i)–(iii))
- **IEPs and Districtwide Assessments:**   Benchmarks that align alternate standards to the alternate assessments must be included in the IEP of a student with a disability taking such assessments. The IEP must contain all accommodations that are needed on any district- or statewide assessment. A statement of rationale must be provided for a student taking alternate assessments. (§ 614(d)(1)(A)(I)(cc)); (VI)(aa), (bb)

serious emotional disturbance (hereinafter referred to as "emotional disturbance"), orthopedic impairments, autism, traumatic brain injury, other health impairments, or specific learning disabilities, and, who, by reason thereof, needs special education and related services. (Pub L. No. 108-446, § 602(3))

Although vigorous debates centered on the definition accompanying each disability term, the overall definition just cited has remained generally unchanged since 1975. For instance, efforts have been made to recast the definition of *serious emotional disturbance* because it is too clinically based and too focused on severity. A small nod was given by Congress with the inclusion of the phrase "hereinafter referred to as 'emotional disturbance'"—but the accompanying definition remained substantially intact.

Where are the specific definitions for each of the disability terms contained in the overarching definition of a child with a disability just cited? With the exception of the definitions of specific learning disabilities and developmental delay, the descriptions are contained not in the law, but rather in the federal regulations (34 C.F.R. § 300.8(c)). In addition, readers should know that the regulations added definitions for *deaf-blindness* and *multiple disabilities* because these terms were deemed to be appropriate extensions of the definition in the law. What follows are examples of these definitions from the regulations:

> *Mental retardation* means significantly subaverage general intellectual functioning, existing concurrently with deficits in adaptive behavior and manifested during the developmental period, that adversely affects a child's educational performance. (34 C.F.R. § 300.8(c)(6))

> *Speech or language impairment* means a communication disorder, such as stuttering, impaired articulation, a language impairment, or a voice impairment, that adversely affects a child's educational performance. (34 C.F.R. § 300.8(c)(11))

> (i) *Autism* means a developmental disability significantly affecting verbal and nonverbal communication and social interaction, generally evident before age three, that adversely affects a child's educational performance. Other characteristics often associated with autism are engagement in repetitive activities and stereotyped movements, resistance to environmental change or change in daily routines, and unusual responses to sensory experiences.

> (ii) Autism does not apply if a child's educational performance is adversely affected primarily because the child has an emotional disturbance. . . . (34 C.F.R. § 300.8(c)(1))

During the 1990–1991 IDEA reauthorization deliberations, vigorous debate focused on the question of whether Congress should add attention deficit disorder (ADD) and attention deficit/hyperactivity disorder (AD/HD) to the categories in the statutory definition of a child with a disability. Many lawmakers and advocates argued that children with ADD or AD/HD would fall under the existing categories of learning disability and emotional disturbance and that adding a new category to the law was both unwarranted and unhelpful in the delivery of appropriate instruction. Ultimately, the push for a new category in the IDEA statute was rejected, but allowance was made for students with ADD and AD/HD by refining the regulatory definition of other health impairment. The definition of other health impairment now reads:

> *Other health impairment* means having limited strength, vitality, or alertness, including a heightened alertness to environmental stimuli, that results in limited alertness with respect to the educational environment, that—

> (i) Is due to chronic or acute health problems such as asthma, attention deficit disorder or attention deficit hyperactivity disorder, diabetes, epilepsy, a heart condition, hemophilia, lead poisoning, leukemia, nephritis, rheumatic fever, sickle cell anemia, and Tourette syndrome; and

> (ii) Adversely affects a child's educational performance. (34 C.F.R. § 300.8(c)(9))

An intense and continuing dialogue, both professional and lay, has surrounded the category of *specific learning disability* since its inclusion in 1975. While generally acknowledged as a legitimate disorder, learning disability invites varying convictions and opinions regarding a number of issues, including the size of the affected population, the criteria and methodologies of eligibility determination, the best practices for instruction and amelioration, and the circumstances under which special education is appropriate for a particular child. The fact that these issues have been current for some 30 years is amply reflected in Congress's original decision to make learning disability one of the two terms defined in the law, rather than the regulations. That statutory definition reads:

(A) In general.—The term "specific learning disability" means a disorder in 1 or more of the basic psychological processes involved in understanding or in using language, spoken or written, which disorder may manifest itself in the imperfect ability to listen, think, speak, read, write, spell, or do mathematical calculations.

(B) Disorders included.—Such term includes such conditions as perceptual disabilities, brain injury, minimal brain dysfunction, dyslexia, and developmental aphasia.

(C) Disorders not included.—Such term does not include a learning problem that is primarily the result of visual, hearing, or motor disabilities, of mental retardation, of emotional disturbance, or of environmental, cultural, or economic disadvantage. (Pub. L. No. 94-142 , § 602(26).

Although Congress included this definition in the original 1975 statute, lawmakers instructed the administering agency to further consider appropriate criteria to refine the category of learning disability. The end result of that deliberation, the so-called discrepancy formula, can be found in the current regulations at 34 C.F.R. § 300.541. In determining whether a child has a specific learning disability, the regulation requires the eligibility evaluation team to find that ". . . a child has a severe discrepancy between achievement and intellectual ability . . ." in one or more of the following domains: oral expression, listening comprehension, written expression, basic reading skill, reading comprehension, mathematics calculation, or mathematics reasoning. Though this definition continues as current national policy, one may safely assert that the parameters of learning disability are ever evolving due to on-going research and enhanced practice.

Congress also addressed concerns related to very young children with disabilities in the law. For children ages three through nine, states and school districts may agree to forego designation of a diagnostic category for a child and instead apply the more general designation of developmental delay. The law states that this category may be applied to a child "experiencing developmental delays, as defined by the State and as measured by appropriate diagnostic instruments and procedures, in 1 or more of the following areas: physical development; cognitive development; communication development; social or emotional development; or adaptive development . . . " (Pub. L. No. 108-446, § 602(3)(B)(i)). This policy, applying to children in preschool through the early grades, is based on the premise that designation in the more specific categories is both inappropriate and unnecessary for many young children. However, this option is totally discretionary and must be approved by both the state and the school district. In addition, states and school districts electing to use this approach may continue to make the other diagnostic categories available for certain young children where deemed appropriate.

INTERCONNECTION OF THE ELIGIBILITY DECISION-MAKING PROCESS

- Is the child's educational performance being adversely affected because of a disability?
- Does the child have a disability?
- If a disability is determined, does the child require special education, or will some other interventions or accommodations in educational programming be appropriate and effective?
- If special education is deemed necessary, the child is now eligible under the IDEA.

A fundamental tenet of the IDEA is that special education proceeds from the educational objectives of public education for all children and, therefore, is wedded to the outcomes sought in general education. As a corollary, special education should be viewed for many, if not most, children participating as no more or less than the "special" component of their overall educational program. This concept will be further explained later in the text.

Fairly early in their deliberations on Public Law No. 94-142, lawmakers determined that a vast number of children would require one or more *related services* in order to benefit meaningfully from special education. Some lawmakers and advocates argued for a generic definition, while others pushed for an actual listing of related services. The end result? The IDEA includes both. The statutory definition can now be found at Public Law No. 108-446, § 602(26). And similar to the approach taken in defining a child with a disability, the law merely names eligible related services, while the regulations define the services (34 C.F.R. § 300.34).

Two baseline facts should be kept in mind when considering the requirement of related services:

1. The statutory definition of related services and its near mirror image in the regulations do *not* offer an all-inclusive listing of services. Note carefully the verb "includes" in the regulation. Also, before the listing of services in both the statute and the regulation, note the generic "developmental, corrective, and other supportive services."
2. Under the IDEA, a child is *not* entitled to a related service unless that child is receiving special education. Phrased another way, related services are required by the IDEA only when necessary to assist the child in benefiting from the concurrent

special education program. However, as is often the case with national public policy, one exception to the rule is included, namely, the need for early identification and medical services to determine if there is a disability.

With these aspects in mind, now consider the regulatory definition:

Related services means transportation and such developmental, corrective, and other supportive services as are required to assist a child with a disability to benefit from special education, and includes speech-language pathology and audiology services, interpreting services, psychological services, physical and occupational therapy, recreation, including therapeutic recreation, early identification and assessment of disabilities in children, counseling services, including rehabilitation counseling, orientation and mobility services, and medical services for diagnostic or evaluation purposes. Related services also include school health services and school nurse services, social work services in schools, and parent counseling and training. (34 C.F.R. § 300.34(a))

SUMMARY

For both regular education and special education students, educators use evaluations to monitor progress, make educational decisions, measure achievement, and determine when a student may require additional support services, such as those provided under the IDEA or Section 504. Assessment includes informal and formal methods and is both formative and summative. Assessments should be a component of the problem-solving process when students progress at a slower pace, do not achieve at the level of their peers, or display behaviors that interfere with their learning. Once interventions are implemented, however, assessment should continue. For students who require special education interventions, school districts should use assessments to monitor progress so that these students can be returned to the general education curriculum when appropriate.

Applying the Law in the Classroom

Lupito is a six-year-old first-grade student of Mexican-American descent who comes from a Spanish-speaking home. Lupito was introduced to English when he entered a church preschool setting at the age of four. He began his public school education in kindergarten. His kindergarten teacher reported that Lupito was able to use English in the school setting and communicated with his peers in both English and Spanish.

Lupito made adequate progress in the initial acquisition of preacademic skills in kindergarten. He struggled somewhat in learning the phonemic awareness skills that were expected of a student in kindergarten. His teacher reported that Lupito's difficulties were not very noticeable in the kindergarten setting because the school population included approximately 80 percent bilingual Hispanic children from homes in which Spanish was the primary language.

Lupito had several good friends in his kindergarten class and seemed to get along very well with both his peers and adults. His kindergarten teacher described him as well behaved and eager to participate in activities.

Lupito progressed to the first grade, where he continued to struggle with the acquisition of early reading skills. He was able to make the associations of letters to sounds in Spanish more easily than he was able to do in English. His first-grade teacher believed that Lupito was having a little more difficulty than his grade-peers. She contacted the IEP team to request a consultation to determine if Lupito required a referral for assessment.

The IEP team at Lupito's school was experienced in dealing with students from diverse cultural and linguistic backgrounds. The team discussed Lupito's case and reviewed the work samples and data collected by the classroom teacher. Ultimately, the team suggested that intensive reading intervention be implemented for Lupito, rather than initiating a referral for assessment. The team set a meeting date to review Lupito's progress in one month. During that time period, the school psychologist and the reading specialist would consult with the teacher to ensure that the interventions were implemented consistently.

The interventions were implemented, and the team met again the next month. During that meeting, it was determined that Lupito was making better progress, but not as quickly as the team had hoped. The first-grade teacher requested the assistance of the English as a Second Language (ESL) teacher to administer similar interventions in Spanish and to complete an informal assessment of Lupito's progress in acquiring early reading skills in Spanish. The team agreed and set another meeting date in six weeks.

Application Questions

1. Should Lupito have been referred for a full evaluation during the first grade? Why or why not?
2. What issues will likely complicate an initial individual evaluation in this case?
3. Consider the use of informal and formal assessment methods in this case. Is one method more fair than the other? If so, which method might be more fair? Explain why you selected this method.

4. In Lupito's case, the kindergarten teacher did not believe that Lupito required intervention for early prereading skills. What was her reasoning for this opinion? Is her reasoning within the requirements of the IDEA?

5. When is it appropriate or fair to consider local norms in determining when students require additional assessment?

6. What was the purpose of requesting interventions in reading in Spanish and an informal assessment by the ESL teacher?

7. If the Spanish reading interventions and assessment indicate adequate progress, what will this mean?

8. If the Spanish reading interventions and assessment indicate that Lupito is not making the progress as expected, what would you recommend?

CRITICAL THINKING QUESTIONS

1. For the purposes of this text, differentiate between *assessment* and *evaluation*.
2. Describe the traditional model of assessment.
3. Describe the key components of the evaluation process.
4. What professionals need to be a part of the evaluation process?
5. Name types of assessments that may be necessary in the evaluation process.
6. In order for an assessment tool to be appropriate, what is required?
7. Explain the difference between the traditional and the contemporary models of assessment.
8. What significant changes were included in the 2004 amendments to the IDEA? Why do you think they were added?
9. How has NCLB affected the assessment process for students with disabilities?

REFERENCES

Algozzine, B., Christenson, S., & Ysseldyke, J. (1982). Probabilities associated with the referral-to-placement process. *Teacher Education and Special Education, 5*, 19–23.

Algozzine, B., Ysseldyke, J. E., & Christenson, S. (1983). An analysis of the incidence of special class placement: The masses are burgeoning. *Journal of Special Education, 17*, 141–147.

Andrews, T. J., Wisnieswski, J. J., & Mulick, J. A. (1997). Variables influencing teachers' decisions to refer children for psychological assessment services. *Psychology in the Schools, 34*, 239–244.

Bender, W. and Shores, C. (2007). *Response to intervention: a practical guide for every teacher.* Thousand Oaks, CA: Corwin Press.

Crawford v. Honig, 37 F.3d 485 (9th Cir. 1994).

Del'Homme, M., Kasari, C., Forness, S. R., & Bagley, R. (1996). Prereferral intervention and students at risk for emotional and behavioral disorders. *Education and Treatment of Children, 19,* 272–285.

Evanston Community Consolidated School District No. 65 v. Michael M., 356 F.3d 798 (7th Cir. 2004).

Fitzgerald v. Camdenton R–III School District, 439 F.3d 773 (8th Cir. 2006).

Harvey, V. (1991). Characteristics of children referred to school psychologists: A discriminant analysis. *Psychology in the Schools, 28,* 209–218.

Holmes v. Millcreek Township School District, 205 F.3d 583 (3d Cir. 2000).

Individuals with Disabilities Education Act (Education for All Handicapped Children Act of 1975), Pub. L. No. 94-142, 89 Stat. 773.

Individuals with Disabilities Education Improvement Act of 2004, Pub. L. No. 108-446, 118 Stat. 2652.

Larry P. v. Riles, 495 F. Supp. 926 (N.D. Cal.), *aff'd in part, rev'd in part,* 793 F.2d 969 (9th Cir. 1986).

Lora v. Board of Education, 587 F. Supp. 1572 (E.D.N.Y. 1984).

McIntyre, L. (1988). Teacher gender: A predictor of special education referral? *Journal of Learning Disabilities, 21,* 382–384.

Mellard, D. and Johnson, E. (2008). *RTI: A practioner's guide to implementing response to intervention.* Thousand Oaks, CA: Corwin Press.

No Child Left Behind Act of 2001 (NCLB), 20 U.S.C. §§ 6301–7941.

Parents in Action on Special Education (PASE) v. Hannon, 506 F. Supp. 831 (N.D. Ill. 1980).

Park ex rel. Park v. Anaheim Union High School District, 464 F.3d 1025 (9th Cir. 2006).

Reschly, D. (1986). Functional psychoeducational assessment: Trends and issues. *Special Services in the Schools, 2,* 57–69.

Seals v. Loftis, 614 F. Supp. 302 (E.D. Tenn. 1985).

Shelby S ex rel. Kathleen T v. Conroe Independent School District, 454 F.3d 450 (5th Cir. 2006).

Soodak, L. C., & Podell, D. M. (1993). Teacher efficacy and student problems as factors in special education referral. *Journal of Special Education, 27*(1), 66–81.

U.S. Department of Education. (2000). *Twenty-second annual report to Congress on the implementation of the Individuals with Disabilities Education Act.* Washington, DC: Author.

10

The Individualized Education Program

Facts at a GLANCE

- The development of educationally and legally sound individualized education programs (IEPs) is essential to ensuring a free appropriate public education in the least restrictive environment for every student with a disability.
- The IEP is intended to ensure that all necessary individuals are aware of the specific needs, requirements, services, and accommodations deemed essential to meeting the child's individual educational needs.
- Since the IDEA's inception in 1975, IEPs have been problematic (Huefner, 2000).
- Congress now allows IEP team members to be released in whole or part from IEP meetings if the local education agency (LEA) and the parents agree.
- In an attempt to eliminate unnecessary meetings after the annual IEP has been completed, the IDEA now permits adjustments to the IEP to be made without a formal meeting.
- In order to further reduce work for the schools, Congress determined that benchmarks or short-term objectives are no longer required in an IEP unless the child is taking an alternate assessment linked to alternate achievement standards.
- In order to further clarify the provisions regarding parental rights and informed consent, Congress stipulates that if a parent does not grant informed consent for the LEA to provide special education and related services to an eligible child, the school may not provide services by invoking due process.
- The point at which a statement of transition services is required has been changed from age 14 to age 16.
- Under the IDEA 2004, the U.S. Secretary of Education is permitted to authorize up to 15 states to pilot three-year IEPs.

■ For students changing schools intra- or interstate, the IDEA 2004 requires that the new LEA provide services comparable to those in the previous IEP until a new IEP, if necessary, is developed.

■ As a part of the procedural safeguards, parents should be given notification of meetings at which the IEP will be developed, reviewed, or revised.

Multiple metaphors have been used over the years to express the importance of the individualized education program (IEP). Bateman (1998) states: "The heart of the law is the child's written Individualized Education Program (IEP) and the core entitlement of the child is to a free appropriate public education (FAPE)" (p. 3). In *Honig v. Doe* (1988), the IEP is referred to as the "Keystone" of the Individuals with Disabilities Education Act (IDEA). The IEP serves as the legal roadmap for the development and implementation of every major component of the educational program for a child with a disability. It provides prescriptive measures for the how, when, where, why, who, and what of each child's educational program. Schools are bound by law to comply with the requirements of the IEP. Therefore, the development of educationally and legally sound IEPs is essential to ensuring a FAPE in the least restrictive environment (LRE) for every student with a disability.

INTENT OF THE IEP

The IEP is intended to ensure that all necessary individuals are aware of the specific needs, requirements, services, and accommodations deemed essential to meeting the child's individual educational needs. The IEP must be developed in such a way that the student will receive educational benefit and progress reasonably in his or her educational program via a FAPE in the LRE.

The importance of the IEP cannot be overstated. When the IDEA was passed in 1975, the IEP was by far its most prescriptive and far-reaching mandate. It is important to note that the IEP was seen by advocates as such a critical element of the IDEA because of the long history of discrimination against and failure to provide an appropriate education to students with disabilities that had been established. The advocates wanted a legally binding document that schools were required to implement.

In relation to meetings, the IDEA mandates (1) an eligibility meeting to share the results of the evaluation; (2) an initial IEP meeting to develop the educational program and determine student placement; and (3) at a minimum, a yearly review of the student's level of performance, goals, and objectives (if included) and a three-year (triennial) evaluation. Additional meetings may be held at the request of any member of the IEP team if there is a need to revise the current IEP. IEP meetings may be among the most time-consuming and costly parent conferences held within the school district. As a result, it is incumbent upon the team to develop the IEP in such a way that it complies with federal law and addresses the needs of the individual student.

COMMON ISSUES AND LITIGATION

Since the law's inception in 1975, IEPs have been problematic (Huefner, 2000). Federal law clearly defines the procedural and substantive requirements of the IEP and highlights the importance of meeting these requirements in a timely and appropriate manner. Nevertheless, these well-defined procedures for developing the IEP are oftentimes viewed as arduous and cumbersome. Unfortunately, both special and regular educators are frequently frustrated by the IEP process. And even though the IDEA is very specific about the IEP components, many school systems fail to meet the requirements of the law, which results in litigation (Martin & Marshall, 1996).

According to Hudgins and Vacca (1999), the recorded causes of complaints concerning the IEP fall into seven categories: (1) improper committee composition, (2) improper development procedures, (3) failure to observe the timeliness requirement for development, (4) omission of required portions of the IEP, (5) failure to provide included services, (6) delay in implementation, and (7) failure to provide included services on a cost-free basis.

It is paramount that special education administrators ensure that these kinds of mistakes are avoided, that all components of the IEP are included, and that these components comply with federal law. To avoid legal action regarding the IEP, Hudgins and Vacca (1999) suggest that school personnel follow every step in the IEP planning procedures, including identification, testing, and parental involvement. In the process, school personnel must state goals and objectives (if included) in broad terms, avoid guarantees of student progress, and make a good-faith effort to carry out the educational program outlined in the IEP.

According to Hollis (1998), as a result of increased litigation, school professionals and parents can no longer sit around the table comfortably assuming that their decisions will never be the subject of a due process hearing or some form of administrative or judicial review. Further, the issue of which of these parties—the school district or the parents—bears the burden of proof when an IEP is challenged in an administrative hearing has been a significant one since IEPs were first litigated. Prior to 2005, the burden of proof was often placed on the school district regardless of who brought the grievance. The underlying assumptions were that the district had an inherent advantage and that it was the responsibility of the district to justify and defend the IEP. However, in *Schaffer v. Weast* (2005), the U.S. Supreme Court determined that under the IDEA the burden of proof is properly placed on the party seeking relief, whether that is the child with a disability or the school district.

Over the past two decades, researchers and scholars have identified several mistakes in the development or implementation of the IEP that have resulted in litigation. According to Yell (2006), Huefner (2000), Lombardo (1999), Martin (1996), Bateman & Linden (1998), Lynch and Beare (1990), and Smith (1990), some of the most common errors that have come under legal scrutiny include the following: (1) Present levels of performance are incomplete (*P.N. v. Seattle School District No. 1*, 2007; *M.S. ex rel. S.S. v. Board of Education of City School District of the City of Yonkers*, 2000); (2) goals and objectives are insufficient (*Burlington School District*, 1994); (3) evaluation procedures do not meet regulatory requirements (*Frank G. v. Board of Education of Hyde Park*, 2006; *Knable ex rel. Knable v. Bexley City School District*, 2001); (4) essential IEP team personnel are not in attendance; (5) placement decisions do not match or are not based on the current IEP (*Nack ex rel. Nack v. Orange City School District*, 2006; *T.F. v. Special School District of St. Louis County*, 2006); and (6) students lack access to the general curriculum (*Pachl v. Seagren*, 2006). In addition, considerable litigation addresses whether or not IEPs are reasonably calculated to result in students receiving educational benefit or a FAPE (*Cerra v. Pawling Central School District*, 2005; *Kenton County School District v. Hunt*, 2004; *Alex R. ex rel. Beth R. v. Forrestville Valley Community Unit School District #221*, 2004; *L.T. and T.B. ex rel. N.B. v. Warwick School Committee*, 2004; *Todd v. Duneland School Corporation*, 2002).

As indicated above, the IEP requirement of the IDEA presents the practitioner with many potential issues and challenges. The concept of the IEP and its intricate development process are the focus of this chapter. Because all of the identified mistakes and common errors are linked to critical components of the IEP—whether procedural or substantive—we will address these critical components and the legal requirements that are associated with each. As well, we will emphasize the development of educationally useful IEPs. The 2004 IDEA amendments provide several notable adjustments to the IEP process and the document itself.

THE 2004 IDEA AMENDMENTS AND THE IEP

Congress made several adjustments to the requirements of the IEP process and the document itself with the intent of making both more practical and less cumbersome to practitioners. In order to minimize the amount of time that educators must spend at long IEP meetings, Congress now allows IEP team members to be released in whole or part if the local education agency (LEA) and the parents agree. If excused in whole, the member may be required to provide a written report to the team (Pub. L. No. 108-446, § 614(d)(1)(C)). This new provision allows members such as teachers to return to the classroom when their presence is not needed or necessary.

In an attempt to eliminate unnecessary meetings after the annual IEP has been completed, the IDEA now permits adjustments to the IEP to be made without a formal meeting. With agreement from the LEA and the parents, written documents may now be submitted to make minor adjustments to an IEP (Pub. L. No. 108-446, § 614(d)(3)(D)). In addition, triennial evaluations may be held during annual IEP meetings (§ 614(d)(3)(E)).

Teachers and school personnel have very little time to meet outside of their instructional duties and other responsibilities. These provisions are very helpful in decreasing unnecessary meetings. It is recommended, however, that providing written reports in place of personal appearances not become common practice. The intent of the IDEA is still for all stakeholders to come together and meet on behalf of the student. As a general rule, it is recommended that individuals attend the meetings to deliver their reports and to answer any parent questions. Upon agreement, it is certainly appropriate for the team member to be released following the report. A written report cannot replace the personal touch of a teacher (or other team member) or answer questions.

In order to further reduce work for the schools, Congress determined that benchmarks or short-term objectives are no longer required in the IEP unless the child is taking an alternate assessment linked to alternate achievement standards (Pub. L. No. 108-446, § 614(d)(1)(A)(i)(I)(cc)). Schools are required to provide only broad annual goals. They are still required to report on the progress made toward these annual goals on the same schedule as grades are reported for the entire school.

As noted above, Congress did include specific provisions for students taking alternate assessments. If the IEP team determines that an alternate assessment is necessary, the team must explain why this is necessary and appropriate (Pub. L. No. 108-446, § 614(d)(1)(A)(i)(VI)(bb)). Both short-term objectives and annual goals are still required for students taking alternate assessments.

In order to further clarify the provisions regarding parental rights and informed consent, Congress has stipulated that if a parent does not grant informed consent for the LEA to provide special education and related services to an eligible child, the school may not provide services by invoking due process (§ 614(a)(1)(D)(ii)(II)).

The point at which a statement of transition services is required has been changed from age 14 to age 16 (Pub. L. No. 108-446, § 614(d)(1)(A)(i)(VIII)). In addition, the 2004 amendments require postsecondary goals related to education, training, employment, and, where appropriate, independent living skills (§ 614(d)(1)(A)(i)(VIII)(aa)). Important to note in relation to the beginning of a transition program at age 16 is the fact that the 2004 amendments dropped the language "or younger, if determined appropriate by the IEP team" and the requirement for interagency linkages in the provision of transition services.

In order to reduce redundancy, a rule of construction for the IEP was added, stipulating that information provided in one component of the IEP does not need to be duplicated in another component (§ 614(d)(1)(A)(ii)).

Under the IDEA 2004, the U.S. Secretary of Education is permitted to authorize up to 15 states to pilot three-year IEPs. The extended IEP is optional and may be implemented only with the informed consent of the parent(s) (Pub. L. No. 108-446, § 614(d)(5)). The three-year IEP is to be reviewed annually and at "natural transition points." Although a pilot for only a handful of states, this is a critical provision in that it may be an indicator of the future of all IEPs.

Further, as families continue to become increasingly mobile, it is critical that gaps in educational services be minimized. Congress addressed this issue by mandating that, for students changing schools intra- or interstate, the new LEA provide services comparable to those in the previous IEP until a new IEP, if necessary, is developed (§ 614(d)(2)(C)(i)).

The IEP

Special education law has defined the responsibility of the school in developing the IEP. According to the IDEA, after permission to evaluate is received, evaluations are completed, and an eligibility decision is made, it becomes the duty of the school to hold a meeting to develop an IEP. This IEP can be described as a management tool for ensuring that the educational design for the student is appropriate to his or her special needs and that services are delivered and monitored. In developing the IEP, the IEP team must consider the strengths of the child; the concerns of the parents for enhancing the education of their child; the results of the initial evaluation or the most recent evaluation of the child; and the academic, developmental, and functional needs of the child (Pub. L. No. 108-446, § 614).

The Function of the IEP

According to Hudgins and Vacca (1999), the IEP is a written agreement—reached through the total participation of parents, designated school personnel, and the student, when appropriate—that presents all aspects of the student's FAPE. They describe its functions as follows:

1. setting and controlling the goals of the student's educational program,
2. establishing the educational setting,
3. defining the length of the program,
4. detailing instructional methodologies (accommodations/modifications) to be employed,
5. identifying the evaluation system,
6. documenting the mode of discipline,
7. determining related services, and
8. setting the standards of progress.

It should also be noted that an IEP is not designed to tell parents what to do or mandate their involvement. It is a legally binding agreement developed primarily to describe what the school system will do to educate an individual student with a disability and how it will be accomplish this. The IEP must address the who, what, when, where, how, and why of the student's educational program. The *who* in the IEP describes which individuals were involved in the development of the program and which individuals will deliver the services in the program. The *what* of the IEP describes the content and skills the student will learn. The *when* includes the amount time allocated for special education services and the duration of those services. The *where* describes the location for the delivery of those services. The *how* describes the instructional methods, modifications, accommodations, and evaluation methods that will be used to address the student's educational needs. Finally, the *why* is the justification for developing the program and delivering the services, which is based on the individual needs of the student.

In addition, federal law mandates that the following issues be considered during the meeting held to develop the IEP. Even though there is no one formal format for the IEP, to ensure that these issues are considered, many school districts have developed checklists within their IEP procedures to document that these issues are discussed.

THE IEP TEAM

Whether it is an initial IEP meeting, which must be held within 30 calendar days of the eligibility meeting, or a meeting called to complete an annual review of or requested revision to the IEP, Part B of the IDEA and its implementing regulations specify the IEP team members and define their roles. A more detailed description of each member's role and responsibilities follows.

PARENTS OR GUARDIANS

One or both parents or legal guardians should take part in the IEP meeting. Parents or guardians are among the most important members of the IEP team and are expected to be equal participants in developing, reviewing, and revising the IEP for their child. It is vital to remember that parents or guardians are the most knowledgeable about their child. They provide critical information regarding the strengths of their child and should have the opportunity to express their concerns for enhancing their child's education. They participate in the discussion about their child's needs for special education, related services, and supplementary aids and services. They join with other members of the team in deciding how the child will be involved and progress in the general education curriculum and participate in state assessments. Ultimately, parents or guardians must give permission for placement. Thus, it is recommended that practitioners avoid educational jargon and acronyms with which parents or guardians might not be familiar in order to maximize their understanding of the discussion and the resulting IEP.

REGULAR EDUCATION TEACHER

The student's regular education teacher should be present if the student is participating or might participate in the general education curriculum. The regular education teacher's role in the IEP process increased with the 1997 amendments to the IDEA, which emphasize the involvement and progress of the student in the general education environment. Prior to this reauthorization, regular education teachers had limited involvement in IEP development. Many regular education teachers felt their role ended after the initial referral and eligibility processes. However, if the intent of the legislation is to provide students with disabilities increased involvement in, access to, and progress in the regular educational program, then the regular education teacher must be involved. This teacher provides expertise regarding the general education curriculum, state standards, grade-level expectations, and day-to-day instructional environment.

SPECIAL EDUCATION TEACHER

The special education teacher who will be responsible for implementing the IEP should participate in the meeting. Oftentimes IEP development is viewed as a special education teacher function. However, the development of the IEP is a team process and should never be done primarily by the special education teacher. The special education teacher is responsible for facilitating the IEP development process, including chairing the meeting, facilitating discussion, and handling the paperwork involved in the documentation of the program. He or she may come to the IEP meeting prepared with evaluation findings and proposed recommendations regarding the IEP content, but must make it clear to the parents at the outset of the meeting that the services proposed by the agency are only recommendations for review by and discussion with the parents. The special education teacher may even bring drafts of some or all of the IEP content to the meeting, but there must be a full discussion with the child's parents before the child's IEP is finalized regarding its content, the child's needs, and the services to be provided to meet those needs. The special education teacher should be knowledgeable about special education procedures, especially those developed for use by the local school district; teaching strategies; and types of accommodations and modifications available to address the child's individual disability.

SCHOOL DISTRICT OR LEA REPRESENTATIVE

A representative of the local education agency must be present. This person can be the principal or his or her designee, and in many schools, this role is fulfilled by the assistant principal or special education coordinator. In situations involving private placement, authorization of a service involving considerable expense, or a prior history of contention, it is common for a central office (superintendent's) representative to be present. The district's administrator of special education or his or her designee should be knowledgeable about special education and due process procedures and guidelines and be authorized to commit school funds and resources to address the needs of an individual student. Also, they are responsible for the administration and supervision of the IEP.

PROFESSIONAL QUALIFIED TO DISCUSS EVALUATION RESULTS

This person can be the special education teacher or the administrative designee, each of whom is already involved as a member of the IEP team, or a specialist that was involved in the eligibility process, such as the school psychologist, social worker, or educational diagnostician. The individual's main function is to interpret, clarify, and discuss any information that was gathered by assessments during the evaluation process and that is included in the current level of performance in the IEP.

OTHER NECESSARY PROFESSIONALS

Other individuals, at the discretion of the school and the parents, can be involved in the IEP development process. These individuals must have knowledge of or special expertise regarding the child. The determination as to whether an individual has knowledge or expertise must be made by the person who invites the individual.

STUDENT

The student, when appropriate, should participate in the IEP development process. Prior to the 1997 amendments to the IDEA, there was little to no student involvement in the IEP development process, and in many cases, students were left in the dark about their disability, which often led to student denial, low-self esteem, and limited academic success. Decisions concerning educational programs for students with disabilities were made on their behalf by their parents and the school. The 1997 amendments strengthened student involvement by requiring that a student with a disability by the age of 14 attend his or her IEP meeting if the purpose of the meeting was to plan transition services. In 2004, Congress changed the age to 16. Involving students in the development of their IEPs, at least by the age of 16, gives them an opportunity to have input into the types of services they need to support their current and future educational and career goals. It also increases their understanding of their disability and better prepares them to advocate for their needs at school and in a variety of other settings.

It is recommended that the IEP team be kept as small as possible to encourage and facilitate decision making and communication. Once the IEP team is formed, the mandate of this group is to develop annual goals (and short-term objectives for a student taking alternate assessments) for the period covered in the IEP—based on the student's current level of educational performance. The IEP should include a list of services to be provided, detailing who will provide the services and where they will be provided. It should include related services, such as transportation, occupational therapy, adapted physical education, modifications for regular classroom participation, and testing accommodations. The IEP team should work toward consensus; making decisions based on a majority vote is inappropriate.

If the team cannot reach consensus, every effort should be made to resolve differences between the parents and the school staff through voluntary mediation or other informal steps. However, the parents and the school have the right to seek resolution through a due process hearing.

IEP DEVELOPMENT: COMPONENTS OF THE IEP

As a part of the procedural safeguards, parents should be given notification of meetings at which the IEP will be developed, reviewed, or revised. This notification should be given a reasonable period of time in advance of the meeting and indicate the purpose of the meeting. This notice can be given in writing, by telephone, or in person with proper documentation. A good rule of thumb is to telephone the parent prior to sending the meeting notification. This allows you to share some potential dates and times and hopefully to schedule the meeting at a time that is convenient for the parents. Once a mutually convenient time and date are established, complete the notification form, indicating the purpose of the meeting; the time, date, and place of the meeting; and who will attend the meeting. It is also very helpful if the meeting notification form has space available for parents to share concerns and make suggestions that can be included in the initial draft of the IEP. If possible, have parents sign the form or a copy of the form and return it to the special education teacher. This provides additional documentation that the parents have been given proper notification and an opportunity to have input into the process. This notification should be included as a part of the IEP.

The following are the eight primary components of the IEP mandated by the IDEA. In addition, other components may be necessary based on individual circumstances. For example, a child who is experiencing significant disciplinary issues will need a behavior intervention plan (BIP). In addition, extended school year services should be reflected in the IEP of the child who needs continuous services.

COMPONENT 1: THE PRESENT LEVEL OF PERFORMANCE

In the present level of performance, the team should describe the child's current level of academic performance and how the disability impacts the child's ability to function in the regular classroom setting. If the child is in preschool, how the child participates in appropriate activities should be addressed. For a child taking alternate assessments, benchmarks or short-term objectives need to be described (Pub. L. No. 108-446, § 614).

The present level of performance is the rationale for all of the components developed in the IEP. Teachers and parents should give details on strengths, learning style, instructional methods, accommodations, and modifications that have been successful with the student. It is essential that the present level of performance include all of the components mandated by the law (*P.N. v. Seattle School*

District No. 1, 2007). Far too often the present level of performance becomes a list of weaknesses and negatives. It is critical that the child's strengths be included. This component can become very upsetting for parents when strengths are not addressed.

If teachers are using assessment data and classroom evaluations to support the impact of the disability on student performance, the testing information should be presented in a fashion that can be easily understood. Also, the present level of performance included in the IEP should be descriptive and written in a manner that any special education teacher at any location can understand. The present level of performance should clearly explain the student's disability and its impact on his or her learning.

COMPONENT 2: ANNUAL GOALS

The team must develop measurable annual goals that address both academic and functional areas. These goals must address the specific needs that have resulted from the impact of the disability. They must be designed so as to result in the child's being included and progressing in the general education curriculum. Further, they must address all issues and needs that are directly linked to the disability.

It is important to note again that the 2004 IDEA amendments removed the general requirement for benchmarks or short-term objectives. As noted earlier, Congress narrowed the requirement, mandating benchmarks or short-term objectives only for students with disabilities taking alternate assessments aligned to alternate achievement standards. Errors commonly made during the development of goals and benchmarks or short-term objectives include (1) including items that are too broad and not measurable, (2) including items that are not linked to the present level of performance, and (3) failing to include critical goals. If an IEP does not address one or more clearly identified areas of deficit, the IEP may be deemed inappropriate (*Burlington School District*, 1994).

The team should compare the present level of performance with the annual goals. Each annual goal should be addressed in the present level of performance, and each need specifically noted in the present level of performance should be addressed by an annual goal.

COMPONENT 3: REPORTING OF STUDENT PROGRESS

Parents must be informed of the methods that will be used to assess their child's progress on the annual goals and must be provided with a report that documents their child's progress toward these goals. This report must be provided to parents as often as the parents of nondisabled students receive a report card. The issue of reporting progress should be discussed at the IEP meeting and documented in the meeting minutes. A good practice for reporting progress to parents is to physically attach the progress report to the report card.

COMPONENT 4: ACCOMMODATIONS, MODIFICATIONS, AND SUPPORT SERVICES

A statement defining the research-based accommodations, modifications, and support services that will be provided to the student with a disability to enable him or her to participate in the general education curriculum, make progress toward annual goals, and be educated with regular education peers as much as possible must be included in the IEP. One method of increasing the student's success in and access to the general education curriculum is providing accommodations and supports or services. It is very important for practitioners to note that the accommodations must address not only academic needs, but also extracurricular and nonacademic activities. Every aspect of the child's school activities must be addressed.

Accommodations should allow the student to demonstrate knowledge of the curriculum without a significant change in instructional level or content. These supports can include, but are not limited to, calculators, graphic organizers, electronic spellers, oral administration of tests, and other forms of assistive technology. Modifications are changes in the curriculum and performance expectations, as when a fifth-grade student is provided reading material on a third-grade level. Also, support services should be provided for the general education staff. These services can include staff development activities such as workshops in instructional strategies and behavior management techniques. Again, these supports, accommodations, and modifications should be based on information from the student's present level of performance. In addition, the team should identify the locations and curriculum areas in which the supports will be used, as well as the frequency and the time period/duration of their use.

COMPONENT 5: LEAST RESTRICTIVE ENVIRONMENT AND RELATED SERVICES

Students with disabilities should be educated with their peers to the maximum extent possible and should be removed from the regular classroom setting only if the nature and severity of their disabilities necessitate the move—that is, if their educational needs cannot be addressed with supplementary aides and services in the regular classroom. The IEP team must determine the extent to which each student with a disability will participate in the general education curriculum and nonacademic activities. The team must provide a statement of justification if the student will not participate with nondisabled students in any part of his or her educational program.

The services provided to the student may include monitoring of the student's progress in general education classrooms or special instruction designed to meet the student's special needs. The team must also decide which related services the student needs in order to make progress on his or her annual goals. Examples of these services include, but are not limited to, adaptive physical education, psychological services, occupational therapy, interpreting services, speech-language pathology and audiology services, and special transportation (see Chapter 3 for related services).

In order to address the varying needs of students with disabilities and to ensure that each student is receiving services in the least restrictive environment, the school must offer a continuum of services that may include such models as consultation, collaboration, resource, self-contained, hospitalization or homebound, special day school, and residential placement. Extended school year services should be considered if the team feels that the lack of specialized instruction during summer breaks and holidays will adversely impact the student's level of achievement or create an irreversible loss of skills. As one can see, no single service delivery model will meet the requirement of a continuum of placement options. These services can be provided for as little as 1 percent up to as much as 100 percent of the student's day, depending on the severity of the student's disability and his or her individual needs.

COMPONENT 6: PARTICIPATION IN STATE- AND DISTRICTWIDE ASSESSMENTS

The component on participation in state- and districtwide assessments was refined in the 2004 amendments to conform to the stipulations of the No Child Left Behind Act of 2001 (NCLB). A statement of level of participation in the state or local assessment must be included in the IEP. Thus, the IEP team must determine how the student will participate in the mandatory state or local assessments and which accommodations and modifications are necessary. Further, the IEP team must make sure that these accommodations and modifications are appropriate and reflect those that the student receives during classroom instruction and evaluations. If the IEP team determines that a child will participate in an alternate assessment, the team must include in the IEP an explanation of why an alternate assessment is necessary. The IEP team has two distinct options regarding the alternate assessment: (1) an alternate assessment linked to the same achievement standards as those of the regular assessment and (2) an alternate assessment linked to alternate achievement standards. If the alternate assessment with alternate achievement standards is deemed necessary by the IEP team, short-term objectives or benchmarks must be included in the goals section of the IEP.

COMPONENT 7: FREQUENCY AND DURATION OF SERVICES

The IEP team must determine and document the beginning date and the projected ending date for services, the frequency with which the services will be provided, and the location at which the services will be delivered. A statement justifying the student's limited participation in the general education program or the provision of services outside the student's home school is required.

COMPONENT 8: TRANSITION SERVICES

If the student is 16 years old, he or she must be invited to any IEP meetings on transition services, and a statement concerning the student's transition needs or services must be included in the IEP. This requirement stresses the importance of planning for the student's life after the completion of secondary education. The team must consider issues such as appropriate education (including specific courses of study), training, supported employment, integrated employment, adult services, community participation, and independent living skills. Also, if community agencies are needed to support the transition services, they should be invited to participate in IEP meetings. These transition services should be provided at no cost to the student and the parents.

DOCUMENTATION OF PARTICIPATION, CONSENT, AND PRIOR NOTICE

Because consensus is required, members of the IEP team should sign the IEP as participants in its development. Parental consent must be obtained for the initial or annual IEP, IEP revisions, changes in placement, and initiation and termination of any special education services. Services cannot be provided or removed without parental consent. In addition, parents must be provided prior notice in writing of any proposed change in a student's services or placement and any refusal to implement a recommended change. This prior notice must describe the action and explain why the school has decided on this action, the options that were considered and the reasons for their rejection, and the data that were used to support the action.

ADDITIONAL COMPONENTS OF THE IEP

The IEP team may have to consider an extended school year plan for a student who needs continuous services, a behavioral intervention plan for a student with behavior concerns, or a service plan for a student who attends a private school. A description of each follows:

   ■ *Extended school year (ESY)* services are provided if necessary to meet the needs of the individual child; they are not a necessary consideration for every child with an IEP. The main purpose of the ESY provision is to deliver services to a student beyond the normal school year, such as during the summer, on weekends, or during holiday breaks. ESY services should be considered if the IEP team determines that the lack of services during nonschool periods will result in significant academic or skill regression.

■ A *behavioral intervention plan (BIP)* becomes a necessary component of the IEP when a student has a behavior disability that impedes his or her learning or that of others. The development of the BIP becomes important when long-term suspension and alternative placement are being considered. The BIP should be developed based on a *functional behavior assessment (FBA)*. This assessment should include the collection and analysis of data prior to and following inappropriate behaviors. Intervention strategies and consequences should then be developed to address these behaviors.

■ A *service plan* should be considered and developed for the child with a disability who attends a private school. The school district must initiate and conduct the meetings to develop, review, and revise the service plan with parents and representatives of the private school. The plan should describe the specific special education and related services the school district will provide; who will provide the services; and the amount, frequency, duration, and location of the services. It is important to note that a school system is not required to provide the same amount of services that it would provide or that the child would receive if the child were enrolled in a public school. In some cases, transportation may need to be provided.

Again, these plans are based on the individual needs of the student and are not included as a regular component of the IEP. Each individual school district will have specific instructions for their development and implementation.

PROGRAM PLANNING

The individual components of the IEP converge to make a comprehensive, individualized, and measurable educational program for children with disabilities. Although the components are specific and should be consistently utilized, personal perceptions and variances in levels of expertise affect the development of the IEP. A broad spectrum of educational programming exists in relation to IEPs in the United States. As a baseline for practitioners to follow, Bateman & Linden (1998) provides the dos and don'ts of educational programming:

Dos: Program Planning

■ Do individualize the child's program.

■ Do specify all necessary special education, related services, and modifications. If no modifications are needed in the regular class, one might question the child's eligibility.

■ Do address behavior/discipline for every child for whom there is any reason to believe it may be an issue.

■ Do base IEPs on the individual child's needs, not on present availability of services in the district.

■ Do observe all procedural requirements of the law. Ensure meaningful parent participation, and remember that the parent has 50% of the decision-making power (p. 7–8).

Don'ts: Program Planning

■ Don't confuse the memberships or functions of the evaluation team, the IEP team, and the placement team. They are three teams, not one or two.

■ Don't use lack of funds as an excuse for failure to provide a FAPE.

■ Don't worry that what is provided to Sarah, for example, will set "precedent" for what must be provided to Jennifer. It won't. Services must be individualized. A child is entitled only to what she or he needs, not to what someone else needs.

■ Don't clutter IEPs with reading, mathematics, and language arts goals and objectives that (1) are not individualized, (2) do not reflect unique needs, and (3) have little to do with special education. Save the paper and the energy. If you feel compelled to include this, do it as a multicopied add-on.

■ Don't use more than two or three behavioral objectives for each goal. All objectives should describe "how far by when" relative to progress toward the goal.

■ Don't ever provide services categorically (p. 8).

SUMMARY

The IEP is often described as the heart of the IDEA. The purpose of the IEP is to ensure that all necessary individuals are aware of the specific needs, requirements, services, and accommodations deemed essential to meet the child's individual educational needs.

Since its inception, the IEP has proven difficult for educators to develop and implement in accordance with federal regulations. Some of the most common errors made in the development and implementation of IEPs include the following: (1) Present levels of performance are incomplete, (2) goals and objectives are insufficient, (3) evaluation procedures do not meet regulatory requirements, (4) essential IEP team personnel are not in attendance, (5) placement decisions do not match or are not based on the current IEP, and (6) students lack of access to the general curriculum. These errors have resulted in a voluminous amount of litigation. To avoid legal trouble, experts recommend that school personnel follow every step in the IEP planning procedures, including identification, testing, and parental involvement. School personnel should state goals and objectives in broad terms, avoid guarantees of student progress, and make a good-faith effort to carry out the educational program outlined in the IEP.

The IDEA mandates that each IEP team comprise the following members: parents or guardians, the regular education teacher, the special education teacher, a district or LEA representative, an individual qualified to discuss evaluation results (e.g., school psychologist), other necessary individuals, and the child, if appropriate. Major IEP decisions such as placement should not be made by majority vote; rather, the team should come to a consensus.

The IEP comprises eight essential components: (1) present level of performance; (2) annual goals; (3) reporting of student progress; (4) accommodations, modifications, and support services; (5) least restrictive environment and related services; (6) participation in state- and districtwide assessments; (7) frequency and duration of services; and (8) transition services. In order to be legally and educationally sound, each IEP must include each of these eight components. It is critical that practitioners take great care and time when developing an IEP. The IEP is the single most important document protecting the educational rights of a child with a disability.

Applying the Law in the Classroom

Brooks Hundler is a seventh-grade student at Robias Middle School (RMS). In fourth grade, Brooks was found eligible for special education services as a student with a specific learning disability in reading and writing. More specifically, Brooks has significant difficulty with reading comprehension, composition, and handwriting (dysgraphia). Brooks works hard and has supportive parents who help with homework and organization.

Brooks has always been placed in regular education classes with accommodations and modifications. He attends a study skills and learning strategies resource class every other day for students with specific learning disabilities. Brooks is a solid "B" student. Brooks's IEP contains the following accommodations and modifications: (1) extended time on quizzes and tests, (2) teacher copies of all notes, (3) extended time on long writing assignments, and (4) oral administration of quizzes and tests. Until recently, his IEP has always been appropriately implemented, and his parents have been very supportive of the teachers and the school.

During the annual review of Brooks's IEP, Mr. and Mrs. Hundler expressed their concern regarding Brooks's English teacher, Mr. Riley. The parents shared documentation of five different times Mr. Riley failed to provide their son with specific accommodations. As requested by the parents,

Mr. Riley was in attendance for this meeting. The parents claimed that Mr. Riley's failure to comply with Brooks's IEP led to failing quiz and test scores, increased frustration, and an overall denial of FAPE.

In response, Mr. Riley noted that he could not confirm or deny the specifics of the five alleged times he did not comply with the IEP. He continued, however, to note that Brooks is in middle school now and that if he does not have legible notes, he should request a copy from another student. Furthermore, he stated that it is very difficult to read every quiz and test to Brooks while he has 26 other students to attend to. Mr. Riley told the parents that if Brooks does not learn to do certain tasks on his own, he will never develop the skills necessary to be successful in the regular education classroom and curriculum. He further commented that the IEP was enabling Brooks and that he should not be provided with a copy of Mr. Riley's notes. Mr. Riley finished by asserting that since Brooks's needs are so significant, he would be better served in a special education English class.

Application Questions

1. How do you think Mr. and Mrs. Hundler will respond to Mr. Riley's comments? Be specific.
2. Under the IDEA, does a teacher have the professional right and discretion to choose which accommodations or modifications he or she will implement?
3. Is it appropriate for a teacher in this situation to recommend another placement? Why or why not?
4. Is the school in compliance with the IDEA?
5. Is Mr. Riley possibly compromising Brooks's right to a FAPE? Why or why not?
6. If you could talk to Mr. Riley, what legal and professional advice would you give him?

CRITICAL THINKING QUESTIONS

1. Why is the IEP considered by many to be the heart of the IDEA?
2. Which component of the IEP is the most critical and why?
3. Why is it so important to advocates that a legally binding educational program be developed for each child with a disability?
4. Why is the involvement of parents so critical to the development of a strong IEP?
5. Discuss the positives and negatives of the IEP in relation to students, teachers, parents, administrators, and school districts.

REFERENCES

Alex R. ex rel. Beth R. v. Forrestville Valley Community Unit School District # 221, 375 F.3d 603 (7th Cir. 2004).

Bateman, B., & Linden, M. (1998). *Better IEPs: How to develop legally correct and educationally useful programs.* Longmont, CO: Sopris West.

Burlington School District, 20 IDELR 1303 (SEA Vt. 1994).

Cantor, R., & Cantor, J. (1995). *Parents' guide to special needs schooling.* Westport, CT: Greenwood.

Cerra v. Pawling Central School District, 427 F.3d 186 (2d Cir. 2005).

Chairez-Vasquez, M., & MacMillan, R. (1989). Meeting special education needs through collaborative consultation. *Thrust, 42–44.*

Cohen, S., Thomas, C., Sattler, R., & Morsink, C. (1997). Meeting the challenge of consultation and collaboration: Developing interactive teams. *Journal of Learning Disabilities, 30,* 427–432.

Cruickshank, W., Morse, W., & Grant, J. (1990). *The individual education planning committee: A step in the history of special education.* Ann Arbor: University of Michigan Press.

Dettmer, P., Dyck, N., & Thurston, L. (1999). *Consultation, collaboration and teamwork for students with special needs.* Boston: Allyn & Bacon.

Frank G. v. Board of Education of Hyde Park, 459 F.3d 356 (2d Cir. 2006).

Friend, M., & Cook, L. (1992). *Interactions: Collaboration skills for professionals.* New York: Longman.

Gascoigne, E. (1995). *Working with parents as partners in SEN.* London: David Fulton.

Hollis, J. (1998). *Conducting individualized education program meetings that withstand due process.* Springfield, IL: Thomas.

Honig v. Doe, 479 U.S. 1084 (1988).

Hudgins, H., & Vacca, R. (1999). *Law and education: Contemporary issues and court decisions.* New York: Matthew Bender.

Hudson, T., & Glomb, N. (1997). It takes two to tango. Then why not teach both partners to dance? Collaboration instruction for educators. *Journal of Learning Disabilities, 30*(4), 442–448.

Huefner, D.S. (2000) *Getting comfortable with special education law: a framework for working with children with disabilities.* Norwood, MA: Christopher-Gordon Publishers, Inc.

Individuals with Disabilities Education Improvement Act of 2004, Pub. L. No. 108-446, 118 Stat. 2652.

Kenton County School District v. Hunt, 384 F.3d 269 (6th Cir. 2004).

Knable ex rel. Knable v. Bexley City School District, 238 F.3d 755 (6th Cir. 2001).

L.T. and T.B. ex rel. N.B. v. Warwick School Committee, 361 F.3d 80 (1st Cir. 2004).

Lynch, E., & Stein, R. (1987). Parent participation by ethnicity: A comparison of Hispanic, Black and Anglo families. *Exceptional Children, 54*(2), 105–111.

Martin, J., & Marshall, L. H. (1996). *Self-directed IEP.* Longmont, CO: Sopris West.

M.S. ex rel. S.S. v. Board of Education of City School District of the City of Yonkers, 231 F.3d 96 (2d Cir. 2000).

Nack ex rel. Nack v. Orange City School District, 454 F.3d 604 (6th Cir. 2006).

Pachl v. Seagren, 453 F.3d 1064 (8th Cir. 2006).

P.N. v. Seattle School District No. 1, 474 F.3d 1165 (9th Cir. 2007).

Schaffer v. Weast, 546 U.S. 49 (2005).

Smith, D. (2001). *Introduction to special education: Teaching in an age of opportunity.* Boston: Allyn & Bacon.

Snell, M., & Janney, R. (2000). *Collaborative teaming.* Baltimore, MD: Brookes.

T.F. v. Special School District of St. Louis County, 449 F.3d 816 (8th Cir. 2006).

Todd v. Duneland School Corporation, 299 F.3d 899 (7th Cir. 2002).

Turnbull, A., & Turnbull, R. (1990). *Families, professionals, and exceptionalities: A special partnership.* Columbus, OH: Merrill.

Vaughn, S., Bos, C., Harrell, J., & Lasky, B. (1988). Parent participation in the initial placement/IEP conference ten years after mandated involvement. *Journal of Learning Disabilities, 21*(2), 82–89.

White, R., & Calhoun, M. (1987). From referral to placement: Teachers' perceptions of their responsibilities. *Exceptional Children, 53*(5), 460–468.

Will, M. (1986). Educating children with learning problems: A shared responsibility. *Exceptional Children, 52,* 411–415.

11

Procedural Safeguards

Facts at a GLANCE

- In *Pennsylvania Association for Retarded Citizens v. Pennsylvania* (1972), the court affirmed the basic principle that districts have to provide parents or guardians notice regarding a change in educational placement for a student with special needs.
- The procedural safeguards section of the IDEA provides rights that must be accorded to the parents of a child whenever a substantive change (or one perceived as substantive) in the educational status or program for the child is contemplated.
- Districts are required to provide parents with two standard notifications: the prior written notice and the procedural safeguards notice.
- The procedural safeguards contained in Section 615 of the IDEA are triggered when parents file a complaint or *dissent*.
- A rule of thumb for practitioners: Any information relevant to the IEP and/or relevant to the provision of FAPE constitutes information that must be available to the parents either as routine sharing or upon request.
- The IDEA regulations allow for a *foster parent* to have the legal standing of a *parent*.
- The mediation provisions require that the state and local educational agencies maintain procedures to "allow all parties to dispute"—including disagreements that have not triggered a formal due process complaint notice—to resolve their disagreements through a mediation process.
- The *impartial due process hearing* is the sine qua non of the procedural safeguards under the IDEA and is typical of the type of due process proceedings occurring throughout the country at the administrative rather than the judicial level.
- In *Schaffer v. Weast* (2005), the U.S. Supreme Court ended the debate over which party bears the burden of proof. The burden falls on the party bringing the grievance.

- The 1986 amendments to the IDEA included the parents' right to seek attorneys' fees.
- In circumstances where schools must suspend or expel a child with a disability beyond ten days, the law mandates that specific procedures and policies be followed.
- A violation of the student code of conduct may be a criminal offense.

In large measure, the spirit of the Individuals with Disabilities Education Act (IDEA) is rooted in the guarantee of procedural protections for children, their families, and the professionals who serve them. But unlike other provisions in the IDEA, procedural safeguards appear throughout and are not simply confined to just one section on the statute. For instance, the law's individualized education program (IEP) requirements are replete with procedural safeguards.

So why is there a section of the IDEA—namely, Section 615, which is titled "Procedural Safeguards"—devoted exclusively to the topic? Part of the answer is found in a historic 1972 consent decree—a judicial order that can be characterized as the precursor to enactment of the IDEA some three years later. In *Pennsylvania Association for Retarded Citizens v. Pennsylvania* (1972), the U.S. District Court for the Eastern District of Pennsylvania affirmed the basic principle that districts have to provide parents or guardians notice regarding a change in educational placement for a student with special needs—with no less than 23 provisions guaranteeing due process. The consent decree included the following fundamental right: "The notice shall inform the parent or guardian of his *right to contest the proposed action at a full hearing . . .* " (emphasis added) (Weintraub et al., 1976, p. 86). Later court actions across the nation would carry forward this guarantee of procedural safeguards as stipulated in the above decree, state legislation, and Public Law No. 94-142 (IDEA), after it was enacted in 1975.

The procedural safeguards section of the IDEA provides rights that must be accorded to the parents of a child whenever a substantive change (or one perceived as substantive) in the educational status or program for the child is contemplated. Thus, a sort of due process umbrella covers any change from general to special education or vice versa, any change of placement along the continuum of instructional environments, any change sought because a program is deemed insufficient or inappropriate, or any change sought because of the alleged failure to provide a free appropriate public education (FAPE) to the child.

The underlying principle is that when lawmakers provide certain rights or benefits for a vulnerable segment of the citizenry, especially when provided as a constitutionally guaranteed necessity, they must accompany that action with due process protections to guard against any improper denial of those rights or benefits. Now let's explore the rights guaranteed in the procedural safeguards section of the IDEA and, as we do, keep in mind a fundamental tenet of American culture: *the right to be heard.*

THE RIGHT TO BE NOTIFIED

Districts are required to provide parents with two standard notifications: the prior written notice and the procedural safeguards notice. Both forms of notice are vital; the initial notice reveals what is under consideration by the local educational agency (LEA), while the second notice provides a listing of available procedural options.

In addition, *prior written notice* is a key element in triggering the entire educational process as prescribed in the IDEA. The statutory language—essentially unchanged since the original enactment of Public Law No. 94-142—requires prior written notice to the parents of the child

> whenever the local educational agency—
>
> (A) proposes to initiate or change; or
> (B) refuses to initiate or change,
>
> the identification, evaluation, or educational placement of the child, or the provision of a free appropriate public education to the child. (Pub. L. No. 108-446, § 615(b)(3))

The LEA must provide the prior written notice in the native language of the parents unless doing so is clearly unfeasible, a standard requirement throughout the law when communicating with parents. The notice must describe the district's action and explain the basis for proposing or refusing. The law also requires the district to describe each evaluation, assessment, record, or report used as a basis for its proposed or refused action. Further, the LEA must alert the parents to the other procedural safeguards and how to obtain a description of them, along with sources for parents to contact to obtain assistance in understanding all the provisions of the law.

The *procedural safeguards notice* is meant to offer a full explanation of all available procedural safeguards contained in the IDEA's due process section (Pub. L. No. 108-446, § 615), as well as those contained in any federal regulations accompanying that section. The IDEA requires that the district list and describe all the pertinent elements of the procedural safeguards package, including the student's initial right to an independent educational evaluation, the student's right to a due process hearing, and the student's right to pursue a civil action in a court of law after all due process options have been exhausted.

In a move to curb postal and email overkill, the 2004 amendments to the IDEA (Pub. L. No. 108-446) stipulate that the procedural safeguards notice need be given to parents only once a year. However, a copy must be given to the parents on three occasions: at the initial referral or parental request for evaluation of the child, the first time a complaint is filed, and when a parent requests a copy. Notice that the word *complaint* offers a bridge to the next section.

THE RIGHT TO DISSENT

The cherished right of its citizens to dissent remains the core of American due process. The basic trigger for the procedural safeguards contained in Section 615 of the IDEA is the filing of a complaint or *dissent* by parents. This filing opens the door for conflict resolution—the most well known method being the impartial due process hearing. The 2004 amendments to the IDEA added three new features to the complaint mechanisms within Section 615. The right to present a complaint now exists not just for parents, but also for *any party*, including the school system. Further, Congress added a new phrase to the terminology in the IDEA: *due process complaint notice*. Finally, lawmakers included a statute of limitations of *two years* for bringing an action; this change has been welcomed widely as fair to all parties despite early reluctance by some advocates.

Observers will evaluate the impact of the change to *any party*, although school districts have always triggered due process, for example, when they believe a child requires the support of special education, but the parents have withheld consent.

The due process complaint notice was added in an effort to better organize the flow of the Section 615 procedures through three major notices—*prior written*, *procedural safeguards*, and *due process complaint*. The law provides

> An opportunity for any party to present a complaint—
>
> (A) with respect to any matter relating to the identification, evaluation, or educational placement of the child, or the provision of a free appropriate public education to such child; and
> (B) which sets forth an alleged violation that occurred not more than 2 years before the date the parent or public agency knew or should have known about the alleged action that forms the basis of the complaint, or, if the State has an explicit time limitation for presenting such a complaint under this part, in such time as the State law allows. . . . (Pub. L. No. 108-446, § 615(b)(6))

The law requires that the due process complaint notice include a description of the nature of the child's problem as it relates to whatever it is that the LEA proposes or refuses to initiate or change, including all relevant facts relating to that problem, and a proposed resolution of the problem. At this point, the non-complaining party can challenge the "sufficiency" of the complaint notice, and the complaining party can respond to any such challenges, with a hearing officer ruling as needed. At the same time, the non-complaining party must—within ten days of the issuance of the complaint notice—transmit to the complaining party a response that addresses the issues raised in the complaint notice. Moreover, if the LEA has not sent a prior written notice to the parent regarding the matters included in the parent's complaint, the agency must—within ten days of receiving the complaint—issue a response that includes an explanation of why the agency proposed or refused to take the action raised in the complaint, along with a discussion of other options considered by the IEP team and why those options were rejected; a description of each evaluation procedure, assessment, record, or report used by the LEA as the basis for its action or refusal; and a description of the factors deemed relevant to the LEA's decision.

After taking these actions, the district has opened the door to formal and less formal conflict resolution, provided the complaint notice has been deemed sufficient.

THE RIGHT TO BE FULLY INFORMED

Built into all aspects of the IDEA—and central to the procedural safeguards of Section 615—is the parents' right to know whatever substantively affects educational decision-making for their child. In order for parents to give fully informed *consent* or engage in fully informed *dissent*, individual schools and their corresponding LEAs are required to commit to transparency. A rule of thumb for practitioners: Any information relevant to the IEP and/or relevant to the provision of FAPE constitutes information that must be available to the parents, either as routine sharing or upon request. See also the discussion titled "Confidentiality of Information" in Chapter 3.

Parents also have the right to solicit professional opinions beyond what is offered by the school district. The law provides parents the right to an independent educational evaluation of their child—that is, an evaluation conducted by a qualified professional not employed by the district. In fact, the regulations require that the district provide information about where parents can obtain such an evaluation, as well as the district's criteria for such an evaluation. Further, the district must provide that independent educational evaluation at public expense if so requested by the parents; this requirement stands unless the district initiates a due process hearing at which it demonstrates that its evaluation is appropriate or that the evaluation obtained by the parents did not meet agency criteria. The parents retain the right to an independent educational evaluation, whether paid for by the district or not, and even if the evaluation is paid for by the parents, the district must consider the results of that evaluation in any decision affecting FAPE for the child if the evaluation meets district criteria (34 C.F.R. § 300.502).

In addition to the parents' right to review all educational records and demand an independent educational evaluation, Section 615 stipulates that parents have the right to participate in meetings involving the identification, evaluation, and educational placement of their child *and the provision of FAPE to their child.* Although the IDEA guarantees the right to participate in a number of specific activities (e.g., IEP meetings, placement meetings), the language of this section includes the long-standing "boilerplate" opportunity for parent involvement—a vital element if parents are to be fully informed.

However, the IDEA's regulations include an important qualifier (one that many see as based on common sense) for parental participation in meetings.

A meeting does not include informal or unscheduled conversations involving public agency personnel and conversations on issues such as teaching methodology, lesson plans, or coordination of service provision. A meeting also does not include preparatory activities that public agency personnel engage in to develop a proposal or response to a parent proposal that will be discussed at a later meeting. (34 C.F.R. § 300.501(b)(3))

THE RIGHT TO A SURROGATE

Since the first enactment of the IDEA through Public Law No. 94-142, the law has included the requirement that the state or local educational agency (SEA or LEA) or other state agency assign a surrogate parent for educational purposes when

- no parents can be identified,
- the public agency is unable to locate a parent, or
- the child is a ward of the state under the laws of the particular state. (Pub. L. No. 108-446, § 615(b)(2))

But who is a *parent*? The IDEA regulations state:

Parent means—

(1) A biological or adoptive parent of a child;
(2) A foster parent, unless State law, regulations, or contractual obligations with a State or local entity prohibit a foster parent from acting as a parent;
(3) A guardian generally authorized to act as the child's parent, or authorized to make educational decisions for the child (but not the State if the child is a ward of the State);
(4) An individual acting in the place of a biological or adoptive parent (including a grandparent, stepparent, or other relative) with whom the child lives, or an individual who is legally responsible for the child's welfare); or
(5) A surrogate parent who has been appointed in accordance with § 300.519 or section 639(a)(5) of the Act. (34 C.F.R. § 300.30(a))

(*Note:* The last category cites the surrogate now under discussion, with Section 300.519 being the surrogate parents section of the regulations.)

The IDEA regulations allow for a *foster parent* to have the legal standing of a *parent*. Specifically, the IDEA regulations state:

Unless State law prohibits a foster parent from acting as a parent, a State may allow a foster parent to act as a parent under Part B of the Act if—

(1) The natural parents' authority to make educational decisions on the child's behalf has been extinguished under State law; and

(2) The foster parent—
- (i)   Has an ongoing, long-term parental relationship with the child;
- (ii) Is willing to make the educational decisions required of parents under the Act; and
- (iii) Has no interest that would conflict with the interests of the child. (IDEA Regulations, Sec. 300.20(b))

Allowing for the need for such legally precise language because of the complex nature of familial arrangements in contemporary society, the reader now may consider a simplification. If the preceding definitions of *parent* (except #4) and *foster parent* still fail to generate a parent for the child, then the agency must assign a surrogate parent for educational purposes.

In assigning a surrogate, the school district must ensure that the person is not an employee of the SEA, LEA, or other agency that is involved in the education or care of the child—a condition that establishes the obvious separation needed for advocacy purposes. An agency may, however, assign a surrogate who is an employee of a *nonpublic* agency if that agency provides only non-educational care for the child. In addition, a person appointed as a surrogate must not have an interest that conflicts with the interest of the child and must have knowledge and skills that assure adequate representation for the child (34 C.F.R. § 300.519(d)(2)(ii)).

Under the IDEA, a surrogate speaks for the child only on matters relevant to identification, evaluation, special education support services, and the overall guarantee of FAPE. The surrogate is not empowered to represent the child in any other domains—for instance, housing or welfare support. Phrased differently, the surrogate stands in for the parent with respect to educational issues alone. Due to considerable variance across the states in laws governing parentage, adoption, and guardianship, special education practitioners are encouraged to consult state and local policy and procedures.

THE RIGHT TO NONADVERSARIAL CONFLICT RESOLUTION

During the 20-year period following the enactment of Public Law No. 94-142, experts increasingly acknowledged that the procedural safeguards process under the IDEA had become—in too many instances—unduly confrontational and highly legalized. Both parents and schools now deemed hired attorneys necessary more often than not; due process hearings often resulted in highly charged, mini–courtroom dramas, with the best interests of the child, the parents, and the professionals who serve frequently submerged in the fervid pursuit of legal victory for its own sake. Though practitioners and parents considered the procedural mechanisms of the IDEA to be sound, necessary, and largely effective in a constructive way, school districts across the nation piloted alternate, less adversarial approaches to conflict resolution.

This movement toward a less confrontational approach led to the universally approved incorporation of a mediation process in the 1997 amendments to the

IDEA. The mediation provisions require that the SEAs and LEAs maintain procedures to "allow all parties to dispute"—including disagreements that have not triggered a formal due process complaint notice—to resolve their disagreements through a mediation process. Mediation sessions allow for low-key, nonconfrontational, nonjudicial discussions to work out differences. Confidentiality is the central ingredient in making such sessions work. As the old saying goes, "Nothing leaves the room."

Using mediation to resolve disputes under the IDEA is entirely voluntary on the part of all parties, and though mediation is an opportunity to avoid a formal due process hearing, a district cannot use it to deny or in any way delay the parents' right to such a hearing. A mediator who is professionally trained for the function and can implement mediation techniques effectively must conduct the mediation. While the mediator must meet the same general test to assure impartiality as the hearing officer, the mediator conducts himself or herself differently than the hearing officer. The mediator steers all parties through the discussion and moves them into problem solving and resolution. The hearing officer may do the same, but is essentially an arbiter who listens to all the facts and delivers a ruling.

Both the cost and the general management of the mediation function must be borne by the SEA; the law requires that the state maintain an up-to-date list of qualified mediators who are also required to be conversant in federal and state laws and regulations governing special education and related services. Because the IDEA requires SEAs to bear the cost, they are allowed to use a portion of their reserved funds for mediation activities. Further, the law stresses the need to schedule mediation sessions in a "timely" manner and at locations "convenient" to the parties involved, both directives having the parents clearly in mind (Pub. L. No. 108-446, § 615(e)(2)(E)). Discussions occurring as part of a mediation session are confidential, and neither education officials nor parents may use them in any later due process hearing or judicial proceeding.

If the parties are able to reach a resolution through mediation, the IDEA instructs the mediator to execute a legally binding agreement that pledges confidentiality by all. The agreement must be signed by the parent and someone officially representing the agency and is "enforceable in any State court of competent jurisdiction or in a district court of the United States" (Pub. L. No. 108-446, § 615(e)(2)(F)).

If parents elect not to pursue mediation, the law includes a gentle enticement to convince them otherwise. The SEA or LEA may afford the parents an opportunity to meet with a "disinterested" party to hear the benefits of mediation. The IDEA specifically cites the federally supported parent training and information centers and community parent resource centers, as well as "an appropriate alternative dispute resolution entity," as such disinterested parties (Pub. L. No. 108-446, § 615(e)(2)(B)). Of course, the parents can once again say, "Thank you—but no."

In the 2004 amendments to the IDEA, Congress added yet another venue for relatively nonadversarial problem solving before a due process hearing. Within

15 days of the filing of a complaint notice, the local educational agency is required to convene what is termed a *resolution session*. The resolution session affords all parties a means to avoid launching into a formal due process hearing by grappling with and attempting to resolve the issue(s) that generated the complaint notice. The statute requires that the district hold the resolution session unless *both* the parents and the LEA agree, in writing, to waive this meeting or agree to the mediation venue instead.

Those attending the resolution session must include the parents, members of the IEP team who have knowledge pertinent to the facts addressed in the complaint notice, and a person who can exercise decision-making authority on behalf of the LEA. Of special note: An attorney representing the LEA may not be present unless the parents are themselves accompanied by an attorney. The IDEA states that the parents should discuss the complaint and the facts that form the basis of the complaint during the resolution session and that the LEA should make an effort to resolve the complaint.

If the parties reach a resolution, then stipulations similar to those required at the end of successful mediation apply. The parties execute a legally binding agreement—signed by both the parents and the LEA representative—that is enforceable in any state court of competent jurisdiction or in a federal district court. A three-day window allows any party to void the written settlement agreement. On the other hand, if no resolution has been reached 30 days after the filing of a complaint, the parties may proceed to an impartial due process hearing.

The Right to a Hearing

The *impartial due process hearing* is the sine qua non of the procedural safeguards under the IDEA and is typical of the type of due process proceedings occurring in this country at the administrative rather than the judicial level. The writings concerning aspects of the American due process hearing—beyond those pertaining just to the IDEA—amount to a library, which is a tribute to the importance attached to this essential forum for "the right to be heard." However, out of necessity, coverage in this volume will be limited to a summation of major requisites stipulated in the IDEA.

Until enactment of the 2004 amendments, the IDEA referred only to the parents' right to a due process hearing. Regardless, the statute made it clear that an LEA could, under certain circumstances, indirectly provoke a hearing through unilateral action. The IDEA now guarantees parents *and* LEAs the opportunity for a hearing after the submission of a complaint notice, logically mirroring the ability of *any party* to file a complaint notice (as already noted in this chapter).

The IDEA always has deferred to state policy with respect to which agency—the LEA or the SEA—will conduct the hearing. When Congress enacted Public

Law No. 94-142, Vermont required all hearings to be held at the state level, while other states utilized a two-tier system that began locally. Pennsylvania also conducted hearings at the regional level through its "intermediate educational units." The framers wanted to tread softly on this matter of local choice.

As with the complaint notice, the time line for requesting a hearing now contains a *statute of limitations*. The agency or the parent must request a hearing within two years of the date the agency or the parent "knew or should have known about the alleged action that forms the basis of the complaint" (Pub. L. No. 108-446, § 615(f)(3)(C)). The IDEA time line language, again mirroring that of the complaint notice, allows an existing state-based time limitation to supersede the federal time line. As a protection for parents, the statute allows two exceptions to the time line: (1) for parents who may have been unable to request a hearing because of misrepresentations by the LEA about the status of the issue at question and (2) for parents who may have been stymied by the LEA's withholding information that it is required to give parents under the IDEA (§ 615(f)(3)(D)).

Another new stipulation inserted as an amendment to the IDEA in 2004 requires that a hearing officer make a decision only on *substantive grounds*. This provision clearly targeted decisions reached on the basis of nothing more than technical procedural violations. Anyone observing courtroom dramas in contemporary American society has witnessed the effect of simple technical objections on crucial judicial decisions. However, accurately making the distinction between *substantive* and *procedural* can be delicate and tricky. Hence, the law includes the following clarification:

> In matters alleging a procedural violation, a hearing officer may find that a child did not receive a free appropriate public education only if the procedural inadequacies—
>
> (I)   impeded the child's right to a free appropriate public education;
> (II) significantly impeded the parents' opportunity to participate in the decisionmaking process regarding the provision of a free appropriate public education to the parents' child; or
> (III) caused a deprivation of educational benefits. (Pub. L. 108-446,
>   § 615(f)(3)(E)(ii))

Another significant addition made in the 2004 amendments prohibits the party requesting a due process hearing from raising issues at the hearing that were not raised in the complaint notice itself unless the other party permits that action. This requisite had been long sought by certain legal experts and may be characterized with a simple "No surprises, please." Further, no less than five business days before a hearing, all parties must share any evaluations of the child or recommendations associated with the evaluations if the party intends to use them at the hearing.

Whether it be a hearing or an appeal after a hearing, all parties, with special regard to the parents, have always been guaranteed a number of safeguards. These include the right to be accompanied and advised by counsel or by individuals with special knowledge of or training in the law and the practice of special education; the right to present evidence, "confront, cross-examine," and require the presence of witnesses; the right to a written or electronic record of the hearing; and the right to written or electronic findings of fact and decisions (Pub. L. No. 108-446, § 615(h)).

BURDEN OF PROOF

The IDEA does not address which party carries the burden of proof when someone challenges the effectiveness of an IEP. As with other areas that the law does not directly address, dissenting parties often ask the courts to determine the intent of Congress. For the IDEA's first 30 years, the courts provided no definitive answer as to which party bears the burden of proof in a challenge to an IEP.

Beginning in 1988, however, a number of circuit courts weighed in on the issue. Ultimately, four major cases emerged: *Kerkam v. McKenzie* (1988); *Roland M. v. Concord School Committee* (1991); *Oberti v. Board of Education* (1993); and *Clyde K. v. Puyallup* (1994). The U.S. Courts of Appeals for the District of Columbia Circuit (*Kerkam*) and the First Circuit (*Roland*) placed the burden of proof on the party that challenged the school district or agency.

In direct contrast, the U.S. Court of Appeals for the Third Circuit, in *Oberti*, placed the burden of proof squarely on the shoulders of the school district. The Third Circuit noted that when a school moves a child with a disability from the regular education setting to a more restrictive environment, the onus of justifying why the child is not being fully included falls on the district. A year after the *Oberti* decision, the U.S. Court of Appeals for the Ninth Circuit sided with the District of Columbia and First Circuits, finding that the burden of proof lies with the party that files the complaint. The Ninth Circuit found that no specific language in the IDEA placed the burden of proof on the district or administrative agency.

In *Schaffer v. Weast* (2005), the U.S. Supreme Court ended the debate over which party bears the burden of proof. The parents of Brian Schaffer, a student with learning disabilities and speech-language impairments, brought suit against Jerry Weast, superintendent of Montgomery County (Maryland) Public Schools (MCPS). Brian's parents had unilaterally placed him in a private school from prekindergarten through the seventh grade—during which time he struggled academically. The school officials of the private school recommended that Brian move to a school that could better meet his specific and unique needs. In 1997, the Schaffers approached MCPS and requested placement for Brian. After evaluating Brian, MCPS wrote an IEP with input from his parents and proposed a placement in one of two local middle schools. The parents disagreed with the options and enrolled him in a private school. The parents did not believe the public school district could provide a program designed to best meet Brian's needs (e.g., small classes and intensive support).

After enrolling Brian in the private school, the parents challenged the IEP and requested reimbursement. MCPS, believing the IEP to be appropriate, refused to reimburse the Schaffers. The Schaffers then filed a complaint notice and invoked their due process rights. The administrative law judge who presides over IEP hearings in Maryland found in favor of the school district, noting that the burden of proof resides with the party filing the complaint.

In a 6–2 decision written by Justice Sandra Day O'Connor, the Supreme Court held that the burden of proof resides with the party filing the complaint and questioning the effectiveness of the IEP. In the majority decision, Justice O'Connor noted: "The Act is silent, however, as to which party bears the burden of persuasion at such a hearing. We hold that the burden lies, as it typically does, on the party seeking relief." Thus, the Supreme Court set the national precedent that nullified any earlier decisions in lower courts (e.g., *Oberti*) that automatically placed the burden of proof on the school district or agency.

THE RIGHT TO A QUALIFIED AND IMPARTIAL HEARING OFFICER

Now we compare both the number and the content of the words addressing the credentials of the hearing officer included in the original IDEA (Pub. L. No. 94-142) and in the 2004 rendering of the IDEA (Pub. L. No. 108-446). Public Law No. 94-142 stated: "No hearing conducted pursuant to the requirements of this paragraph shall be conducted by an employee of such agency or unit involved in the education or care of the child" (§ 615(b)(2)). The 2004 amendments to the IDEA added more clarity:

A hearing officer conducting a hearing pursuant to paragraph

(1) (A) shall, at a minimum—
   (i)   not be—
      (I)   an employee of the State educational agency or the local educational agency involved in the education or care of the child; or
      (II) a person having a personal or professional interest that conflicts with the person's objectivity in the hearing;
   (ii) possess knowledge of, and the ability to understand, the provisions of this title, Federal and State regulations pertaining to this title, and legal interpretations of this title by Federal and State courts;
   (iii) possess the knowledge and ability to conduct hearings in accordance with appropriate, standard legal practice; and
   (iv) possess the knowledge and ability to render and write decisions in accordance with appropriate, standard legal practice. (Pub. L. No. 108-446, § 615(f)(3)(A))

Readers should note readily that (I) and (II) pertain to the need for the highest achievable degree of impartiality for hearing officers and that only one additional consideration has been added in the nearly three decades following enactment of Public Law No. 94-142. Congress developed the remaining requisites in recent reauthorizations and addressed other qualifications now desired of the hearing officer. These requirements clearly illustrate the evolution of that function from one performed by a generally knowledgeable lay professional to one performed by a heavily prepared and trained legal professional—or, more to the point, by an attorney. This, in turn, illustrates the evolution of the hearings, which shifted from relatively non-confrontational meetings for sorting out and ruling on facts to highly legalistic, often adversarial quasi–court proceedings. In the early years, a hearing officer typically may have been a competent educator, human services provider, or other professional who was subsequently trained in the basic rules and procedures of a hearing. Not so today—now thorough legal expertise is the paramount qualification.

THE RIGHT TO APPEAL

Generally speaking, the IDEA regulations stipulate that a final decision shall be made by the hearing officer within 45 days of when a party filed a due process complaint notice—although this time line can be lengthened if options for resolution in addition to the formal hearing are chosen. Some general leeway also is afforded hearing officers if a party to the dispute requests an extension of time. In any event, the rule of thumb as of this writing stands at 45 days.

The IDEA clearly states that a hearing officer's ruling shall be considered final. However, if the due process hearing was conducted by any agency other than the SEA (typically, an LEA-conducted hearing), the losing party may appeal the hearing decision to the SEA. In such cases, the SEA has 30 days from receipt of a request for a review to deliver its final decision, although the reviewing officer at the state level may also grant an extension of time to either party. The individual conducting the SEA review must examine the hearing record, making certain all hearing procedures were correct, and seek additional evidence when needed. If necessary, the state reviewer may convene a hearing, giving the parties an opportunity to submit oral or written testimony or both. Following the full review, the state's agent must make an independent decision (34 C.F.R. §§ 300.514(b)(2)(v). The SEA's decision is final under the law unless one of the parties files a civil action after the completion of all due process procedures.

Since the IDEA's inception in 1975, both parents and educational agencies—with particular emphasis on parents—have had the right to pursue a judicial remedy in court. Unsatisfied parties may file such civil actions in a state court of competent jurisdiction or a federal district court.

The disputants must bear in mind two basic constraints when considering a court action. First, the 2004 amendments to the IDEA added a statute of limitations similar to the time restrictions applied to the filing of a complaint notice and the request for a due process hearing. The aggrieved party must file the judicial appeal within 90 days of the hearing officer rendering his or her decision (again, with deference to state law if a state has a different time frame). Second, in most cases, a party may not bring a civil action until the procedural process outlined in Section 615 has been completed. Phrased more concisely in what legal experts call *exhaustion of remedies*, the aggrieved party may not bypass the law's due process mechanisms and proceed straight to the court system.

THE RIGHT TO REIMBURSEMENT

After a highly charged debate among stakeholders, the 1986 amendments to the IDEA included the right to attorneys' fees. In essence, if a parent of a child with a disability obtains a favorable verdict in his or her court action, the court—at its discretion—may require the losing party (the district) to pay the cost of the parents' attorneys throughout the appeals process. Congress thus opened the door to increased participation by attorneys in special education disputes at all levels of the appeals process and routine special education procedures. Although an interesting topic that warrants further exploration, space and content constraints make it impossible to discuss the debate surrounding the recovery of attorneys' fees or the notably legalistic details in the statute and the regulations. The specific language may be found in the law at Section 615(i)(3) of Public Law No. 108-446 and in the regulations at 34 C.F.R. § 300.517.

Of special note, however, is the fact that the 2004 amendments to the IDEA authorized the court to award attorneys' fees to SEAs and LEAs when either prevails against the attorney of a parent. The law created a caveat, however, which limited the states' and districts' opportunities to recoup attorneys' fees to instances where the court deems the parents' lawsuit to be frivolous, unreasonable, or without foundation—or where the parents' attorney continues to litigate after the action clearly has become frivolous, unreasonable, or without foundation. Further, the court may levy an award against the parents' attorney or *against the parents* if the parents' complaint or subsequent cause of action was presented for any improper purpose, such as to harass, cause unnecessary delay, or needlessly increase the cost of litigation.

DISCIPLINE

Disciplining students with disabilities is one of the most debated and contentious areas surrounding the IDEA and special education in general. The alleged "dual disciplinary standard" has fostered strong emotional response across a spectrum of constituents. A significant misperception regarding students with disabilities has been perpetuated, however, as a number of advocates and practitioners mistakenly assert that students with disabilities cannot be disciplined to the same degree as regular education students due to the protections of the IDEA. Although procedural safeguards ensure that students with disabilities are not unilaterally removed, the safeguards do not provide immunity from consequences. In circumstances where schools must suspend for more than ten days or expel a child with a disability, the law mandates that specific procedures and policies be followed. But the only major difference in long-term removals or expulsions for students with disabilities is that the IDEA allows for "no cessation of services." The law says that schools must provide students with disabilities who are removed for a long period or are expelled with educational services outside of the regular education setting. This chapter will explain in depth the specific procedures and policies that must be followed when disciplining students with disabilities.

In the *Honig v. Doe* (1988) case, two students with emotional disabilities were expelled for violating the district's code of conduct (engaging in violent and disruptive behavior) without a continuation of educational services. The High Court ruled that the school district's indefinite expulsion of the boys violated the "stay put" provision and resulted in a "prohibited change in placement." This case set the precedent that students with disabilities may not be unilaterally removed for disciplinary reasons beyond ten days without educational services or an alternative educational placement. In addition, students with disabilities may not be excluded from their educational placements due to dangerous or disruptive conduct growing out of their disabilities during the pendency of review proceedings.

In the last part of the twentieth century, a previously uncommon reality suddenly gripped the consciousness of American society: violence in the nation's schools. Following the horror of the Columbine High School massacre, communities across the nation rightly demanded that a greater emphasis be placed on safe and drug-free schools. But as schools pondered potential methods for reducing violence on their campuses, another question immediately rose to the surface: What if the student charged with a violation is a child with a disability? The pendency clause and related due process protections guaranteed in the IDEA now became problematic in light of the asserted need to immediately remove a student with special needs from his or her current learning environment.

In writing Public Law No. 94-142, Congress included a critical provision in the procedural safeguards section; this measure is generally referred to as the *pendency clause* or, more pointedly, as the *stay put provision*. That stipulation provides that

> during the pendency of any proceedings conducted pursuant to this section, unless the State or local education agency and the parents otherwise agree, the child shall remain in the then-current educational placement of the child, or, if applying for initial admission to a public school, shall, with the consent of the parents, be placed in the public school program until all such proceedings have been completed. (Pub. L. No. 108-446, § 615(j))

Lawmakers inserted this requirement to keep school authorities from arbitrarily removing a child from his or her current educational placement during disagreements over the student's placement until after the procedural safeguards process runs its course. Congress also included this requirement as a guarantee of the initiation and maintenance of a public school program while a due process dispute resolution is occurring. The IDEA refers to this stipulation as the "Maintenance of Current Educational Placement."

Allegations of misbehavior or misconduct and their corollary, a presumption of disruptive behavior, have been an all too common basis for a school to recommend that a child with a disability be removed from the general education classroom—or the regular school environment altogether. Thus, advocates originally perceived and continue to perceive the pendency clause as a vital protection of the child's right to an education in the least restrictive educational (LRE) environment.

A highly charged debate among policy makers and stakeholders during the 1997 IDEA reauthorization led Congress to add a new subsection to Section 615, titled "Placement in Alternative Educational Setting." This subsection is commonly referred to in the field as the *discipline provisions* of the IDEA. Nonetheless, the change prompted another highly charged response focusing on the mind-numbing complexity and undue paperwork attendant to the discipline provisions; Congress responded by writing a streamlined and more coherent revision of these provisions in the 2004 amendments to the IDEA. What follows is a description of the most current discipline provisions in the law.

BASELINE CONSIDERATIONS

The trigger for action by school authorities governing all of the discipline provisions centers on a violation of the school's code of student conduct. The IDEA offers a number of options, with suspension followed by a possible placement in an interim alternative educational setting. The determinant in decision making for school personnel contemplating a change in placement *may* be (not *must* be) "any unique circumstances on a case-by-case basis" (Pub. L. No. 108-446, § 615(k)(1)(A)). What constitutes a "case-by-case basis" is not made clear in the legislative history and thus should be approached with caution. Professionals are advised to make every effort to maintain harmony in all decision making with the child's parents. With no disagreement, there is no need for the discipline requirements of the IDEA, except as general guidance.

THE 10-DAY SUSPENSION

School personnel under this subsection may remove a child with a disability who violates a code of student conduct from their current placement to an appropriate interim alternative educational setting, another setting, or suspension, for not more than 10 school days (to the extent such alternatives are applied to children without disabilities). (Pub. L. No. 108-446, § 615(k)(1)(B))

Experts sometimes refer to this as the student's "time in no man's land." Included to provide the authority to engage in immediate—typically, emergency—removal, this provision allows for up to ten school days of suspension, during which no educational program has to be provided (but only to the extent this form of suspension is the same policy as that applied to all other students in the school). Removal to an interim educational setting during this ten-day period is indirectly encouraged, as can be witnessed in the statutory language just cited.

Maximum caution, however, should be exercised when utilizing the ten-day suspension. One should think in terms of not more than ten *consecutive* school days and *further* suspensions—whether ten *consecutive* school days or a lesser number of days—that might be applied to the same student over an entire school year. Can there be an eleventh *consecutive* day of suspension without an educational program? The law says no. But can there be suspensions over the course of a school year that cumulatively amount to more than ten days? Possibly, according to the IDEA, but only if the pattern of removals does not effectively constitute a change in placement. While allowing discretion for suspensions of short durations of time in the interests of school safety and discipline, the law also directs schools to prevent so-called revolving-door suspensions, which can discourage the child from his/her educational program. Careful attention should be paid to the length of each suspension, the proximity of the suspensions to each other, and the cumulative amount of time the student has been removed. From the standpoint of both adherence to the IDEA and best professional practice on behalf of the student, educators are well advised to reinstate an educational program for the student with a disability—with appropriate involvement of the IEP team—when a pattern of suspensions under the ten-day rule develops, whether or not the school is pursuing a change of placement.

THE GUARANTEE OF FAPE

Congress deemed the bedrock guarantee of no cessation of educational services, regardless of the disciplinary action taken, of such fundamental importance that the above reference to suspension or expulsion was added in the 1997 amendments to the requirement of FAPE contained in the opening sections of the IDEA. The *only* exception to this requirement is the ten-day suspension just discussed:

> (1) Free Appropriate Public Education.—
>> (A)   In general.—A free appropriate public education is available to all children with disabilities between the ages of 3 and 21, inclusive, including children with disabilities who have been suspended or expelled from school. (Pub. L. No. 108-446, § 612(a)(1))

Under the IDEA, districts must guarantee FAPE to children with disabilities regardless of whether or not the conduct in question is a manifestation of the child's disability, whether there is removal to an interim alternative educational setting, whether disciplinary procedures may be applied to the child in the same manner and for the same duration as they are applied to children without disabilities, or whether the school system chooses to use the word *expelled*.

To make the message abundantly clear, federal policy makers inserted language related to FAPE guaranteeing that the child continues to receive educational services for a number of reasons, including (1) enabling the child to continue to participate in the general education curriculum; (2) helping the child progress toward meeting the goals in the child's IEP; and (3) receiving, when appropriate, a functional behavior assessment, behavioral intervention services, and modifications designed to address the behavior violation so that it does not recur (Pub. L. No. 108-446, § 615(k)(1)(D)).

AUTHORITY FOR CHANGE OF PLACEMENT

The IDEA allows two circumstances when school authorities can seek or unilaterally make a change in placement beyond ten consecutive school days of suspension: (1) when the behavior deemed to have caused the violation is found *not* to be a manifestation of the child's disability and (2) when specific violations named in the law have occurred regardless of whether the violations are a manifestation of the child's disability.

In the first circumstance, the lawmakers carefully wrote the statutory language to state: "If school personnel seek to order a change in placement. . . ." Congress used this specific wording because it intended for a manifestation determination to occur *before* this option could be exercised by school authorities. If the designated persons (as described in the next section) decide that the violation is not a manifestation of the child's disability, disciplinary procedures may be applied "in the same manner and for the same duration" as they are applied to children without disabilities (Pub. L. No. 108-446, § 615(k)(1)(C)).

Due to allegations of a dual discipline standard—one for children without and another for children with disabilities—Congress created this option. However, four important factors must be kept in mind regardless of the local interpretation of "in the same manner and for the same duration." First, this option applies only when the violation is not a manifestation of the disability. Second, the district still must provide educational services under the rubric of FAPE that adhere to the individual IEP, as previously discussed. Third, logic compels that there be a placement for the student since FAPE must be provided. Fourth, parents may disagree with the placement and trigger the procedural safeguards process if proper regard and attention have not been afforded them. This last factor is reinforced by the legal requirement that the specific alternative placement under this option be determined by the IEP team.

In the second circumstance, school personnel may move a student to a new educational placement when a violation occurs regardless of whether the behavior is a manifestation of the student's disability. Such action may be taken

in cases where a child—

(i) carries or possesses a weapon to or at school, on school premises, or to or at a school function under the jurisdiction of a State or local educational agency;

(ii) knowingly possesses or uses illegal drugs, or sells or solicits the sale of a controlled substance, while at school, on school premises, or at a school function under the jurisdiction of a State or local educational agency; or

(iii) has inflicted serious bodily injury upon another person while at school, on school premises, or at a school function under the jurisdiction of a State or local educational agency. (Pub. L. No. 108-446, § 615(k)(1)(G))

School authorities may exercise this option with the following qualifications:

1. The child may be removed to an interim alternative educational setting for not more than 45 days.
2. Not later than the date on which a decision to take disciplinary action was made, the parents must be notified of the decision and be given a copy of the procedural safeguards available to them. See "The Right to Be Notified" in this chapter.
3. While under this option the decision to remove the student to an interim alternative educational placement is made by school authorities, the determination of the specific alternative setting must be made by the IEP team, which, of course, includes the parents, just as required in the first circumstance.

The IDEA defines *serious bodily injury* as

bodily injury which involves—

(A) a substantial risk of death;
(B) extreme physical pain;
(C) protracted or obvious disfigurement; or
(D) protracted loss or impairment of the function of a bodily member, organ, or mental faculty. (18 U.S.C. § 1365(h)(3))

Further, the statute states that *illegal drug* means

a controlled substance but does not include a controlled substance that is legally possessed or used under the supervision of a licensed health-care professional or that is legally possessed or used under any other authority under [the Controlled Substances Act, 21 U.S.C. § 812(c)] or under any other provision of Federal law. (Pub. L. No. 108-446, § 615(k)(7)(B))

MANIFESTATION DETERMINATION

Despite the complex and heated professional and policy debate surrounding the concept of violence as a manifestation of a disability, the manifestation standard has been maintained in the law since the 1997 amendments to the IDEA. Congress intended this behavioral linkage to the disability of the child—or lack thereof—to be the gatekeeper between discipline applied "in the same manner and for the same duration" as that applied to all children and the time limitation on alternative placements applied when a violation is judged to be a manifestation of the disability. To appreciate the import of this gatekeeper function, the reader is encouraged to re-read and reference the immediately preceding paragraphs.

So whom does the IDEA tap to perform this Solomon-like function? As in all major decisions under the law, the IDEA requires that the IEP team perform this vital function. However, a stipulation in the law qualifies that only relevant members of the IEP team should be involved, with the parents and the LEA choosing the participants. Nonetheless, the IDEA requires that the parents and an LEA representative participate. The statute also mandates that a review and determination occur within ten school days of any decision to change a child's placement, whether that change develops from either the first or the second circumstance discussed in the previous section.

So what responsibilities does the IDEA charge the IEP team with completing? First, all information in the student's file must be reviewed, with particular attention to the student's IEP, teacher observations, and information provided by the parents. Next, the panel must answer two questions:

- Was the conduct at issue *caused* by or did that conduct have a *direct and substantial* relationship to the student's disability?
- Was the conduct at issue the *direct result* of the LEA's failure to implement the IEP?

If the IEP team finds itself answering either of these questions in the affirmative, the law charges the IEP team with determining whether the conduct was a manifestation of the student's disability. Conversely, if the team does not answer either question in the affirmative, then the team must rule that the conduct was not a manifestation of the student's disability.

If the members of the IEP team determine that the behavior in question was a manifestation of the disability, their work is not finished. The team must (1) conduct a functional behavior assessment (FBA) and (2) develop and implement a behavioral intervention plan (BIP) for the child if the LEA had not done so before the violation occurred. If the IEP team had developed and implemented a BIP for the child prior to the violation, the team then must review the BIP and modify it to address the behavior. The lone exception occurs when school personnel are faced with the second circumstance under the heading "Authority for Change of Placement" in this chapter (where specific types of violations are at issue); then the district must return the child to the placement from which he or she was removed—unless the parents and the LEA agree to a change in placement resulting from a modification of the BIP. The team's third task illustrates the delicate balance between the child's rights and the need to ensure a safe school environment for all students and staff. The reader may locate the manifestation determination provisions at Public Law No. 108-446, § 615(k)(1)(E) and (F).

At this point in the chapter, we can concisely summarize the IEP team's overall responsibilities in the IDEA discipline provisions. The IEP team is responsible for conducting manifestation determinations, setting the specific characteristics of all interim alternative educational placements, and deciding on the exact nature of the educational services provided—whatever the placement. Still, a major question remains: What happens if the parents and the LEA disagree on how a district should handle a child who has violated the code of student conduct?

APPEAL: DISSENT, HEARING, DECISION

Both the parents and the LEA can request a hearing, but for different reasons. If the parent of a child with a disability disagrees with any decision regarding either the educational placement or the manifestation determination, the parent may request a hearing. If the LEA believes that maintaining the child in the current educational placement is *substantially likely to result in injury to the child or to others*, the LEA may demand a hearing to argue for a change in placement. Readers should note, however, that this situation is different from the violations previously listed in the second circumstance under the heading "Authority for Change of Placement." The IDEA empowers the LEA to request a hearing based on an anticipated occurrence. Under this scenario, the LEA may make an actual change in placement based on an actual occurrence—namely, when the student inflicts serious bodily injury (Pub. L. No. 108-446, § 615(k)(3)(A)).

The hearing officer may take any of the following steps, depending on the issue that triggered the hearing:

- uphold the manifestation determination or reject it;
- return the child to the original placement from which he or she had been removed or maintain the interim alternative education placement; and
- order a change of placement for the child to an interim alternative education placement if the officer decides such action is necessary; such a decision must be based on the possibility that staying in the current placement is *substantially likely* to result in injury to the child or others.

But readers should not confuse this period under the IDEA discipline provisions—the period when a hearing is requested and in process, known as a period of appeal—with the state-level appeal available under the IDEA's overall procedural safeguards. Unlike appeals provided in the broad section on procedural safeguards, this process must conform to all the rights and procedural guarantees spelled out in Section 615 and discussed earlier in this chapter, including the right to state-level appeal. The law mandates one self-evident difference: The hearing, in this case, is expedited and must occur within 20 school days of the original request—with a ruling following no more than ten school days later. This provision also necessitates shortened timelines for the resolution session required prior to a hearing.

So what is the child's educational setting during this appeal period? Regardless of who requested the hearing—and unless the parent and the state or LEA agree otherwise—the law provides that the child shall

- remain in the interim alternative educational setting (the 45-day time period in the second circumstance), or
- remain in the alternative setting until the expiration of the time period designated by school personnel or when the team determined that the behavior was not a manifestation of the disability (the first circumstance), whichever comes first (e.g., the hearing officer's decision or the alternative setting timeline).

WHAT DID THE LEA KNOW?

Let us consider this situation. The child has violated the code of student conduct. However, the school district has not deemed the child eligible for special education and related services. Do the special discipline considerations of the IDEA nonetheless apply to this child? The IDEA says yes, but only if the LEA *had knowledge* that the student was a child with a disability *prior* to the misconduct that resulted in disciplinary action.

The law says that an LEA had knowledge of the disability before the behavior precipitating disciplinary action if any one of the following has occurred:

- the parent of the child has expressed concern *in writing* to the student's teacher or to supervisory/administrative personnel that the child is in need of special education,
- the parent of the child has requested an evaluation of the child to determine if he or she has a disability, or
- the teacher of the child or other district personnel have expressed *specific* concerns about a *pattern* of behavior evidenced by the child to the LEA's director of special education or to other supervisory personnel.

On the other hand, the law states that an LEA does not have knowledge that a child is a child with a disability if

- the parent of the child has not *allowed* an evaluation of the child to determine if he or she has a disability,

■ the parent of the child has *refused* special education and related services for the child, or

■ the child has been evaluated and the evaluating team has determined that the child is *not* a child with a disability.

If the LEA does not have knowledge, prior to taking disciplinary action, that the child has a disability based on the above criteria, the law requires that the district apply the same disciplinary measures as those applied to children without disabilities.

Finally, when a party requests an evaluation of a child during the time the student is disciplined, the law mandates that the evaluation be expedited. However, the child stays in the educational placement determined by school authorities pending the results of the evaluation. If the child is found to have a disability, the LEA must provide special education and related services. This subsection of the law—Public Law No. 108-446, § 615(k)(5)—is titled, somewhat misleadingly, "Protections for Children Not Yet Eligible for Special Education and Related Services."

LAW ENFORCEMENT

Of course, a violation of the student code of conduct also may be a criminal offense. The IDEA's statutory language makes it abundantly clear that a school district is expected to report any criminal offense to appropriate law enforcement and judicial authorities—whether or not the offense is committed by a child with a disability. Further, the LEA must transmit copies of the special education and disciplinary records of the student to the authorities when a crime is reported.

SUMMARY

The guarantee of due process is among the most basic and essential components of a free and democratic society. Since the founding of the United States, the assurance of due process has served as the bedrock of our judicial system. The rights to dissent, disagree, and receive a hearing in a fair and an impartial forum remain core components of due process in this country. To ensure civil rights for students with disabilities, Congress embedded procedural protections throughout the IDEA, while also including a separate and distinct section on such protections in the law.

Procedural safeguards are a set of rights guaranteeing both parents and students a mechanism for resolving disagreements. Due process ensures that parents are informed, involved, engaged, and given the authority to permit or refuse actions by the school. In addition, the IDEA offers parents a number of other guarantees, including the right of notification, the right to dissent, the right to be fully informed, the right to nonadversarial conflict mediation, the right to a hearing, the right to a qualified and impartial hearing officer, the right to appeal, and the right to reimbursement. The law requires that educators not only follow procedural safeguards, but also fully inform parents of their rights.

Applying the Law in the Classroom

Mia began sixth grade at Richmond Middle School—her local neighborhood school. The district had found Mia eligible for special education services as a child with a serious emotional disturbance (SED) in April of her fourth grade year at Midlothian Elementary. Mia had been mainstreamed, with the exception of a resource and social skills class in fifth and sixth grades. Her teachers have reported consistent growth and improvement regarding academic and social skills.

In September of her sixth-grade year, Mia's parents requested an IEP meeting to discuss her placement. Together, the parents and the school agreed to meet on October 2 to discuss the parents' concerns. The school did not send out a letter of prior notice indicating the agreed-on date and time of the meeting. However, the parents arrived on time along with the remainder of the IEP team. Mia's parents requested that the district place Mia in Old Dominion—a private day school for students with behavioral and emotional disorders. The parents presented the IEP team with a letter from her physician noting that Old Dominion represented the best placement for Mia. The doctor claimed the severity of her emotional disability necessitated the services provided by Old Dominion. In light of the extent of the request (which meant a representative from the central office would need to be present) and the submission of the new report, the school principal requested another meeting the following week. The parents agreed and a time and location were set. At the end of the initial meeting, the parents verbally indicated their intention to place Mia in the private day school the following day; they also made it clear verbally that they intended to seek financial reimbursement from the school district. The parents did not submit their intentions to seek reimbursement or their rationale in writing. Although the parents had received several copies of their procedural safeguards in other meetings, the school did not present the parents with a new copy during the October 2 meeting.

Both parties—the parents and school staff—agreed to meet again on October 8 to address the issue of placement. The district sent prior notice on October 3. On October 6, the school staff who served as part of Mia's IEP team met informally to review the doctor's note, Mia's academic and disciplinary records for the past three years, her IEP, and her teacher's observations—all of which had been requested immediately following the October 2 meeting. Based on the collective information, the staff members felt strongly that placement in the neighborhood school with her regular education peers was appropriate for Mia. The principal believed that the team members would be in violation of the LRE mandate if they agreed to pull the child out of the school and place her in a private setting. The staff members expressed concern about the nature of the doctor's note. The staff specifically addressed two issues: (1) The doctor had met with Mia only one time, according to the records provided with the letter, and (2) the doctor did not recommend a specific treatment or type of setting—rather, he named the specific school the parents had mentioned at the prior meeting.

On October 8, the IEP team reconvened to discuss the placement. The principal began the meeting by summarizing the prior meeting and the purpose of the current meeting. She provided copies of Mia's cumulative file and the material collected by the school staff earlier in the week. The team engaged in a discussion that ultimately led to an impasse. The principal asked each member of the team to offer his or her opinion about the placement. The parents supported the private day placement, and each member of the school staff supported the current IEP and placement. At the close of the meeting, the parents said that they planned to keep their daughter enrolled at Old Dominion and would invoke their due process rights. As a result, the parents filed for a hearing with the local and state education agencies.

Application Questions

1. What was the school's first procedural error? Did the violation appear to have an impact on the parents or the child?
2. If the violation has little to no actual substantive impact—but represents a procedural error—will it have an impact during a due process hearing?
3. Is the school legally obligated to follow the recommendation of a physician?
4. What is the legal responsibility of the school regarding the use of medical or other information provided by professionals via the parents?
5. Do you think the concerns of the school staff regarding the doctor's letter are correct? Why or why not?
6. Even though the parents verbally stated their intention to seek financial reimbursement, could the absence of a written statement, including the rationale for the private placement, impact the parents' ability to win reimbursement in a due process hearing or lawsuit?
7. Do you feel the school violated the parents' due process rights in a substantive manner?
8. Do you think the hearing officer will find in favor of the school district or the parents? Why?

CRITICAL THINKING QUESTIONS

1. With procedural protections embedded throughout the IDEA, why was there a need for a separate section placed in the law for procedural safeguards?
2. Do educators have an ethical or professional responsibility to help parents when they dissent or invoke due process, even when the educators disagree with the parents?
3. What do you see as the most essential changes of the 2004 amendments in relation to procedural safeguards and their potential implications?
4. What is going to be the realistic effect of the statute of limitations?
5. What is the significance of the new provision that an SEA or LEA may seek an award of attorneys' fees because a suit is found to be frivolous? Do you think it will be difficult for LEAs or SEAs to prove a suit is frivolous?
6. What are the similarities and differences between a mediation and a resolution session? Why are both included in the law?
7. What is the difference between administrative due process and judicial due process? Should administrative due process be exhausted prior to engaging in judicial due process?
8. Why is it considered combative for parents to invoke due process if the original intent of the IDEA was to bring parents and educators together to amicably resolve issues? What has happened to change the culture of due process?

REFERENCES

Clyde K. v. Puyallup, 35 F.3d 1396 (9th Cir. 1994).

Honig v. Doe, 479 U.S. 1084 (1988).

Individuals with Disabilities Education Act (Education for All Handicapped Children Act of 1975), Pub. L. No. 94-142, 89 Stat. 773.

Individuals with Disabilities Education Improvement Act of 2004, Pub. L. No. 108-446, 118 Stat. 2652.

Kerkam v. McKenzie, 862 F.2d 884 (D.C. Cir. 1988).

Oberti v. Board of Education of the Borough of Clementon School District, 995 F.2d 1204 (3d Cir. 1993).

Pennsylvania Association for Retarded Citizens v. Pennsylvania, 334 F. Supp. 1257 (E.D. Pa. 1972).

Roland M. v. Concord School Committee, 910 F.2d 983 (1st Cir. 1990).

Schaffer v. Weast, 546 U.S. 49 (2005).

Weintraub, F., et al. (1976). *Public policy and the education of exceptional children*. Reston, VA: Council for Exceptional Children.

Epilogue: Future Implications

The contents of this epilogue are offered in the spirit of collaboration and collective thought. As I pondered the best approach to addressing both current and future issues regarding special education law, it seemed only appropriate to view the epilogue through two lenses—one rich with historical, legislative, and policy-oriented experiences and one with practical, hands-on knowledge of current, daily special education issues. I quickly concluded an epilogue written by two pens—one belonging to Joe Ballard and the other mine—would provide the most balanced and informed approach. The following epilogue represents the combined efforts, thoughts, and perspectives of Joe Ballard and Kurt Hulett.

ADVOCACY

This text has placed heavy emphasis on the importance of informed citizen advocacy, both individual and organized, in the development and enactment of the Individuals with Disabilities Education Act (IDEA). It has often been observed that political success requires developing an absolute passion for the achievement of a clear, tightly defined objective. While that axiom was validated in the realization of Public Law No. 94-142 in 1975, the authors would contend that the "absolute passion" must be sustained, and sustained permanently.

After some 30 years since the IDEA's original enactment, an attitude can take hold that regards the IDEA as so deeply embedded in our legal culture as to be unassailable. Further, complacency can develop that takes for granted the guaranteed permanence of the six pillars of the IDEA, a major focus of this text. However, one need only observe the continuing national debates and challenges surrounding such macro issues as citizen privacy, personal choice, and minority discrimination to see that a heavy dose of caution is in order, even for the IDEA.

Further, the best evidence of the need for sustained vigilance and caution lies in the history of the IDEA itself in the decades after the 1975 enactment. To borrow from the vernacular, it was not "easy street" after the IDEA became law. Within two years of the ink drying on President Gerald Ford's signature, powerful (primarily state-level) interests were on Capitol Hill pleading for at least postponement, and at best cancellation, of major features of the IDEA. Unmoved, Congress held firm; the final regulations were published in August of 1977, and full implementation of the law proceeded in earnest during the 1977–1978 school year.

Lest anyone be found dozing on his watch, the Reagan administration was installed in 1981 with a public agenda to basically reverse the direction of national education policy. The administration proposed, on the more symbolic level, to abolish the U.S. Department of Education in its infancy and, on the obviously very concrete level, to liquidate what were now the two centerpiece federal programs in elementary and secondary education—Title I of the Elementary and Secondary Education Act and the IDEA—and replace them with gigantic, no-strings-attached block grant to the states. In 1981, what was a breathtaking summer of point/counterpoint resulted in bipartisan action (Senate-Republican, House-Democrat) in which Congress gave the administration its block grants, but preserved Title I and the IDEA. Also during this period, the administration considered lessening the provisions of the IDEA through major revisions to the IDEA regulations, only to eventually abandon this exercise as well. In fairness, it should be observed that, in its later years, the Reagan administration, if not friendly toward, at least seemed accepting of the mission of the IDEA.

Later in the 1980s, the U.S. Supreme Court ruled in *Smith v. Robinson* that, in effect, only the IDEA, and not Section 504 of the Rehabilitation Act of 1973 as well, could be the legal basis when bringing a grievance where the issue was solely a special education matter. Such a decoupling of the IDEA and Section 504 was deemed critically damaging to the child and to the family tool chest of procedural safeguards, and the Court's action was eventually reversed through congressional legislation.

The late 1980s and the 1990s brought yet another severe test of the IDEA in what may be described as the stirrings of a backlash nationally over the costs and requirements of the IDEA, along with attacks on the nature of special education itself. Memorable examples from the media include a report on the popular *60 Minutes* television program, viewed by millions, presenting on camera a young person with a disability being transported daily to and from his special education program by Leer jet at public expense. The magazine *U.S. News and World Report* published an edition with a front cover declaring "Special Education—Separate and Unequal."

The flames of backlash were barely tamped when yet another hurdle appeared. The issue of the IDEA as an underfunded program when actual annual federal appropriations were compared to the original fiscal commitment made at IDEA enactment had been frustrating for organizations such as the Council for Exceptional Children, not to mention local and state school governance, for at least two decades. Rather abruptly, Congress in 1995–1996 seriously considered either funding or repealing laws that had not realized their full original fiscal promise. Under the sometimes explosive mantra of "unfunded mandates," the IDEA seemed yet again grievously challenged. However, at roughly the same time, the first truly powerful bipartisan coalition of members of Congress was at last cobbled together on the money issue, putting the IDEA on track toward truly substantial yearly increases in actual dollars obligated to the program. Through all of these potential detours and ambushes, the IDEA has remained, its fundamental policy components unsullied. The question is "Why?"

Let it first be acknowledged that the IDEA has generally enjoyed solid bipartisan support in Congress throughout its existence, despite periods of negative clamoring. However, Congress needs to be regularly reminded of what it is supporting and why. Thus, a permanent advocacy is required, routinely providing information on the funding and operation of the program and regularly bringing individual and collective success stories of real children in real time to the attention of the elected representatives on Capitol Hill. Though this task can often be grueling and tedious, it has to be done and it was done. Who did that work and is still doing that work? Throughout 30 years of sustained advocacy, that task has been performed by a determined, no-nonsense coalition of organizations. This coalition comprises parent, special education, some general education, other professional, and disability advocacy interests.

What refinements in advocacy are in order for this twenty-first century? Since the seismic explosion of digital electronic communication (especially the Internet) that accompanied mankind into the new century, Congress is no longer inundated with just cards, phone calls, and letters; members receive literally millions of emails and other forms of electronic communication. And these are accompanied by volumes of unsolicited information, on a previously unimaginable multiplicity of subjects. To put it simply, one particular subject can instantly be buried in the daily avalanche pouring into Capitol Hill offices. Further, members and staff are finding ways to psychologically tune out so they don't drown. But while what is being styled as the Information Age brings new problems in effective advocacy, it also brings exciting opportunities. One must add to all of this the fact that another era is also well under way, the age of accountability in education. Regardless of the future of the accountability banner—namely, the No Child Left Behind Act (NCLB)—the demand for concrete accountability is here to stay. But, again, new problems also frequently convey new opportunities.

Following are a few modest recommendations for the future of advocacy. *Note:* Given space constraints in this overall text, recommendations in this epilogue will be brief, hopefully concise, and without expatiation. Whether specific proposals are accepted or not by the reader, the authors' intent is to assist in sparking creative thinking about the future of the IDEA and special education in the twenty-first century. After all, the future is indeed now.

ADVOCACY UNIFICATION

Given the realities of mass digital communication, the IDEA advocacy community must stop being so notably inbred and isolationist. It must reach out to a broader range of parent and professional education and human service clusters representing other subgroups of students, both at risk and not at risk. These can include clusters such as those representing all students (PTAs), educationally disadvantaged students, ethnically diverse and minority students, gifted and talented students, English language learners, economically and socially disadvantaged students, and students otherwise challenged in such content areas as reading, mathematics, and science. Such a coalition of organizations should cross-fertilize its collective advocacy—every cluster pitching in to advocate for any one cluster when needed. The alliance should be highly organized over time, with a carefully developed system of call-to-action protocols. Its motto could be a paraphrase of Ben Franklin's famous warning: Either we all hang together, or we may each hang separately.

PUBLIC PRESENCE

A well-planned, systematic infusion of information about children with special needs, their challenges, and their personal success stories needs to be plotted and provided to the mass media (radio, television, and Internet and print publications) on a sustained schedule throughout each year. Financed by multisourced contributions and operated by the major IDEA and special education advocacy groups, this information sharing should be "Madison Avenue" excellent, but low-key; entertaining and positive; and regular, but spaced periodically. If the goal is really to become part of the fabric of America, not a single year of this methodical infusion should be neglected for the foreseeable future.

MAXIMIZATION OF TECHNOLOGY

With respect to the Internet, websites with the information mission described above should be established, maintained, and brought to the attention of the ever-burgeoning population that acquires most of its information through that medium.

CELEBRATING SUCCESS

"Our Exceptional Citizens" week (or month) should be made an American institution, including "Our Exceptional Students" day (or week), with appropriate activities methodically planned throughout.

NCLB—A WATCHFUL EYE

Being already well versed in all the particulars of the IDEA, the special education advocacy network of groups must become equally well versed in all components of NCLB. Though NCLB may undergo many alterations and refinements, it is unlikely to vanish. Advocates will need to walk the halls of Congress on behalf of children with disabilities during reauthorizations of NCLB just as they do for the IDEA—since the policy integrity of the IDEA is now shadowed by the stipulations of NCLB.

A DEMOGRAPHIC UPHEAVAL

In March of 2006, the nation was taken aback when 500,000 peaceful Hispanics marched in Los Angeles. By mid-May, literally millions of Hispanics, both documented and undocumented, had marched in demonstrations in cities across the country. At issue was congressional consideration of comprehensive immigration legislation. But issues aside, a review of history indicates that America, a nation of immigrants, had nonetheless never witnessed an outpouring in such staggering numbers by relatively new arrivals to American soil.

The political and societal ramifications of changing demographics are not subjects of this text. For special education, the current ethnic, racial, and linguistic changes in the school population are especially pressing. Readers are referred to the findings of Congress that accompanied the 2004 IDEA amendments (at the beginning of Chapter 7). Of course, inappropriate designation for special education and high dropout rates are, regrettably, long-standing challenges. See also the "Facts at a Glance" at the beginning of Chapter 9, which spotlights court decrees. But the unprecedented numerical increase over the last 15 years of English language learners in the school population, plus the alarming increase in the percentage of students who are deemed socially and economically disadvantaged in the same time frame, has intensified the overall challenge. The nondiscriminatory testing provisions of Public Law No. 94-142 reflected primarily a concern for the misclassification of African-American children. The reality of Spanish-speaking children was barely over the horizon, except for the expert few. Thirty years later that original concern still festers, while new imperatives join in.

The self-directive for special education has always been twofold: to avoid inappropriate referral and designation of ethnically diverse and minority children for special education and to provide diagnostically and culturally effective special education to appropriately designated diverse children. Though much is being done, the following additional national priorities are recommended.

A UNIFIED NATIONAL DIALOGUE

The professional and civic groups representing ethnically and linguistically diverse children must coalesce with similar groups representing children with disabilities in a permanent national-level dialogue on mutual education and problem solving. Nothing even close to an organized approach is currently under way, and special education professionals and parents should provide the initiative. The general topic should be the intersection of disability, culture, and language in American public education.

A PROFESSIONAL ACADEMY

A permanent national professional academy should be instituted, with appropriate staff, to work on a sustained basis in the domain of ethnic, cultural, and linguistic aspects of American education as they relate to special and compensatory public education. The academy should be independent of political interference (such as the National Academy of Sciences). Immediate charges to this body would be (1) grappling with referral, evaluation, and assessment issues and protocols and (2) exploring elements of what would constitute responsive and effective special education for diverse learners.

MANDATORY CROSS-CULTURAL PREPARATION

Content covering all major aspects of diversity and diverse children should become required course work at all levels of professional preparation for both special and general educators.

NATIONAL COMMISSION ON ENGLISH LANGUAGE IMMERSION

A frank and candid national dialogue, with commission status, should commence on the relative merits of the gradualism of the bilingual approach to learning English versus the total immersion in English by the second or third grade. Aside from the very real danger that the United States could well become two nations with different languages occupying the same piece of real estate by the mid-twenty-first century, the earliest possible student command of English would greatly reduce the nagging pitfalls and routine misfires of referral and evaluation. And it should be remembered that very young children are the best language learners.

THE TROUBLESOME NCLB

NCLB has triggered the same protest banner, "teaching to the test," that was unfurled by parents and educators during the competency-based testing movement of the early 1980s, and with good reason. Academic proficiency is critical, but so is development of the whole person during the schooling years, the latter being a particularly sensitive matter for children with disabilities.

Chapter 6 addresses the parameters of the intersection of the two laws and the modestly successful effort to conform the IDEA to NCLB in the 2004 IDEA amendments. Much may be said positively of NCLB—notably, its "tough love" attention to school and school system accountability, its focus on the success of *all* children enrolled in *each* and *every* public school in the nation, and its mandate of a high achievement bar for all students. But a nagging reality will continue to fester—NCLB focuses on achievement for *subgroups* of students in a given school, whereas the IDEA is structured for the *individual* development of each student participating. Since this reality is a classic instance of the proverbial "round peg in a square hole," a harmonizing of the two laws through both NCLB amendments and best practices must occur during the coming years. The authors wish to stress that the IDEA need not and should not undergo any structural amending, but NCLB should. Toward that end, the following specific suggestions are offered.

STATUS AND GROWTH

Increasing evidence suggests that NCLB rules fail to include a critical measurement, relative growth. Suppose that two schools have both passed muster under NCLB in a given year, scoring identical status levels. But one of the schools has doubled the overall collective growth in learning for its students; the other has shown no student growth at all. Do these two schools still look the same? Let us further hypothesize that the school that doubled collective growth is designated as failing because it still did not reach the NCLB scorecard numbers. Is this fair? Should this school move to the debit column? NCLB needs assessment protocols that measure both *status* and *growth*.

DOMAINS OF LEARNING

Chapter 6 includes discussion of the 1 and 2 percent caveats allowed in assessments of certain students with disabilities. In point of fact, NCLB should include a broader framework of learning measurements for all students in our schools, assessing growth in social, emotional, and creative domains, to mention three.

A RETURN TO TRACKING

Danger signals are surfacing that the NCLB structure may be bringing a return of the student track system to our schools—namely, inadequate, adequate, and proficient. That, in turn, resurrects the low-expectation syndrome and potentially life-long labels for students. This requires immediate monitoring and, if necessary, NCLB course corrections.

POLICY CREEP

Interestingly enough, the *highly qualified* content area requirements for special education teachers, however worthy in theory, have the "policy creep" potential of diminishing integration of children with disabilities in the regular classroom—as well as the opposite, restricting placement options along the continuum. This issue requires ongoing national samplings and surveys. NCLB requirements could be engendering actions that are illegal under the IDEA.

INDIVIDUALIZED APPROACH TO EDUCATION

Finally, Congress should order a national study and report. The charge: How and to what degree the IDEA principle of *individualized education* can be applied to all students in the nation toward the achievement of proficiency by the NCLB date of school year 2013–2014.

IN LITIGIOUS AMERICA

Chapter 11 reviews the protections provided to families that are both embedded throughout the IDEA and placed in a separate section when disagreements or misunderstandings occur. While the due process procedures of Section 615 are vital safeguards, efforts are now under way to make them less confrontational in practice.

In a nation that seems sometimes to manufacture new lawyers faster than new automobile tires, confrontation in administrative due process proceedings exists in numerous sectors nationwide, not just in the realm of special education disputes. Of course, lawyers perform important functions in society, having been influential in the culture of the English-speaking world since at least the early Middle Ages. Moreover, parents should always have the right to attorney counsel, as should the schools. But every lawyer knows that one of the hallmarks of a good American law school is intensive training in the fine arts of courtroom sparring and debate, a natural by-product of which is an almost reflexive penchant for confrontation.

In the most recent reauthorizations of the IDEA, proposals banning lawyers from mediation sessions and hearings have always been offered and considered. The underlying notion seems to be *"You* can't bring your lawyer if they don't bring *their* lawyer." Such proposals ultimately die of their own weight. And maybe they should. Actually, Congress—again, in recent reauthorizations—has made considerable progress in providing tools to reduce the potential for confrontation. Examples include the mediation and resolution session options; the requirement that hearing decisions be made on substantive, not procedural or technical, grounds; and the prohibition of complaints that are frivolous, unreasonable, or otherwise without foundation. The authors offer this further modest proposal.

SOLUTION ORIENTATION

Professional development at the school level toward avoidance of parental confrontation has been neglected in too many school districts since the inception of the IDEA. This situation needs to be reversed through aggressive in-service preparation. The instructional and administrative leaders in the schools are the principals, who should be the primary recipients of this preparation (and who would be, by and large, grateful to receive it if credibly packaged and delivered by experts). The justification for such in-service preparation might be this: "When the lawyers arrive, you have just admitted failure." The in-service content should address establishing a long-term atmosphere of trust with all parents having children with disabilities; listening studiously and reacting appropriately to parental concerns; performing one's ethical and professional responsibilities to help parents, even when differences of opinion obtain; and initiating and maintaining a climate of mutual problem solving, even when the air gets heavy with emotion. This continuing education content may look like nothing more than plain common sense, but the evidence suggests that it is far from common practice.

PROTECTING THE SIX PILLARS

As noted earlier, the six pillars of the IDEA are symbiotic elements; the loss or serious diminution of any one pillar could be fatal to the efficacy of the others. At the close of this text, we address these elements with a few brief comments, laced with warnings. Of the six, procedural safeguards have already been touched on in the immediately preceding segment.

THE IEP: THE HEART OF SPECIAL EDUCATION

Like so many powerful, but controversial instruments of policy, the IEP will always have its detractors. The most serious threat, however, might come through a gradual reduction of this mechanism's core ability to do its work for the child—bringing about its eventual death not with a bang, but with a whimper. At least two actions taken in the 2004 IDEA reauthorization serve as a clear warning: the regression to age 16 for the initiation of transition planning and services and the weakening of the stipulations for general education teacher involvement in the IEP process. Further, the pilot experiments with the three-year IEP should be subjected to rigorous monitoring and analysis in concert with vigorous national debate.

FREE AND APPROPRIATE PUBLIC EDUCATION

Chapter 7 addresses the historic guidepost provided by the U.S. Supreme Court in its 1982 decision in *Board of Education of the Hendrick Hudson Central School District v. Rowley* (458 U.S. 176). "Basic floor of opportunity" and "some educational benefit" became the educational program markers under the IDEA. Forgotten by many now, advocates were in anguish over *Rowley* being the case before the High Court on the parameters of a free appropriate public education. Why? Though matters turned out reasonably well, *Rowley* was actually a case involving the provision of a related service, not special education. Numerous other professions and interests are highly adept at carefully steering the best possible lower court cases to the U.S. Supreme Court. The IDEA community of interest is not adept at such promotion, having never even organized a coordinated effort. Cases on aspects of the IDEA will continue to be heard by the nation's highest nine justices. Monitoring these cases in order to identify and promote the most desirable ones as they wend their way up the judicial ladder needs to become a coordinated, ongoing task.

Further, Chapter 7 addresses the dangerous waters the courts are stepping into regarding the educational methodologies attendant to autism. Given the explosive increase in autism-related diagnoses in recent years, the IDEA community needs urgently to address this tendency through such vehicles as amicus curiae (friend of the court) briefs at every opportunity. The same sort of designated experts assigned to the previous task might shoulder this activity as well.

LEAST RESTRICTIVE ENVIRONMENT

This text, and particularly Chapter 8, addresses the inherent tension built into the IDEA because the required starting point for the child is presumed to be education in the regular classroom (with supplemental aids and services), moving along the continuum of placement options only when educationally appropriate for the child. But here everyone must guard against moving to the extreme point in either direction. In national, state, and local movements at various times throughout the history of the IDEA, full-inclusion movements sometimes seem to be dismantling the continuum in certain locales. At other times and places, placements in the regular classroom have been greatly reduced in the interest of administrative, budgetary, and professional convenience. Two tenets must be kept in mind simultaneously by all education professionals: First, failure to begin with a presumption of the regular classroom is illegal under the IDEA; second, failure to make the *full* continuum of placements available as options is also illegal under the IDEA.

APPROPRIATE EVALUATION AND ASSESSMENT

Racial, ethnic, cultural, and linguistic issues, central to present and future directions in evaluation, have been touched upon already. Also of special note, the framers of the 2004 IDEA amendments have clearly added the option of determining learning disabilities through *response to intervention (RTI)*, which has taken up residence with the discrepancy formula, enshrined in the IDEA regulations since the late 1970s. Will it lead to an increase or a reduction in the cohort of children designated as having learning disabilities? Will RTI survive a long-term testing as "research and scientifically-based"? While RTI protocols should certainly proceed, so should intensive monitoring and analysis of their effectiveness during at least the next two decades.

PARTICIPATION: PARENT AND TEACHER

The authors have only the following warning to add, and it is addressed to all our teachers, especially special education teachers. Do not ever let anyone or any movement—whether anti–public education zealots, presumed legal eagles, bosses above you who may have grown weary and callous, private school program hustlers, or just all-around naysayers—drive a wedge between you and the parents. Your partnership with the parents is sacred; it is the very heartbeat of the educational enterprise and the very soul of effective special education for yours and their special children. Without your partnership, there is nothing, as the saying goes, "but the sound of one hand clapping." One of the authors was present throughout the original development of the IDEA. He can tell you, without fear of credible contradiction, that the intent from the beginning was to place the child, the parents, and the teachers *at the top* of the educational pyramid.

It will happen, that reversal of the pyramid. Maybe not today, or tomorrow, but it will happen. An ancient Judaic salutation of hope is apropos. *"Next year*, in Jerusalem."

Glossary

ADA	The Americans with Disabilities Act of 1990
Appellate court	A court that hears cases on appeal from lower courts (e.g., the U.S. Court of Appeals for the Fourth Circuit)
AYP	Adequate yearly progress (term used in the No Child Left Behind Act of 2001)
BIP	Behavioral intervention plan
Case law	Law that is created through the courts—also referred to as judge-made or common law
C.F.R.	Code of Federal Regulations
DOE	Department of Education (may refer to federal or state)
FAPE	Free appropriate public education
FBA	Functional behavior assessment
FERPA	Family Educational Rights and Privacy Act
Full inclusion	The philosophy of placing children with disabilities *only* in regular education classes; the practice implies that the continuum of placements outside of the regular education classroom is not utilized or considered
IDEA	The Individuals with Disabilities Education Act
IEP	Individualized education program
LEA	Local education agency
LRE	Least restrictive environment
Mainstreaming	The practice of placing children with disabilities in regular education classes as much as appropriate
NCLB	No Child Left Behind Act of 2001
OSEP	Office of Special Education Programs (federal)
OSERS	Office of Special Education and Rehabilitative Services (federal)
SEA	State education agency
U.S.C.	United States Code
Zero reject	The philosophy under the IDEA that no student with a disability—regardless of the severity of the disabling condition—may be denied a FAPE

INDEX